Understanding C++
for
MFC

Understanding C++
for
MFC

Richard F. Raposa

CRC Press
Taylor & Francis Group
Boca Raton London New York

CRC Press is an imprint of the
Taylor & Francis Group, an **informa** business

Supplementary Resources Disclaimer

Additional resources were previously made available for this title on CD. However, as CD have become a less accessible format, all resources have been moved to a more convenient online download option.

You can find these resources available here: https://www.routledge.com/9781138436374

Please note: Where this title mentions the associated disc, please use the downloadable resources instead.

CRC Press
Taylor & Francis Group
6000 Broken Sound Parkway NW, Suite 300
Boca Raton, FL 33487-2742

© 2001 by Taylor & Francis Group, LLC
CRC Press is an imprint of Taylor & Francis Group, an Informa business

No claim to original U.S. Government works

ISBN-13: 9781578200689 (pbk)
ISBN-13: 9781138436374 (hbk)

**Visit the Taylor & Francis Web site at
http://www.taylorandfrancis.com**

**and the CRC Press Web site at
http://www.crcpress.com**

*For Susan,
without whom I would have never
had the motivation to finish.*

Table of Contents

Chapter 1

The Fundamentals of C++

Introduction

C++ evolved from C, a procedural programming language developed in the early 1970s by Dennis Ritchie at Bell Laboratories. C was an advanced, versatile programming language that grew to be highly popular. Most of today's popular operating systems are written in C.

In the early 1980s, Bjarne Stroustrup, also of Bell Laboratories, developed an object-oriented programming (OOP) language that extended C called C++. Its name implied an increment of C. (The "++" is called the *increment operator* in C.) OOP was a new way of designing software, and C++ provided a powerful OOP language that used syntax familiar to C programmers. Soon, C++ became a popular language among software developers.

This chapter introduces *procedural* C++. In other words, I will discuss the elements of C++ that do not involve OOP. Much of this chapter will be review for programmers with a proficient C background. However, when learning any programming language, a good understanding of the foundation of that language can go a long way in trying to learn the more advanced features.

Topics discussed in this chapter include the keywords and built-in data types, as well as a discussion of variables, references, and pointers. Structures and arrays are covered, as are the control structures of C++. Functions are discussed in detail, including C++ features like overloading and default arguments. I begin with a discussion of the main() function, and the layout of a C++ program.

The `main()` Function

All programs have an entry point where execution begins. When a user executes a C++ program, the operating system invokes the `main()` function of that program. After the operating system executes all statements within `main()`,the program terminates. (In some cases, programs can end for other reasons however.) The `main()` function has the following outline.

```
int main()
{

        //program statements go here
        return 0;

}
```

The keyword `int` specifies an integer and declares the data type that `main()` returns. The value of this integer is known as the program's *exit code*. When a program executes to completion successfully, the exit code is typically 0. Other exit codes can be useful for debugging purposes.

The `main()` function is created in a text file with either a `*.cpp` or `*.cxx` filename. Using these extensions ensures compilation by a C++ compiler — an important distinction considering much of the syntax of C and C++ is identical. (Source files written in C use the `*.c` filename.)

To illustrate how `main()` works, and to get our first look at a C++ program, the following program displays a message box with the current time. The remainder of this chapter discusses each line of code in this program, and a sample output is shown in Figure 1.1.

```
/* Description: Displays the current time
   Filename:  time.cpp*/

#include <windows.h>
#include <time.h>

int main()
{
  //allocate space to store the time as a string
  char timeString[9];

  //get the current time and store it in timeString
  _strtime( timeString );

  //display the time
  MessageBox(NULL,timeString, "The time is now",
             MB_OK | MB_ICONINFORMATION);

  return 0;
}
```

Figure 1.1   Running the `time.cpp` **program displays a message box with the current time.**

Comments

The first two lines of code are *comments*, which are remarks that can be placed throughout the program to make your code more readable. They have no effect on the size of a program's executable and are ignored by the compiler.

You have two ways to place comments in a program.

1. On a line of code after two forward slashes (//).
2. Between /*, which begins a comment, and */, which ends the comment.

Preprocessor Directives

The `time.cpp` program displays the current time as a string in a message box. To accomplish this, I use the _strtime function, a Windows-specific function declared in the `time.h` header file. We also invoked `MessageBox`, a Windows API function declared in the `windows.h` header file. To use these functions, I included their header files into the source file using the following statements:

```
#include <windows.h>
#include <time.h>
```

The #include statement is an example of a *preprocessor directive*. Before a program is compiled, a preprocessor program scans the source code for directives, which are denoted by the # sign. The include directive copies the given file into the source code. Other common examples of preprocessor directives are #define, #ifdef, and #ifndef.

You frequently use the include directive to insert header files into source files. I discuss header and source files in "Functions" (page 28) and subsequent sections of this chapter.

Message Boxes

Message boxes are windows that display messages to users and possibly retrieve an answer. Message boxes are a common feature of many Windows programs. For example, if you try to exit Microsoft Word without having saved the document on which you are working, a message box appears to warn you and ask if you want to save the document before exiting.

You use the MessageBox function in the Win32 API to display a variety of message boxes. The declaration for MessageBox is found in windows.h and looks like:

```
int MessageBox( HWND hWnd, // handle of parent window
                LPCTSTR lpText, // text in message box
                LPCTSTR lpCaption, // title of message box
                UINT uType // style of message box
            );
```

I discuss the data types of parameters, such as hWnd in the previous code, in Chapter 4, "Advanced Object-Oriented Programming Using C++." Until then, we only need to understand how to use the function. The time.cpp program used the following function call:

```
MessageBox(NULL,timeString, "The time is now",
        MB_OK | MB_ICONINFORMATION);
```

- The first parameter, NULL, makes the Windows desktop the owner of our message box. The second parameter is the message to display, which in our example is the timeString variable initialized from the call to _strtime. The third parameter is a string that displays in the title bar of the message box.

The final parameter specifies which buttons and icons display in the message box. You choose the icon and button styles from the values shown in Table 1.1.

Table 1.1   Message box styles.

Message Box Style	Result
MB_OK	One button: OK
MB_OKCANCEL	Two buttons: OK and Cancel
MB_YESNO	Two buttons: Yes and No
MB_RETRYCANCEL	Two buttons: Retry and Cancel
MB_YESNOCANCEL	Three buttons: Yes, No, and Cancel
MB_ABORTRETRYIGNORE	Three buttons: Abort, Retry, and Ignore
MB_HELP	Adds an additional button, Help, to the above styles
MB_ICONINFORMATION	Icon: an "-i-" inside a quote balloon
MB_ICONEXCLAMATION	Icon: an exclamation point
MB_ICONQUESTION	Icon: a question mark
MB_ICONSTOP	Icon: a stop sign

To use more than one style, you combine them using the *bitwise or operator*, |, as follows:

```
MB_OK | MB_ICONINFORMATION
```

The MB_HELP style can be added to any message box, which displays a Help button. For example,

```
MB_OK | MB_HELP | MB_ICONINFORMATION
```

C++ Syntax Conventions

Notice how the main() function used *curly braces* to denote the beginning and ending of the body of main(). C++ uses curly braces for all blocks of code.

When a new block of code is started, you typically indent the statements in that block. The editor in Visual Studio does this indenting automatically, which makes our code much more readable and less error-prone. The extra spaces and tabs are called *whitespace*, which is ignored by the compiler and has no effect on the size of the executable.

C++ is *case-sensitive*, which means that main() and Main() are two different identifiers. So you must make your main() function all lowercase to tell the compiler that this is the function where the program's execution begins.

C++ Keywords and Identifiers

The *keywords* of a language are those words that have a pre-defined meaning to the compiler. *Identifiers* are the names programmers create for classes, variables, and functions.

Table 1.2 shows the keywords of the C++ language. Note that the keywords preceded by a double underscore are specific to the Microsoft Visual C++ compiler.

Table 1.2 C++ and Visual C++ keywords.

__asm	__assume	auto__
based	bool	break
case	catch	__cdecl
char	class	const
const_cast	continue	__declspec
default	delete	dllexport
dllimport	do	double
dynamic_cast	else	enum
__except	explicit	extern
false	__fastcall	__finally

float	for	friend
goto	if	inline
__inline	int	int8
__int8	__int16	__int32
__int64	__leave	long
main	__multiple_inheritance	__single_inheritance
__virtual_inheritance	mutable	naked
namespace	new	noreturn
operator	private	protected
public	register	reinterpret_cast
return	short	signed
sizeof	static	static_cast
__stdcall	struct	switch
template	this	thread
throw	true	try
__try	typedef	typeid
typename	union	unsigned
using	uuid	__uuidof
virtual	void	volatile
wmain	while	

We will not discuss all of these keywords in this book, but it is important to know them, because they have special meaning to the compiler and cannot be used in other situations.

When creating identifiers, the following rules apply in C++:

1. An identifier cannot be a C++ keyword.
2. An identifier cannot begin with a digit 0–9.
3. The remaining characters of an identifier can consist of letters, digits, and the underscore character.

For example, x_1 and intValue are valid identifiers, while 1_x and int are not.

Primitive Data Types

Programmers often refer to primitive data types as *built-in* data types, because these data types are an intrinsic feature of a language. Table 1.3 lists the primitive data types of C++ for storing numbers and characters. The actual size of each data type is machine-dependent. This table lists its size on Windows 98/NT/2000. The `sizeof` operator is used to determine the exact size of any data type. (The accompanying CD contains a program in `sizeof.cpp` that was used to determine the values in Table 1.3.)

Table 1.3   C++ primitive data types.

Data Type	Size
char	8 bits
short	16 bits
int	32 bits
long	32 bits
float	32 bits
double	64 bits
long double	64 bits

Primitive data types allow flexibility in the amount of memory used for storing data. For example, if memory is critical, you can use a `short` in lieu of an `int` if the data does not need more than 16 bits of storage.

Each primitive data type in Table 1.3 is signed. This means that the most significant bit is used as a sign bit. You can precede any of the primitive data types with the `unsigned` keyword. This gives you the ability to store larger numbers (by a factor of two) in memory, but the numbers stored in that location can only be positive.

For example, the range of values you can store in a `char` is –128 to 127, because the largest positive `char` is 01111111 in binary, or 127. (Negative values are stored using 2's complement.) However, if you use an `unsigned char`, the largest number would be all binary 1's, which is 256, while the smallest `unsigned char` is 0.

Literals

A *literal* is a constant value used in a program. For example, in the following statement, the value of 3.14 is a literal.

```
double area = 3.14 * radius * radius;
```

Table 1.4 shows the literals in C++ and what data types the computer stores.

Table 1.4 Literal values in C++ and their data types.

Literal	Example	Data type
integer	14	`int`
floating-point	3.14	`double`
floating-point exponential	2.789E12	`double`
character	`'A'`	`char`
floating-point with F suffix	3.14F	`float`
floating-point with L suffix	5.901E34L	`long double`
integer with L suffix	987109847598L	`long`

Notice in Table 1.4 how you can assign F and L suffixes to alter the default behavior of literals. For example, you can use the F suffix to store a floating-point literal as a `float` instead of a `double`, which is the default data type for floating-point literals.

Also, notice the use of E in Table 1.4 for expressing floating-point literals in scientific notation. The example 2.789E12 is the value 2.789 times 10 to the power of 12.

Variables

A *variable* in C++ represents an identifier for a memory address. The data stored at the memory address is called the variable's *contents*. For example, in the following declaration the variable x identifies a memory address whose contents are the value 12. Creating variables of a specific data type is how we allocate and keep track of our data in memory.

```
int x = 12;
```

When the x variable is used in a program, it will be the value 12. Because x is a variable, we can also change the contents at any time using the assignment operator (=). For example, the following statement changes x to the value -41.

```
x = -41;
```

C++ takes advantage of two other techniques for representing data: references and pointers. This is an important feature of C++ and is often a source of confusion for beginners of the language. However, after you begin to use references and pointers, you will quickly learn how useful and versatile they can be.

References and pointers are still variables; but instead of containing specific data, they correspond to other variables in a program. This technique is useful when passing data back and forth between functions, among other benefits. The next sections discuss references and pointers as alternatives to using variables.

References

A *reference* in C++ is a variable that acts as an alias for another variable. To declare a reference, precede the reference variable with an ampersand, &, to initialize the reference to the variable for which it is an alias.

The following statements declare a variable x and a variable r, which refers to x.

```
double x = 3.14;//x is a variable whose contents are 3.14
double & r = x;//r is a reference to x
x = 2.17;//both x and r are now 2.17
r = -9.0;//both x and r are now -9.0
```

You can not reassign a reference to a different variable; so in the code above, r can only refer to x. Because r is a reference to x, you can now access the contents of x either directly by using x or by using r. Changing the value of either x or r changes the value of both of them.

When creating a reference as a local variable, you *must* initialize the reference, as you saw in the preceding code. After the reference is initialized, it cannot refer to any other variable.

However, in some instances, a reference does not need to be initialized when it is declared. Those instances are:

- When using a reference as a parameter to a function, the argument passed to the function initializes the reference.
- When declaring a return value of a function as a reference.
- When variables are members of a class, you do not need to initialize them, because the constructor of the class can assign the reference to its corresponding variable.

Pointers

A *pointer* in C++ is a variable whose contents are the memory address of another variable. Pointers do not need to be initialized like references, and a pointer can be changed to point to a different variable.

To declare a pointer, we use the asterisk, *, after the data type. Here is an example:

```
double * d;
```

This example declares d as a pointer to a double. I have not initialized d, but I can make it point to any variable of type double.

Initializing Pointers

You can initialize the contents of a pointer with a memory address through any of the following three techniques.

1. Use the *address operator*, &, which returns the memory address of an existing variable.
2. Allocate memory for an object using the new keyword.
3. Declare an array, whose identifier points to the first element in the array.

Later in this chapter, arrays are discussed in the "Arrays" section (page 18) and the new keyword is discussed in "The new Operator" section (page 12). The current section discusses the address operator, which you can use on any variable to determine its memory address. For example, the following statements create a pointer to a variable x.

```
long x = 10;
long * p = &x;
```

The variable p contains the address of the variable x. Figure 1.2 shows what the x and p look like in memory.

Figure 1.2 A pointer containing the memory address of a variable.

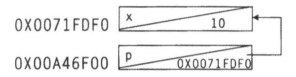

You can also create pointers to objects using the same notation. For example, the following statements create a pointer to a CFrameWnd object, a well-used MFC class.

```
CFrameWnd F;
CFrameWnd * pF = &F;
```

The object F is a large object, consuming hundreds of bytes of memory. However, in operating systems like Windows, the size of a pointer is 32 bits. (This is the size of memory addresses in Windows, which explains the term "32-bit operating system.") This technique makes pointers convenient when dealing with objects that consume large amounts of memory. Instead of copying or moving large objects in memory, you can use relatively small and efficient pointers.

Dereferencing Pointers

Viewing the contents of the object to which a pointer points is called *dereferencing* the pointer. Now that you have seen how to declare and initialize a pointer in the preceding section, I will discuss how to use the operator for dereferencing pointers, which is known as the *dereferencing operator.*

This topic raises an important difference between pointers and references. With a reference, you do not use any special operators or syntax, because the reference is simply an alias for a variable. However, with pointers, you need to make the distinction between when you want the contents of a pointer and when you want the contents of the object being pointed to.

The dereferencing operator in C++ is the asterisk (*), which you use by placing it directly in front of the pointer. The following program demonstrates how to deference a pointer to view and alter the object being pointed to. I use simple if statements and the equals operator (==) for illustration purposes. (I discuss the if statement in "The if Statement" section, page 22, and the equals operator in the "Boolean Expressions and Comparison Operators" section, page 21.)

```
#include <windows.h>

int main()
{
  long x = 10;//initialize x to 10
  long * p = &x;//initialize p to point to x

  if(*p == 10)
      MessageBox(NULL, "p points to a 10", "Success",
                  MB_OK | MB_ICONINFORMATION);
  if(p == &x)
      MessageBox(NULL, "Contents of p is the address of x",
                  "Success", MB_OK | MB_ICONINFORMATION);

  //change the value of x through p
  *p = 20;
  if(x == 20)
      MessageBox(NULL, "x is now 20", "Success",
                  MB_OK | MB_ICONINFORMATION);

  return 0;
}
```

In the accompanying code example, the variable p is initialized to point to x, which contains the value 20. As a result, all three of the if statements will evaluate to true. The following observations can be made:

- The variable p points to a variable whose contents are 10 (that is, *p == 10)
- The contents of p are the address of x (that is, p == &x)
- You can change x by dereferencing p (for example, *p = 20)

In other words, we can manipulate the contents of x without using the variable name x at all. All we need to know about x is its memory address, that is, a pointer to x.

The previous program uses a pointer to a primitive data type, a long. The section "Instantiating Objects" in Chapter 3 shows how to access members of an object using a pointer to the object.

Dynamic Memory

To dynamically allocate and free memory at runtime, C++ provides the new and delete operators, respectively. (I discuss each of these operators separately in the following two sections.)

Dynamic memory refers to the process of creating and freeing memory on the *free store* — a physical location in a computer's memory where programs store data.

C programmers are familiar with the `malloc` and `free` functions. However, these functions are not appropriate in C++ when allocating memory for objects. You will see the specific reasons why when I discuss constructors in Chapter 3, "Fundamentals of Object-Oriented Programming."

The new Operator

The `new` operator is a simple yet powerful technique for allocating memory in the free store. You do not need to know the exact amount of memory being allocated, just the data type or class name of the object you are creating.

The return value of `new` is the address on the heap of the allocated memory, so you need to use a pointer to keep track of this location. The following statements illustrate some of the uses of `new`.

```
double * p1 = new double;        //a new double object
CFrameWnd * p2 = new CFrameWnd;  //a new CFrameWnd object
int * p3 = new int[200];         //an array of 200 ints
```

You can dereference and use pointers created with the `new` operator just like any other pointers. Do not let these pointers go out of scope without freeing the memory, which we discuss in the next section.

Memory allocated on the free store that you do not specifically free will result in a *memory leak* — a common occurrence in C++ programs that use dynamic memory. The next section discusses how to free dynamic memory to avoid memory leaks.

The delete Operator

Every block of memory allocated on the free store with the `new` operator should have a corresponding `delete` operation to free the memory. The `delete` operator can be performed on any pointer to the dynamic memory. The following statements show how to free memory of the objects we created in the preceding section.

```
delete p1;    //free the memory of the double
delete p2;    //free the memory of the CFrameWnd object
delete [] p3; //free the memory of the 200 ints
```

Be careful when freeing memory allocated for an array using `new`. Notice how we used the square brackets when deleting p3. Without them, the result is undefined. For example, the statement

```
delete p3;//undefined!
```

will compile successfully. However, the most we would achieve by deleting just p3 is that the first `int` in the array would be freed. This would create a memory leak of 199 integers!

Note that deleting a pointer that has not been initialized causes a runtime error. Therefore, be sure when declaring a pointer to at least assign it the value NULL. This precaution allows you to delete the pointer, whether you allocated memory to it or not.

The const **Keyword**

C++ uses the const keyword as the mechanism to create constant variables — meaning the contents of the variable can not be altered. You can use the const keyword for variables and for pointers, as discussed in the following sections.

Constant Variables

To create a constant variable, simply precede the declaration with the const keyword and initialize the variable. For example, you might create a constant for the value of pi as follows:

```
const double pi = 3.14159;
```

You must initialize a constant variable, because its contents can not be altered later in the program. For example, the following statements cause a compiler error:

```
const double pi = 3.141;     //pi is a constant
pi = 3.14159;  //we decide to change it: doesn't compile!!
```

Constant Pointers

Using const when creating a pointer requires you to answer the following questions:
1. Do you want the pointer to be constant, meaning it cannot point to any other object, but be able to change the contents of what it points to?
2. Do you want the pointer to be able to point to anything, but not be able to alter the contents of the data it points to?
3. Do you want the pointer to have both of these features?

These are important questions, because the syntax is similar and you want to ensure the pointer you are creating has the correct capabilities.

In the first question, you want a pointer that cannot point to any other memory address. If this is the desired result, then the const keyword is placed directly after the *asterisk* in the declaration. The following statements create a constant pointer and try to reassign the pointer to another memory location.

```
int x,y;
int * const p = &x;      //a constant pointer
*p = 20;                 //Valid, x is now 20
p = &y;                  //Invalid! p can only point to x
```

If you read the declaration of p from right to left, it reads, "p is a constant pointer to an int." Because the pointer is constant, it must be initialized in its declaration.

The second question asks for a pointer that is not constant, but the data being pointed to is. In this situation, the const keyword is placed directly after the data type. For example, compare the following statements with the previous ones.

```
int x,y;
int const * p;          //a pointer to a constant int
p = &x;                 //Valid
*p = 20;                //Invalid! Causes a compiler error
p = &y;                 //Valid
```

Again, reading right to left in the declaration of p we see that "p is a pointer to a constant int." We can make p point to any int, but we cannot change the contents of the int by dereferencing p.

To obtain both of these features as in the third question, simply use the const keyword in both places. Because the pointer is constant, be sure to initialize the pointer in its declaration. For example, the following statement declares p as a "constant pointer to a constant int," reading right from left, and initializes it to point only to the variable x. The pointer p can only point to x, and it can not be dereferenced to the change the contents of x.

```
int const * const p = &x;
```

The Scope Resolution Operator

When declaring variables, a naming conflict can occur when the same name is used for both a local identifier and a global identifier. You can use the *scope resolution operator* (::) to specify the desired identifier.

Consider the following program, which creates a global variable named x and a local variable named x.

```
#include <windows.h>
int x = 0;    //a global variable
int main()
{
  int x = 20;      //a local variable with a name conflict

  x++;             //increments the local variable
  ::x++;           //increments the global variable
}
```

Within main(), the global variable x cannot be seen without using the scope resolution operator preceding the identifier x. This code is an example of the *unary scope resolution operator* — meaning it takes one argument. You will see an example of the binary scope resolution operator in the next section.

Namespaces

A *namespace* in C++ refers to a specific declarative region where variables, functions, and classes can be defined. Every identifier lies within a namespace, with C++ providing a global namespace for those identifiers not belonging to a specified namespace.

The unary scope resolution operator discussed in the preceding section can be used to distinguish between a local and global identifier with the same name. But what if the two identifiers with the same name come from different header files and you need to include *both* header files in your source code? The solution to this scenario is found in namespaces.

The syntax for creating a namespace is the keyword namespace followed by an identifier. Consider the following header file which contains a namespace called cars.

```
// Filename: vehicles.h
namespace cars      //a new namespace identified as "cars"
{
  double cost;        //a variable
  void driveCar();    //a function
} //end of "cars" namespace declarations
```

To use the variable cost or the function driveCar(), you need to include the vehicles.h header file and state which namespace you are using. You can use three techniques to refer to a variable or function that is defined within a namespace:

1. Precede the variable or function name with its namespace and the scope resolution operator.
2. Use the using keyword to declare which namespace you are using.
3. Use the using keyword to use specific variables or functions from a particular namespace.

The following program illustrates the syntax for the first two techniques.

```
// Filename: SomeProgram.cpp
#include "vehicles.h"

int main()
{
  cars::cost = 12000.00;  //from vehicles.h

  using namespace cars;
  driveCar();             //also from vehicles.h

  return 0;
}
```

You can also use the third technique for clarifying which identifier you are using. You can use the using keyword preceded by the desired identifier — demonstrated in the following program. The program contains a naming conflict with the variable cost.

```
// Filename:  AnotherProgram.cpp
#include "vehicles.h"
char cost;
int main()
{
  cost = 'A';      //changes the global variable from this file
  using cars::cost;
  cost = 15000.00;  //changes cost from vehicles.h
  ::cost = 'B';     //changes cost from this file


  return 0;
}
```

After you declare that you are using the cost variable from the cars namespace, any use of the identifier cost corresponds to the cost variable from vehicles.h. You can still access the global cost variable, but you must use the unary scope resolution operator as shown at the end of the program.

Structures

C++ allows you to create user-defined data types called structures. A *structure* is a collection of various data types wrapped into one entity. The data types a structure consists of are called *members*.

You use the struct keyword to create a structure. The syntax looks like the following:

```
struct NameOfStructure
{
  //members of the structure are listed here
};
```

Structures are useful when you need to store data that is more complex than the primitive data types. For example, suppose you need to need to write a program that uses calendar dates. You could use three ints to store their values, as the following statements illustrate.

```
int day = 24, month = 6, year = 2000;
```

This might work if you only had to represent one date in your program. However, suppose you needed to store the values of two dates. You would have to declare six integers, but there would be no correlation between them. For example, a given day would not know its corresponding month or year.

A better alternative would be to create a structure to represent a date. The integers for the day, month, and year would be the members of the structure. This structure would provide you with a new data type to represent dates, and the day, month, and year would be considered one entity instead of three separate integers. Your date structure might look like the following:

```
struct Date
{
  int day,
  int month,
  int year
};
```

This code defines a structure, but does not allocate memory for it at this time. You must instantiate the structure before any Date objects exist. To instantiate a structure, simply declare them in the same fashion as other variables.

```
Date today, newyears;
```

This declaration would create two Date objects in memory. The members of each object are accessed using the *dot operator.*

```
today.day = 11;
today.month = 5;
today.year = 1999;
newyears.day = newyears.month = 1;
newyears.year = 2000;
```

You can also instantiate a structure dynamically using the new operator and a pointer. The following statements create a Date object dynamically and initialize its member variables by dereferencing the pointer.

```
Date * p = new Date;
(*p).day =11;
(*p).month = 5;
(*p).year = 1999;
```

Note that parentheses are required to ensure the proper order of operations. We want to dereference the pointer first, and then access the members of the structure being pointed to by using the dot operator.

C++ provides a different syntax for accessing members of objects through a pointer, which is the *indirection operator* (->). The following statements illustrate how to use the -> operator with a pointer to a Date object.

```
Date * p = new Date;
p->day =11;        //equivalent to (*p).day
p->month = 5;      //equivalent to (*p).month
p->year = 1999;    //equivalent to (*p).year
```

Your choice of technique to access a member via a pointer is purely a matter of style.

Arrays

An *array* in C++ is a collection of elements of the same data type denoted by a single variable name. You distinguish the elements in the array by their *index* — an integer value that determines where they are located in the array. In the following sections, you will see how to declare arrays and access their contents.

Declaring Arrays

C++ uses square brackets to denote that a variable refers to an array of elements. For example, the following declaration creates an array of 80 variables of type double.

```
double grades[80];
```

When declaring arrays, you must declare the size of the array. That number must be a positive constant integer. In the preceding grades array, I used the constant literal 80. Often in programming, you would use a constant variable. For example, we could have created the grades array as follows.

```
const int size = 80;
double grades[size];
```

Note that using a constant integer instead of a literal value is a common technique in C++. Hard-coding the value 80 can create problems later on if we ever need to make grades a different size.

Index element numbering always begins at zero. So, the index of the first element in grades is 0 and the index of the last element is 79. The elements can be accessed using a literal or a variable, as shown in the following statements.

```
grades[0] = 97.5; //use a literal 0 to access an array element
int i = 1;
grades[i] = 72.0; //use a variable to access an array element
```

Array Bounds

As with any programming language, be careful not to go beyond the bounds of an array. The size of an array in C++ is fixed. So if you try to access an element that is beyond the array, the result is undefined. (An undefined result in C++ can be interpreted as, "our program will crash at the most inopportune time.")

A common programming error is to use the size of the array to access the last element in the array.

```
const int size = 80;
double grades[size];
grades[size] = 76.9;                //beyond the array bound
```

To achieve the intended effect in the preceding code, the correct syntax would assign the value of 76.9 to grades[size-1]. Be aware that the invalid code will compile; but at runtime, the program will perform an illegal operation and terminate.

Strings and Arrays of Characters

C programmers have become quite familiar with the concept of a string as an array of characters. The program shown in Figure 1.1 declared a string as an array of 9 characters.

```
char timeString[9];
```

The timeString array can hold a string of up to eight characters, because we always need room at the end of the string for the null character '\0' with which C terminates strings.

However, MFC has a better alternative to using arrays of characters: the CString class. This book emphasizes the use of the CString class, but you will find instances in which arrays of characters are required. For example, many C library functions, such as _strtime(), deal with strings in this fashion. The following sections discuss the creation and formatting of string arrays.

Creating Strings

An important detail of creating a string using an array of characters is to ensure room at the end of the array for a null character. Because they are arrays, the identifier of the string is really a pointer to the first character in the string. You initialize a string by simply assigning a literal value to the identifier.

```
char name[5] = "Rich";
char lastname[10] = "Raposa";
```

The size of the array can be larger than the string, as we see in the lastname identifier. The seventh element in lastname is the null character, and the remaining three characters of the array will contain garbage.

Formatting Strings

Many C library functions manipulate strings as arrays of characters. These functions are not of interest to an MFC programmer, because the CString class contains all of the functions you need for using strings. However, one function that is useful for formatting strings is sprintf. The syntax for the function is unique; but it is used in the CString class, so I will discuss it now.

The sprintf function is found in stdio.h. It formats a literal string and stores the result into an array of characters (often referred to as a *buffer*). The first argument to sprintf is the buffer, which must be an array large enough to contain the string plus the null character at the end.

The second argument is the string in a format notation containing a combination of literal characters and format symbols. The format symbols are preceded by a percent symbol (%), and each symbol represents a particular data type. The remaining arguments to sprintf depend on the number of format symbols used. Each symbol requires a variable of the specified data type. For example, the following program formats a double, which requires the %f format symbol.

```
#include <stdio.h>
#include <windows.h>

int main()
{
  double p = 3.14159;
  char buffer[40];
  sprintf(buffer, "The value %f is referred to as pi", p);
  MessageBox(NULL, buffer, "A formatted string", MB_OK);

  return 0;
}
```

You can place as many variables as you like when formatting a string simply by using the variable's corresponding format symbol. Table 1.5 shows the symbols and the data types they represent.

Table 1.5 Format symbols for the sprintf function.

Format Symbol	Data Type
d	signed integer
u	unsigned integer
f	double
e or E	double in scientific notation (prints "e" or "E")
x or X	unsigned hexadecimal (uses "abcdef" or "ABCDEF")

The f, e, and E symbols in Table 1.5 also allow optional values for width and precision in the format %width.precision. The width includes a decimal and E, and the precision is the number of digits past the decimal to display. The following statements format a string using several double variables. The message box is shown in Figure 1.3.

```
double pi = 3.14159, exp = 2.719, sci = -4.72E21;
char s[40];  //a buffer for the formatted string
sprintf(s, "pi = %4.2f and exp = %9.4f and sci = %7.2E",
      pi, exp, sci);
MessageBox(NULL,s,"A few doubles", MB_OK);
```

Figure 1.3   Formatting numeric values in a string.

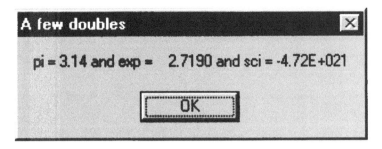

Boolean Expressions and Comparison Operators

A *Boolean expression* is an expression that evaluates to true or false. A common occurrence in programming is the need to compare two values and make a decision depending on the outcome. C++ provides comparison operators for comparing similar data types. Comparing two items is an example of a Boolean expression because the result of all the comparison operators is either true or false.

Table 1.6 shows the syntax for the comparison operators.

Table 1.6   C++ comparison operators.

Operator	Comparison
==	equal to
!=	not equal to
<	less than
<=	less than or equal to
>	greater than
>=	greater than or equal to

Another common task in programming is the need to make a decision based on more than one criteria. For example, you might ask a user of a program to input a number between one and ten. Your program would have to verify that the value was greater than 0 "and" less than or equal to 10. You would use the "and" operator (&&) in C++ to validate the user's input.

```
(x > 0) && (x <= 10)
```

There are two other Boolean operators in C++: the "or" and "not" operators. Table 1.7 shows the syntax.

Table 1.7 C++ Boolean operators.

Operator	Logical Expression
&&	and
||	or
!	not

The Boolean operators short-circuit when appropriate. For example, the second comparison in the following code will not be performed if the first comparison is false. A similar result occurs when using the || operator and when the first expression is true.

```
if(grade >= 80 && grade < 90)
{
    MessageBox(NULL,"You got a B!", "Your grade", MB_OK);
}
```

If the value of the grade in the preceding code segment is not greater than or equal to 80, then grade is not checked for less than 90 because it is a waste of program execution.

Control Structures

Every programming language has a mechanism for making decisions and repeating tasks using loops. C++ offers two techniques for making decisions: the if statement and the switch statement. The looping control structures include for, while, and do/while loops. The following sections discuss the syntax for each of these control structures.

The if Statement

Using if and else statements is the most common and versatile technique for making decisions. The syntax for an if/else statement looks like

```
if (Boolean expression)
{
  //do something when the result is true
}
else
{
  //do something when the result is false
}
```

A Boolean expression can either be some type of comparison or an integer value. If the Boolean expression is false (or zero), the statements in the if block are skipped and the else block executes. Otherwise, the if block executes and the else block is skipped.

The else block is optional, or the else statement can be followed by another if, as the following example illustrates.

```
char lettergrade;
if( grade >= 90)
        lettergrade = 'A';
else if (grade >= 80)
        lettergrade = 'B';
else if (grade >= 60)
        lettergrade = 'C';
else
        lettergrade = 'F';
```

Note that the curly braces can be omitted in the block of code following an if or else when there is only one statement to execute within that block, as the preceding code demonstrates.

The switch **Statement**

A switch statement is like a specialized if expression, in which each comparison is an "equal to" comparison. Switch statements can make your code more efficient and readable.

A switch statement consists of various case statements, as well as an optional default case. The switch variable is compared to each of the case statements. If the two values are equal, the code after the case executes until a break statement occurs.

Each case must be a literal value, and the switch variable must be convertible to an int. The syntax for a switch statement looks like the following:

```
switch(an integer value)
{
  case literal:
        //do something
        break;
  case literal:
      //do something
      break;

  //include as many cases as necessary

  default:   //optional
        //do something if all cases are false
}
```

For example, suppose you want to display a message to a student commenting on his or her grade in a class. The following switch statement compares the character grade to 'A' through 'F' and determines the message and a message box icon for each case.

```cpp
char grade = StudentGrade(); //function that returns a grade
char comment[20];
int icon;
switch(grade)
{
case 'A':
case 'B':
  comment = "Excellent!";
  icon = MB_ICONEXCLAMATION;
  break;
case 'C':
  comment = "Nice job!";
  icon = MB_ICONEXCLAMATION;
  break;
case 'D':
case 'F':
  comment = "See you next year!";
  icon = MB_ICONQUESTION;
  break;
default :
  comment = "Error: Invalid grade";
  icon = MB_ICONSTOP;
}
MessageBox(NULL,comment,"switch demo",MB_OK | icon);
```

Note when grade equals an A, the comment will be "Excellent," although grade does not equal a B. This is an example of what is called *fall through* in a switch statement. Remember, after a case is true, all statements execute until a break occurs.

The default case is always optional and does not require a break. If no default statement is present and no case statements evaluate to true, the switch statement results in no action.

The while **Loop**

The most versatile looping mechanism in C++ is the while loop. In fact, a while loop can be used in lieu of any other loops in C++. The syntax for a while loop includes a Boolean expression, and the body of the while loop repeats until the Boolean becomes false.

```
while(Boolean expression)
{
  //body of the while loop goes here
}
```

The Boolean expression is checked initially and after each iteration, so it is possible to write a while loop that never executes. It is also possibly to write an infinite while loop — either inadvertently or for programs that need to execute indefinitely. For example, the following while loop executes 100 times and computes the sum of the first 100 numbers.

```
int x = 1;
int sum = 0;

while (x <= 100)
{
      sum += x;

      x++;
}
```

The following while loop is an infinite loop, perhaps a mistake by the programmer who forgot to increment the value of x within the body of the while loop:

```
int x = 1;
int sum = 0;

while(x <= 100)
      sum += x;
```

As with the if statement, when the body of the while loop is only one statement, then the curly braces are not required. (Curly braces are permitted in such instances, however, and can often make your code more readable.)

The do/while **Loop**

The only difference between a while loop and a do/while loop is that a do/while is guaranteed to execute at least once. The Boolean expression appears at the end of the body of the loop, so one iteration occurs before the Boolean expression is evaluated.

Here is the syntax for a do/while loop. The curly braces are required only if a loop contains more than one statement. Note the semicolon at the end of the while statement.

```
do
{
    //body of the loop
} while(Boolean expression);
```

Certain algorithms can take advantage of the fact that do/while loops execute at least once. For example, the following loop simulates the rolling of two dice. Assume the random() function returns an integer between 1 and 6.

```
int die1 = random();
int die2;


do
{


    die2 = random();
}while(die1 != die2);
```

The first die is rolled, then the second is rolled until it matches the first die. Because the second die must be rolled at least once, this situation is a perfect opportunity to use a do/while loop. The loop executes an indefinite number of times, but it is guaranteed to execute at least once.

The for Loop

A for loop works well for situations where you know exactly how many times you want to repeat a task. A while loop could be used in these situations, with a loop counter incremented at each iteration. But a for loop is easier to implement and makes code more readable.

The syntax for a for loop includes three statements: an initialization, a Boolean expression, and an update step.

```
for( initialization; Boolean expression; update)
{
    //body of the for loop
}
```

Any of these three statements can be left out by simply leaving it blank, but you must include its semicolon. (At a minimum, a for loop contains two semicolons within the parentheses.) The initialization step occurs first, then the Boolean expression is checked. If the expression is true, the body of the loop executes. After each iteration, control of the program goes to the update step. Then the Boolean expression is checked, and the iterations continue until the expression becomes false (or zero).

The following program uses a for loop to compute the balance of a bank account after a year of compound interest. A message box displays the balance after each month.

```c
#include <windows.h>
#include <math.h>//for the pow() function
#include <stdio.h>

int main()
{
   double principal = 1000.00;//initial balance
   double rate = 0.07;//interest rate
   double balance;//account balance
   int compound = 12;//compounded monthly
   for(int month = 1; month <= 12; month++)
   {
        //compute the new balance
        balance=principal*pow(1+rate/compound,month);

        //display balance after each month
        char buffer[40];
        sprintf(buffer,"Balance = %8.2f after month %d",
                balance, month);
        MessageBox(NULL,buffer,"New balance", MB_OK);
   }

   return 0;
}
```

The for loop in the preceding example executes 12 times, which generates 12 message boxes. The final balance is shown in Figure 1.4.

Figure 1.4   The result of one year's compound interest using a for **loop.**

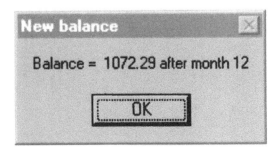

Functions

The most important feature of a procedural programming language is the ability to modularize code into functions or procedures. Though object-oriented programming takes a different approach to solving problems than procedural programming, as we will see in Chapter 3, functions still play a key role. Functions are the foundation of C++, and it is important to understand how to write them and transfer information back and forth between them.

This section will discuss the two steps involved in writing functions: the prototype and the implementation. Once we see how to write a function, much of the remainder of this chapter will focus on passing data to a function using arguments and parameters, and returning a value from a function.

Function Prototypes

To use a function in a program, the compiler needs to know several details about the function. The function needs a name, of course. The compiler also needs to know what type of information gets passed into the function, as well as the data type of any value that the function returns to the function that called it. All of this information is found in the declaration of the function, known as the *function prototype* (sometimes called the *function signature*.)

In C++, you should prototype the function *before* you invoke the function. Otherwise, the compiler will complain about an undefined function. Also, you want functions to be as reusable as possible — perhaps to use them in other source files.

To facilitate these needs, C++ uses the concept of a header file. *Header files* are saved in the *.h format, and contain function prototypes as well as other declarations (including classes). Header files are not compiled because they typically do not contain any statements. Instead, they are included in the source files that need them.

A function prototype in a header file has the following format:

```
qualifiers return_value NameOfFunction( parameter list);
```

The *qualifiers* are optional and are often not needed. The *return value* is the data type of the value (if any) that is returned by the function. A function can return only one value and the data type generally must be included in the prototype. (C++ provides a default return data type of int if a return data type is not specifically provided.) The keyword void denotes a function with no return value.

The name of a function can be any valid identifier. (The rules for creating a valid identifier are discussed in the "C++ Keywords and Identifiers" section beginning on page 5.) The parameter list is a comma-separated list, which determines the number of arguments passed to the function as well as their data types. The semicolon at the end of the declaration tells the compiler that this is a function prototype, not the actual implementation of the function.

Consider the following example of function prototypes in a header file named MyFunctions.h.

```
//Filename: MyFunctions.h


double ComputePay(double, double);
void ErrorMessage(CString);
long Factorial(int);
DoSomething();
```

You can tell from a function's prototype exactly what another function needs to pass to the function, and what the calling function receives in return. The ComputePay() function accepts two doubles and returns a double. The ErrorMessage() function accepts a CString object and returns nothing. Factorial() requires an int and returns a long. DoSomething() requires no arguments and returns an int, because no return data type is specified.

Implementing Functions

You place function definitions in an implementation file with a cpp or cxx extension. The header file containing the function's prototype is included at the beginning of the implementation file. After the functions are defined, the implementation file can then be compiled into object (machine language) code, which creates an *.obj file with the same name as the *.cpp file.

A function's definition needs to contain its prototype. The following code shows the implementation file for the functions prototyped in the MyFunctions.h file listed in the preceding section.

```
//Filename:  MyFunctions.cpp
//Description:  Implementation file for functions
//             prototyped in MyFunctions.h


#include "MyFunctions.h"


double ComputePay(double hours, double rate)
{
   double pay = hours * rate;
   return pay;
}


void ErrorMessage(CString message)
{
   MessageBox(NULL, message, "Error", MB_OK | MB_ICONWARNING);
}
```

```
long Factorial(int n)
{
  long result = 1;
  for(int j = 1; j <= n; j++)
      result = result * j;
  return result;
}


DoSomething()
{
  //do whatever
  return 1;  //the default return type is int
}
```

Note that C++ does not require that you prototype a function in a separate header file. You can place prototypes at the top of an implementation file and place definitions later in the same file. In fact, functions are not required to have a prototype at all. However, when not using a prototype for a function, you need to ensure that the function's implementation appears before any invoking of the function. For this reason, prototyping functions in a header file is the preferred technique.

NOTE: A common programming error is to prototype a function, but in defining the function, not matching its definition with its prototype. Perhaps you spelled something differently or forgot a parameter. The compiler does not complain, because it thinks you are simply defining a new function that does not have a prototype. However, a link error results when the program is built into an executable. The compiler only needs to know a function's prototype, while the linker needs to find the actual implementation in an object file. Not finding the implementation is the cause of one of the most common link errors.

Passing Arguments to Functions

A *parameter* is a variable within the scope of the function that receives the data passed to it. In this section, we will discuss how to pass data into parameters. The data passed into a parameter is called an *argument*. Passing arguments to parameters is an important capability of functions, because often the data passed to a function is outside the function's scope or varies each time the function is invoked.

Generally, C++ provides two techniques for passing data to a function: call by value and call by reference. A third technique is a special case of call by value, wherein the argument is a pointer. Each technique has its own benefits and drawbacks, so it is important to understand the differences among them. I discuss each of these techniques in the sections that follow.

Call by Value

Call by value is the simplest technique to implement to pass data to a function, because it involves no special syntax. When an argument is passed by value, the corresponding parameter receives a copy of the data. There is security involved in passing a copy of the data under this technique, because the function can not alter the original data.

Call by value is denoted simply by listing a parameter with its data type. For example, the following Factorial() function has one parameter that uses call by value.

```
long Factorial(int n)
{
   long result = 1;
   for(int j = 1; j <= n; j++)
       result = result * j;
   return result;
}
```

Consider the following function call to Factorial():

```
int x = 10;
Factorial(x);
```

A copy of the variable x is passed to the n parameter of the Factorial() function. Even if n is changed by Factorial(), the value of x in the calling function does not change.

The security of not having to worry about a function inadvertently altering your data involves a certain amount of overhead. If the data passed to the receiving function consumes a large amount of memory, then making a copy of the data is inefficient. Call by value is ideal for small data types; but for larger objects, you probably should use call by reference, which I discuss in the next section.

Call by Reference

The call by value techniques create a copy of a calling function's arguments. By contrast, *call by reference* uses a reference parameter, which means the parameter becomes a reference to the argument. A *reference* is simply an alias for another variable. So if you alter the reference, you alter the original data passed to the function as well.

This technique has many advantages over call by value. Suppose you want a function to actually change the argument that it receives, or suppose the data is large and you do not want the memory overhead of copying it. In either case, using a reference may meet your needs.

The syntax for call by reference is similar to declaring a variable. The parameter's identifier is preceded by an ampersand (&). For example, the following function uses call by reference to change the value of its argument.

```
void ChangeValue(double &d)
{
  d = 1.234;
}
```

When the function is called, whatever double is passed in will be changed to the value 1.234, as in the following statements:

```
double w;
ChangeValue(w);//w becomes 1.234
```

Notice that the function is invoked with the same syntax as through the call by value technique. However, in this example, the parameter d becomes a reference to w so, when the called function changes d, w changes, too.

A key advantage to call by reference is its limited overhead, which is especially important when you pass large objects between functions. However, the lack of security of call by reference might be unacceptable with critical data, because the called function may modify that data.

If a function does not need to alter its argument, then the security of call by value can be accomplished with call by reference by using the const keyword. The const keyword appears in front of the parameter's data type, and the result is a constant reference that cannot be reassigned to a new value.

The following function has two constant reference parameters, hours and rate. Any attempt to alter hours or rate within ComputePay() would generate a compiler error.

```
double ComputePay(const double & hours, const double & rate)
{
  return hours * rate;
}
```

No special syntax is needed to invoke a method with a const parameter. In the following example, the function passes a literal and a variable.

```
double wage = 6.50;
double pay = ComputePay(40, wage);
```

The parameter hours will be 40, and the parameter rate will be a constant reference to the variable wage. In this case, the hours parameter is 40 and the rate parameter is a constant reference to the wage variable.

You can pass in a literal to a reference parameter [such as 40 in the call to ComputePay() in the example in the main text] only if the parameter is constant. In this example, if the hours parameter was not declared as const, then the compiler would generate an error when we attempted to pass 40 as an argument. For this reason, it is important to use the const keyword whenever possible in call by reference, especially if the function does not intend to alter the parameter's content.

Passing Pointers by Value

You have seen how using a reference parameter can avoid the overhead of copying large amounts of data that occurs when using call by value. Another common technique is to pass a pointer to the data.

The pointer can be passed as a call by value or call by reference. If you need to make the pointer point to a different memory location, you can use call by reference. If you want the function to be able to change the data being pointed to, then you can pass the pointer by value.

You use an asterisk for declaring a parameter that is a pointer — just like when declaring a pointer. (See the "Pointers" section, page 9.) The following function has a parameter that is a pointer to a Date object (assuming Date is a structure or class).

```
void InitializeDate(Date *, int, int, int);
```

When invoking InitializeDate(), we need to pass one of the following:

- an existing pointer to a Date object, or
- the address of a Date object.

For example, the following statements invoke InitializeDate() and demonstrate both of these techniques.

```
Date d;
Date * p = &d;
InitializeDate(p,1,1,2000);    //pass an existing pointer
InitializeDate(&d,1,1,2000);   //pass a Date object address
```

In both of the above cases, the parameter of InitializeDate() points to the Date object d. The implementation might look like the following. Notice the use of the indirection operator (->) to access the members of the Date object. (The indirection operator is discussed in the "Structures" section, page 16.)

```
void InitializeDate(Date * pdate, int d, int m, int y)
{
  pdate->day = d;
  pdate->month = m;
  pdate->year = y;
}
```

Notice that the function InitializeDate() can change the contents of the Date object pointed to by pdate, which may or may not be a desired possibility. However, because I used call by value to pass in the pointer p, InitializeDate() can not make p point to a different Date object. The next section shows how to pass a pointer with the added security of not allowing the function to alter the contents of the passed data.

As with call by reference, you can use the const keyword to denote a constant pointer parameter, much like for the constant reference parameters discussed in the "Call by Reference" section on page 31. For example, suppose you want a function to display a Date object in a message box. This function would not need to change the contents of the Date object, and in fact, probably should not be able to do so. The following prototype shows how to implement this objective.

```
void DisplayDate(Date const *);
```

You still need to pass in either a pointer or a memory address of a Date object. However, DisplayDate() can only view the contents of the Date object passed in to it, not alter that object.

Passing Arrays

When a function requires an array as a parameter, passing a copy of the array's data would be extremely inefficient. C++ does not even allow you to do so. When passing an array to a function, you must pass the memory address of the first element in the array.

The syntax for an array parameter is the data type and brackets ([]). Here is the prototype of a function that computes the average of an array of integers, which is passed in as a parameter.

```
double Average(int [], int);
```

The implementation might look like:

```
double Average(int values[], int numberOfElements)
{
    double sum = 0.0;
    for(int j = 0; j < numberOfElements; j++)
        sum += values[j];
    double average = sum/(double) numberOfElements;
    return average;
}
```

When invoking the Average() method, you simply pass the identifier for the array as the first argument.

```
int grades [] = {67, 84, 100, 92, 76};
double percent = Average(grades, 5);
```

The variable grades is essentially a pointer to the first element in its array, which is what you could pass to values in the Average function. The Average() function can now access and alter the contents of the array using the values parameter.

If you do not want the Average() function to be able to alter the data provided by the calling function, you could use the const keyword.

```
double Average(const int []);
```

Returning Values .

You return values in the same manner as parameters, either by value or by reference. When using return by value, a function returns a copy of the object. Similarly, return by reference returns a reference to an object. The next two sections discuss these two techniques.

Return by Value

The syntax for return by value is to simply state the data type of the return value. For example, the following function returns a copy of a long. The return value is a copy of the value of result.

```
long Factorial(int n)
{
  long result = 1;
  for(int j = 1; j <= n; j++)
        result = result * j;
  return result;
}
```

Returning a copy is simple to code and implement. It is also a safe technique to use, considering that returning a reference is not always feasible, as we will see in the next section.

Return by Reference

The syntax for returning by reference is to declare the return item using an ampersand (&), just like when declaring reference variables. Consider the following function prototype:

```
const CString& operator=(const CString& source);
```

This function is invoked when as assignment of two CString objects occurs. The returned value is a reference to a CString object. In particular, operator= simply returns source. This technique is common and allows you to chain assignments together like in the following statements.

```
CString a, b, c = "Hello";
a = b = c;    //calls operator= function twice
```

The first time I invoke the operator= is when b is assigned to c. The CString c is the argument to operator=, and the parameter source becomes a reference to c. The string "Hello" is copied to b and then source is returned. This reference is then used to initialize a when I invoke operator= a second time to also assign a to "Hello".

Default Arguments

Functions in C++ can contain default arguments. A *default argument* lets you invoke a function without passing an argument for each parameter. Instead, these optional arguments default to a specified value, which is declared in the function's prototype.

A function can have any of its arguments default, *as long as the parameters that do not have default arguments appear first in the prototype.* To demonstrate, consider the following prototype.

```
void ErrorMessage(char [], int = MB_ICONWARNING);
```

When implementing a function with default arguments, you do not repeat their default values. You only need to specify the default values in the function's prototype. The ErrorMessage() function might be defined as follows.

```
void ErrorMessage(char message[], int icon)
{
    MessageBox(NULL, message, "Error", MB_OK | icon);
}
```

You can invoke ErrorMessage() by passing a string and an int. However, you can also invoke the function by just passing a string, in which case the second parameter would default to MB_ICONWARNING. Consider the following two examples.

```
ErrorMessage("Something went wrong", MB_ICONSTOP);
ErrorMessage("Something else went wrong");
```

In the first call to ErrorMessage(), the icon is MB_ICONSTOP. In the second call, the icon defaults to MB_ICONWARNING.

Function Overloading

C++ allows functions to be *overloaded,* meaning you can create several functions that have the same name. What makes them distinct is their parameter lists, which must be different for each of the similarly-named functions.

For example, the following prototypes declare a Display() function that is overloaded with different parameters.

```
void Display(char []);
void Display(double);
void Display(char [], double);
```

When invoking the Display() function, the compiler can determine which overloaded function you want by the arguments passed to it. The following statements invoke the various Display() functions.

```
char s [6] = "Hello";
Display(s);         //invokes Display(char [])
double d = 3.14;    //invokes Display(double)
Display(d);         //invokes Display(double)
Display(s,d);       //invokes Display(char [],double)
```

You need to be aware of several rules when overloading functions. First, changing only the return value is not enough to overload a function, because the compiler will not have enough information to determine which function to invoke. The following statements cause a compiler error.

```
void Display(double);
bool Display(double);   //invalid overloading!
```

However, all overloaded functions do not need to return the same data type. For example, the following is legitimate function overloading.

```
void Display(double);
bool Display(char []); //valid, the parameter is different
```

In addition, be careful when using overloading with default parameters. Using default parameters is similar to overloading a function, because it allows a program to call the function in various ways. Always make sure that an overloaded function has something distinct to distinguish it from the other functions that share the same name. For example, the following statements are invalid.

```
void Display(char []);
void Display(char [], double = 3.14);   //error!
```

Either of these functions can be invoked by passing only a string. (In the case of the second Display() function, the parameter that is a double will default to 3.14.) If we called Display() and passed only a string, how can the compiler determine which Display() function we want to invoke? It can't, which is why a compiler error is generated. To solve this problem, you should either use one Display() function, or not have the double parameter default to a value in the second Display() function.

Inline Functions

C++ implements the concept of an *inline function*. A function declared using the inline keyword tells the compiler to replace each function call with the actual code of the function.

This technique can be useful for very small functions (one or two statements) that a program invokes regularly. Instead of having the overhead of a function call, the compiler simply replaces each function call in your program with the actual statements of the function. The program executes faster.

However, the side effect of inline functions is that they increase the size of the executable file. This is strictly a design issue, and you should determine whether or not to use inline functions on a case-by-case basis.

You use the inline keyword to make a function inline. For example, the following inline function computes the average of two integers.

```
inline double Average(int a, int b)
{
   return (a+b)/2.0;
}
```

NOTE: Not all functions can or should be inlined. If a function is more than two or three statements, it is typically too long for inlining. If a function is recursive or virtual, it cannot be inlined. In other, unique circumstances, a compiler can not inline a particular function, even if you use the `inline` specifier. The bottom line is, the compiler can determine not to inline a function, even if you use the inline specifier. Think of "inline" as a *suggestion* to the compiler that you would like the function to be inlined if it is feasible and beneficial to the program.

Chapter 2

Visual Studio

Visual Studio is an Integrated Development Environment (IDE) for writing and developing Windows applications. It allows developers to create applications with different languages, but with the convenience of a common interface. Some of the tools incorporated in Visual Studio include Visual C++, Visual Basic, Visual J++, and Visual InterDev. I will focus on using Visual C++, but many of the features of Visual Studio are identical for all these tools.

Some of the basic features of Visual Studio include:

- A Text Editor that is integrated with the compiler and debugger. Among other things, the Text Editor has the capability to jump right to a compiler error or follow the debugger line-by-line through the source code.
- The ability to navigate quickly through source files, classes, and functions.
- A built-in Resource Editor with a WYSIWYG environment for creating menus, toolbars, dialog boxes, and other resources.

MFC programs consist of many files which would be difficult to manage without an IDE like Visual Studio. Even more difficult would be trying to create a make file for compiling and building an executable from all the different files. Visual Studio simplifies these tasks by providing a simple GUI interface for navigating through source files and changing project settings. No make file is required in Visual C++, although one can be generated if desired.

I focus on MFC applications, but Visual Studio can be used to create a variety of different Windows applications and libraries. Dynamic link libraries (DLLs), ATL/COM objects,

ActiveX controls, and even non-Windows applications can be created in Visual C++ using Visual Studio.

A *complete* discussion on Visual Studio would be a whole other book, so I limit the discussion in this chapter to those topics important to developing MFC applications, such as:

- The Visual Studio Environment
- Projects and Workspaces
- AppWizard and ClassWizard
- The Resource Editor

In addition, resources and AppWizard are covered in further detail in Chapter 7 and Chapter 10, respectively. The present chapter gets you up and running in Visual Studio so you can experiment with the examples used in Chapter 1 and Chapter 3. More importantly, because the programs in those chapters are console applications that do not use MFC, the section "Creating a Console Application" (page 48) shows how to create a proper project for a non-MFC program.

The Visual Studio Environment

Visual Studio consists of essentially three windows:

1. The Text Editor window.
2. The Workspace window.
3. The Output window.

The Text Editor typically displays all the time, while the Workspace and Output windows can be toggled on and off easily. Figure 2.1 shows the default layout of Visual Studio. Use the corresponding toolbar buttons to display or hide the Workspace and Output windows, or you can also use the View menu item.

Figure 2.1   Visual Studio with the Workspace window on the left, the Editor on the right, and the Output window on the bottom.

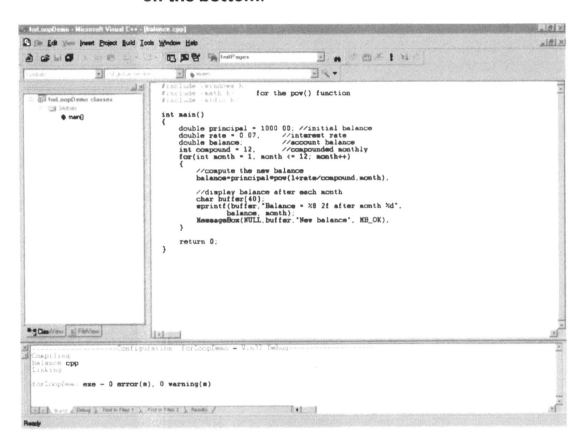

The Text Editor

Source code is displayed and edited in the Text Editor window. C++ keywords and comments are color coded, and the editor has some nice features such as automatically indenting statements within curly braces.

Other features of the Text Editor include the capability to list a function's parameters automatically after you enter the function's name. In addition, the Text Editor displays an object's methods and attributes in a pop-up window after you enter the variable's name — a great feature for saving compile errors and for determining what an object does. Some of these features might seem intrusive at first; but after time, you will find yourself relying on them.

The Workspace Window

Being able to quickly jump to specific source files or lines of code is an important capability of any IDE. The Workspace window provides this capability by displaying the Workspace in three separate views:

1. ClassView
2. ResourceView
3. FileView

The Workspace window in Figure 2.2 shows the ClassView of the currently opened workspace. ClassView contains a tree that displays the classes and global items in each project in the workspace. You can expand each class to display its member variables and methods, and double-clicking on an item takes you directly to its corresponding location in the source code. For other features, try right-clicking an entry in the tree to display a pop-up menu of choices.

Figure 2.2   ClassView with the tree expanded to display the classes and global items of the project.

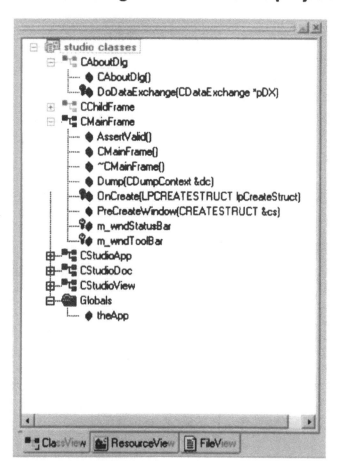

Figure 2.3 shows an example of the ResourceView. You use ResourceView to display and navigate through the various resources of the workspace. One of the most useful aspects of Visual C++ is the Resource Editor, which allows for the creation of resources in a WYSIWYG environment. I discuss the Resource Editor throughout the book, because you can use it in many situations.

NOTE: The ResourceView is only displayed in projects that contain resources.

Figure 2.3 **ResourceView with the tree expanded to display all of the resources of the project.**

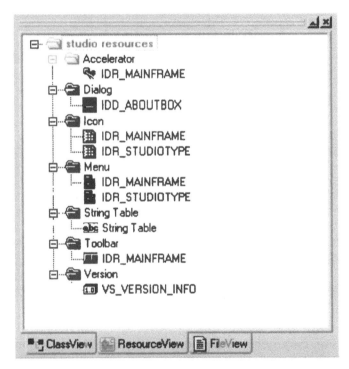

FileView is a view of the workspace in terms of the source files, header files, and other files. Figure 2.4 shows a FileView window. As with the other workspace windows, double-clicking an item in the tree opens the file in the Text Editor window. You can remove files from a project by highlighting them and pressing the Delete key.

Figure 2.4 FileView with the tree expanded to display the files of the project.

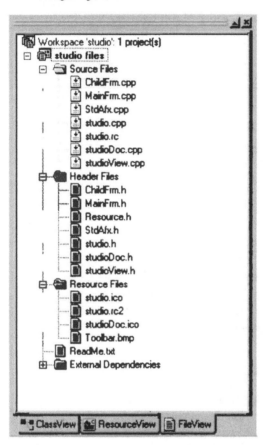

Projects and Workspaces

Visual Studio uses the concept of a project to keep track of the various source files, header files, and resources of an application. A project is created for each Windows executable or DLL, and all the project files are placed in the same folders. The settings of a project are kept in a dsp file. (Earlier versions of Visual Studio were known as Developer Studio; dsp stands for "developer studio project.")

Figure 2.5   The various projects Visual Studio supports.

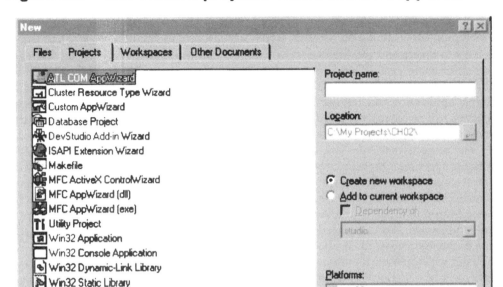

Make files are a common occurrence, and a common headache, in application development. Visual Studio does not use a make file for a project, although Visual Studio can export a make file. The project settings in the dsp file keep track of the make file information for you, and property sheets are used to easily edit the compile and link settings.

When developing a Windows application, you begin by creating a project for the type of application you need. For example, if you were writing an MFC program, you would create an MFC project that has all the required settings for using MFC. If you were developing an ActiveX control, you would create an ActiveX project with all the appropriate settings for building ActiveX controls. Most of the time, you do not need to worry about the details of the project file, as long as you know what type of project you need. You generate projects using AppWizard, a tool that comes with Visual C++ and that is discussed in the next section.

You can think of a *workspace* in Visual Studio as a container to house your projects. You might be developing a program that consists of an executable and several DLLs. Each of these components requires its own project, but these related projects can be combined into one workspace. This concept allows for easier development and debugging of a large application.

Visual Studio saves workspaces in a dsw file. These dsw files are the files that Visual Studio opens and closes, and AppWizard creates them just like project files. You can easily add or remove projects from a workspace. A new project is added by selecting File/New... and choosing the type of project you want. An existing project can be added by selecting Project/Insert Project into Workspace. To remove a project from a workspace, highlight the project in ClassView or FileView and press the Delete key.

AppWizard and ClassWizard

AppWizard and ClassWizard are built-in features of Visual Studio that make the process of developing MFC applications easier. AppWizard is used to create a project, and ClassWizard is used to create and modify classes within your project. Perhaps one of the strongest arguments for using Visual C++ as opposed to other IDEs to create MFC applications is the availability of AppWizard and ClassWizard. MFC applications are not trivial to write, and even a simple application can require hundreds of lines of code in several source files. AppWizard relieves you of having to recreate large chunks of code by generating as much of the source code as it can each time you start a new project.

The projects that AppWizard generates are a foundation to build from, but they actually compile and run. (Of course, they are not very exciting programs, but they are Windows programs nonetheless!) Think of AppWizard as the contractor that lays the foundation and framework for your new house. All you have to do is go in and paint the walls and lay down some carpet. In other words, AppWizard does a lot for you, but you still have some work to do on your own. You also need to understand the code that AppWizard generates for you — one of the main goals of this book.

I discuss AppWizard in more detail in Chapter 10, "MFC AppWizard", as well as in a discussion in the section "Creating a Console Application" (page 48), which explains how to create a project for developing console applications. But if you want to experiment with the AppWizard now, select File/New from the Visual C++ menu bar. A dialog appears displaying the various AppWizard projects available from your particular version of Visual C++.

Not all versions of Visual C++ are created equal. Visual C++ 6.0 is available in three editions: Standard, Professional, and Enterprise. The various projects available from AppWizard vary substantially among editions. As you might expect, the Enterprise Edition contains the most functionality, while the Standard Edition has limited resources. The Professional Edition fits nicely between these two extremes. Figure 2.5 shows the projects that AppWizard can create in the Professional Edition.

ClassWizard is another powerful feature of Visual C++. It also generates code for our MFC applications, particularly in terms of message handling. GUI programming and message handling are inseparable, and ClassWizard provides an easy-to-use interface for linking messages with functions and generating the stubs for these functions in the appropriate source files.

Figure 2.6 shows the ClassWizard, which can be run by selecting View/ClassWizard or by pressing Ctrl+W on the keyboard. You will see how to use ClassWizard throughout Chapters 6–8 which cover the MFC Graphical User Interface controls and windows.

Figure 2.6   MFC ClassWizard.

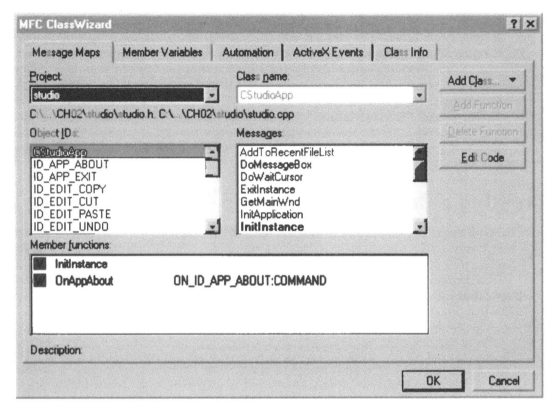

The Resource Editor

Windows programs contain many different types of resources. Because resources are so frequently used in Visual C++, the product ships with a powerful tool called the Resource Editor for creating and editing them. The following is a list of the resources available for a Windows application.

- Dialog windows and property sheet pages
- Menus
- Toolbars
- Icons and other bitmaps
- A version resource for keeping track of versioning
- Cursors
- A table of accelerator keys
- A string table, so strings do not need to be hard-coded into an application

You use the Resource Editor to create all of these resources in a powerful, easy-to-use WYSIWYG environment. You can create resources by hand, but only with much more effort and time.

Resources are defined in a text file with an rc extension, which can be viewed in the Text Editor as well as the Resource Editor. However, because Visual C++ creates the resource file for you and the Resource Editor is simple to use, you rarely need to edit a resource file manually. You will notice when building your projects that the resource file is compiled just like any other source file.

Earlier in the "The Workspace Window" section (page 42), you saw how to view a project's resources using the ResourceView pane of the Workspace window. Double-clicking an item in ResourceView opens the resource in the Resource Editor. I discuss the Resource Editor in detail in Chapter 7, "Windows Resources."

Creating a Console Application

The C++ programs presented in Chapter 1 were not MFC applications and did not use a window. Instead, a C++ application is typically run in an MS-DOS console window, thus the name *console application.*

This section explains the steps necessary to create a workspace and project for a console application using AppWizard. If you have a workspace open in Visual C++, you will want to close it at this time by selecting File/Close Workspace from the menu.

1. Select File/New... from the Visual C++ menu. AppWizard appears as seen in Figure 2.5. Make sure the Projects tab is currently selected.

2. Click Win32 Console Application so that it is highlighted.

3. You need to give your project a name and specify what folder to use for storing all of the project's files. By typing in a name in the Project Name edit window, notice that a folder of the same name appears in the Location window. See Figure 2.7.

4. The Create new workspace radio button should already be selected. If you had an existing workspace open in Visual Studio, you would have the option of adding our new project to the existing workspace.

5. The Platforms list box displays the various platforms targeted for your project. The list that appears varies depending on the various compilers and toolkits you have installed with Visual Studio. Make sure you select the appropriate platforms because it is difficult to add a target platform to an existing project. In this book's examples, we are writing programs for the Windows 32-bit operating systems. So the target platform is Win32, which should be selected already.

6. Select OK when all your choices are made. The AppWizard for creating a Win32 console application will be displayed. See Figure 2.8.

7. Most wizards in AppWizard have several steps, but because there isn't much to a console application, you will notice only one step to this particular wizard. You are given several choices, depending on your version of Visual C++. You want an empty project, so select that option.

8. Click the Finish button.

9. At the end of each wizard in AppWizard is an information window detailing what type of project you selected, the files that will be created, and other choices you made. Select OK to complete AppWizard and have the project created.

You will get a directory with the various project and workspace files in it. In our example, no source files were generated from AppWizard because you selected an empty project. We will need to include the source files ourselves — discussed in the next section.

Figure 2.7 Selecting a project for AppWizard.

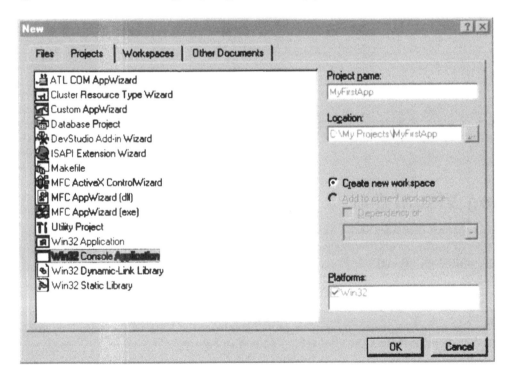

Figure 2.8 AppWizard choices for a console application.

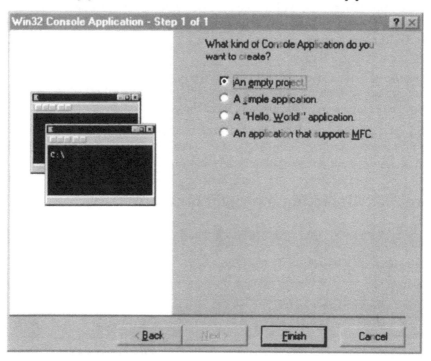

Using Visual C++

This section describes some of the common tasks that occur in Visual C++ beyond the creation of a project and workspace. Topics include adding a file to a project, compiling a file, and building (linking) our executable.

Adding Files to a Project

You add a file to a project by selecting File/New from the Visual C++ menu bar. The New dialog box appears. Select the Files tab, as shown in Figure 2.9.

Figure 2.9   Adding a file to a project.

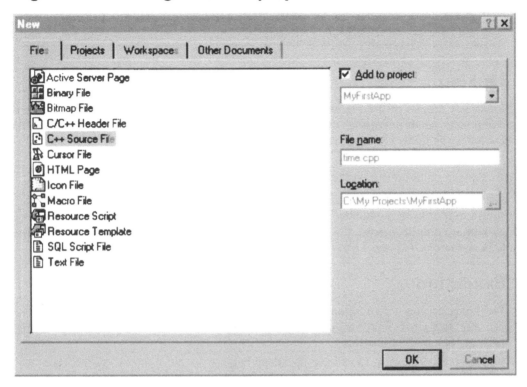

Select the type of file you want (either a C/C++ Header File or a C++ Source File), enter a name for the file, and click OK. Your new file appears in the Text Editor.

Compiling

Once the source file is edited, you need to compile the C++ code into object code. The compiler will scan your source file and make sure your code is valid C++. If the code compiles successfully, an object file is created with the same name as your source file, except with an obj extension. If the compiler is not successful, the errors it generates will appear in the Output window of Visual Studio.

You can start the compiler in Visual C++ in the following ways:

- Select Compile from the Build menu.
- Use its accelerator keys Ctrl+F7.
- Click the Compile button on the Build toolbar.

The Output window displays all output from the compiler. If a compiler error occurs, double-click it in the Output window. The file opens in the Text Editor (if it is not open already) and an arrow appears on the line number where the error occurred.

NOTE: You can click an error in the Output window and press F1 to bring up the Help item for your particular compiler error. Help typically consists of a description of what could have caused the error.

Linking

Linking a project is often referred to as *building* because this is how you actually build the component you are creating (an executable, DLL, ActiveX control, etc.). As with running the compiler, the linker can be started through several methods:

- Select Build/Build *.exe.
- Use the Build button on the Build toolbar.
- Press the F7 shortcut key.

All output from the builder displays in the Output window. Build errors are not as easy to correct as compiler errors, so typically you need to seek help. As with compiler errors, highlight the error and press F1 to display an error's Help item.

Executing

The linker creates a stand-alone executable for your program. You can run your executable just like any other Windows application, or you can run it from within Visual Studio by selecting one of the following:

- Select Build/Execute *.exe from the menu bar.
- Click the exclamation point (!) button on the Build toolbar.
- Press the Ctrl+F5 shortcut key.

NOTE: If the executable is a console application, a DOS window will appear.

Now that you are familiar with the features of Visual Studio and Visual C++, you will be able to recreate the examples in the book and begin writing your own C++ programs using Visual Studio.

Chapter 3

Fundamentals of Object-Oriented Programming

Object-oriented programming involves a different way of thinking. Instead of focusing on the functions and tasks of a program, you design an object-oriented program around the objects in the problem domain. Once you determine these objects, a class is written to define the attributes and behaviors for each object.

This chapter will discuss the details of writing classes in C++ and instantiating those classes to create objects. A well-written class can ensure that its objects have valid and consistent data in them, and you will see how this is accomplished using *encapsulation*. Encapsulation involves adding member functions to a class. Classes can contain a function called a *constructor* that initializes an object when it is instantiated. A similar function called a *destructor* is invoked when the object is destroyed. You will see how to implement constructors and destructors and discover their uses and benefits.

I will finish this chapter with a discussion of the CString class — a utility class in MFC that can be used to represent strings. There are many useful methods in the CString class, which makes it a preferred alternative to using an array of characters for strings.

Classes vs. Objects

Before I begin our discussion on object-oriented programming, you need to understand the difference between a *class* and an *object*. I have used both words frequently — most noticeably in the terms object-oriented and Microsoft Foundation Classes. But what exactly is an object? This section defines both terms and how they are related.

A class is often described as a blueprint of an object. The analogy works well if you compare classes and objects to blueprints and houses. Before a house is built, the building contractor needs a blueprint, i.e., a detailed description of exactly what the house is going to look like. Similarly, a class describes exactly what an object is going to look like. In C++, you write *classes*, not objects. Each class you write can then be used to *build an object*, using your class as a blueprint for what the object should look like. The object built is called an *instance* of the class.

If I have an architect draw up a set of blueprints for a house, does this mean I have a new house? Of course not. Likewise, when I write a class, I do not have an object of this class in memory until I instantiate one. A blueprint for a house can be used again to build as many houses as you want, assuming you have enough locations to build on. Similarly, you can instantiate as many objects as you want from one class, assuming the computer has enough memory to store them.

When programming in C++, you write a class and instantiate objects. I'll discuss how to determine what objects you need in a program in the following section. The section "Defining Classes" (page 57) discusses how to write a class in C++. Once you become familiar with writing classes, I will show you how to instantiate and use objects from your classes in "Instantiating Objects" (page 59).

OOP vs. Procedural Programming

Using a procedural programming language to solve a problem involves partitioning a project into smaller tasks, and writing a function for each task. For example, suppose you needed to implement a payroll application that allowed employees to be paid on a monthly basis. You would probably write functions to compute the pay and taxes, print the check, and mail or deposit the check. Notice that these functions are *verbs*, implying that each function performs a task.

In an object-oriented programming language, the thought process is different. You do not try to solve a problem by breaking it down into tasks (functions). Instead, you analyze the program requirements and determine the objects in the problem domain, which are *nouns*, not verbs.

For instance, in the payroll example, the objects might include the employee and the paycheck. Does this mean you do not need a function somewhere to compute the pay or mail the check? No, certainly not. One of the requirements here is to compute the pay, and the implementation has to be done somewhere. This is not going to be a global function, but a behavior of one of our objects. In this example, you would write a class called `Employee` that contained a member function called `ComputePay()`. I will define the `Employee` class in the section "Defining Classes" (page 57). For now, I want you to realize that such a class is needed — because I want you to start thinking in terms of objects.

Think Objects

An *object* is a person or thing. As the payroll application demonstrated, the objects in a program are the nouns in the problem domain. There is a lot more that can be said about determining the objects in a program and is the topic of many books and courses. *Object-Oriented Analysis and Design* (OOAD) is the term used to describe the process of determining which classes to include in solving a problem, and determining what each class should look like. I will cover OOAD in this section in its simplest form: determining the objects in a problem domain and describing what those objects will look like.

Let us analyze another example thinking in terms of objects. Suppose we needed to write a program to simulate driving a car. There are certainly many tasks involved with this problem, but do not concern yourself with these details quite yet. Instead, focus on the objects that are involved.

We could certainly view the car as an object. However, some other objects involved in driving a car include the steering wheel, gas pedal, brake pedal, seat belt, and radio. We might also decide that the engine and wheels are objects, as well as the headlights, windshield wipers, and so forth. I guess it all depends on how realistic we want our simulator to be.

NOTE: Keep in mind that there is no single, correct solution to writing a program. I will simply illustrate some of the objects that might be candidates for becoming a class. If we were to actually implement the car simulator, more detailed analysis would need to be done initially to determine exactly what each class would look like and do. I am sure that more classes would be discovered, and some initial classes might end up being removed. As with any software development, spending time in the analysis phase is time well spent!

Attributes and Behaviors

Once you have determined the objects for your program, the next step is to determine the attributes and behaviors for each one. This is the point in your design phase where you distribute the tasks your program "performs" to their appropriate objects.

You can view an object as consisting of two components:

- Attributes — the properties of the object. An attribute can be thought of as what the object *has* (or *consists of*).
- Behaviors — the functions of the object, and can be thought of as what the object *does*.

In the car simulator example, you would need to determine the attributes and behaviors of each object in the problem domain. For example, a car would have attributes like a make, model, steering wheel, radio, seat belt, and so on. (Notice that some of the attributes of the car are objects themselves.) Behaviors of the car would include driving and parking.

Attributes of the steering wheel might include its color and whether or not it contains an airbag. The behavior of a steering wheel is that it turns the wheels. Continuing in this fashion, we would determine the attributes and behaviors of each of the objects in our car simulator.

I have discussed in this section what can be thought of as the fundamentals of OOAD. In summary, when solving a problem from an object-oriented point of view, there are two key steps:

1. Determine the objects in the problem domain.
2. Determine the attributes and behaviors of each object from the first step.

Once you have analyzed the problem and followed these two steps, the next task is to write a class for each object.

Members of a Class

Once the attributes and behaviors of an object have been identified, a corresponding class needs to be written. Since a class is a blueprint for an object, the attributes and behaviors of the object need to be described in the class. This is done using member variables and member functions. This section discusses these members of a class and how to declare and implement a class definition.

Member Variables

A *member variable* of a class is an attribute of the object being described. Structures in C++ use the same terminology for member variables, and the meaning is the same for classes. Once you determine the attributes of an object, you need to decide how to represent those attributes using data types that the computer understands. They are either one of the built-in data types, like int or char, or they can be an object of some other class type.

For example, the steering wheel in the car simulator example had two attributes: a color and whether or not it had an airbag. The color of the steering wheel could be represented as a string, and the airbag feature could be represented as a Boolean. Thus, the steering wheel class would have two member variables: a string and a Boolean.

A car has an attribute of type steering wheel, so the car class needs a member variable that is an instance of the steering wheel class. This common situation, where a member variable of a class is an object of another class, is referred to as *composition*.

Member Functions

A *member function* of a class is a behavior of the object being described. Once you have determined the behaviors of an object, you need to decide how those behaviors are going to be implemented in terms of C++ functions. In other words, you need to determine if the function requires any parameters or if it should return a value. You also need to determine how this function is going to accomplish its task. (In other words, the actual code or body of the function.)

What is important to understand about member functions is that they have access to the member variables of a class. This is an essential feature of OOP because it is important for the behaviors of an object to be aware of and be able to change the attributes of an object.

Returning to the car simulator example, the steering wheel had one behavior: it turned the wheels of the car. This would imply there should be a member function in the steering wheel class called TurnWheels(). The car class had two behaviors: driving and parking, so the car class would probably contain Driving() and Parking() member functions. Because member functions of a class have access to their member variables, the Driving() function could have access to the steering wheel object, which could be used to invoke TurnWheels().

Defining Classes

Once the members of a class have been determined, you are now ready to start creating the source files that define the class. There are two steps to creating the source code for a class:

1. Define the class in a header file.
2. Implement the member functions in a source file.

To create these files in Visual C++, you would start with an appropriate Workspace, then add these files using File/New from the menu. Figure 2.9 (page 51) shows the choices for a new file. Notice you can select either a new C/C++ Header File or a new C++ Source File. Let's now discuss what each of these files is used for.

Header Files

The header file contains the *declaration* of the class. A declaration includes the name of the class, its member variables, and the prototypes of its member functions. For example, the following header file declares a class called Employee, which has four member variables and two member functions.

```
//Filename: Employee.h

class Employee
{
public:
    char m_FirstName[20];
    char m_LastName[30];
    int m_Number;
    double m_Salary;
    double ComputePay();
    void PrintCheck();
};
```

The declaration is saved in a header file with the h extension. Common practice is to match the filename with the class name, as we did with Employee.h. Notice Employee.h does not contain any statements, only declarations. For this reason, a header file is not compiled. We simply include this header file into any source file that needs the Employee declaration.

Notice the notation of m_ preceding the names of the member variables. This style is referred to as *Hungarian notation*. I will use the Hungarian notation to be consistent with MFC, which also follows this convention.

Also, notice the use of the keyword public before the member variables and functions. The specifier public means the members of this class are accessible from any other object. I will discuss public and the other options for allowing access to class members later in this chapter.

Source Files

The source file contains the implementation of the class. Here is where all the actual work takes place in terms of the member functions. Each member function needs to be implemented, and the typical process is to define them all in a source file with the same name as the header file. Once the source file is written, it is compiled into object code.

The following code demonstrates an implementation file for our Employee class.

```
//Filename: Employee.cpp
#include "Employee.h"
#include <string>
#include <windows.h>


double Employee::ComputePay()
{
    //Perform the necessary arithmetic here
    return m_Salary/12.0;//monthly pay period
}


void Employee::PrintCheck()
{
    //Print out the Employee's paycheck
    char buffer[40];
    sprintf(buffer,"Pay to the order of %s %s\n$%8.2f",
            m_FirstName, m_LastName, ComputePay());
    MessageBox(NULL, buffer, "Paycheck", MB_OK);
}
```

When defining a member function, you must use the scope resolution operator to let the compiler know to which class the member function belongs. Because ComputePay() and PrintCheck() belong to the Employee class, we declared them as:

```
double Employee::ComputePay()
void Employee::PrintCheck()
```

The return value and any parameters of a member function need to be listed in the same manner as the function's prototype in the header file.

NOTE: Without the scope resolution operator and the corresponding class name, the compiler will treat the function as a global function, *not* as a member function of the class it belongs. This is a common programming error, and the result is not a compiler error but a build error. The linker will complain about not being able to find a member function's implementation.

Notice in the implementation of ComputePay() and PrintCheck() that both member functions had access to the member variables of the class. For example, ComputePay() used m_Salary to determine the employee's pay, and PrintCheck() used m_FirstName and m_LastName to print the employee's check.

Also notice that member functions can invoke each other. This is a common occurrence in OOP, because it allows us to separate an object's behaviors into separate, logical components. For example, printing a paycheck is a specific behavior. If the PrintCheck() function had to compute the employee's pay itself, then the code would have to be repeated because the ComputePay() function already provides that behavior. To avoid this repetition of code, PrintCheck() simply invokes ComputePay(), as you can see in the previous implementation.

Instantiating Objects

You instantiate an object in C++ by simply declaring one, just like you would declare one of the built-in data types. For example, to instantiate an Employee object from the Employee class defined in the previous section, you declare one and give it an identifier.

```
Employee ryan;
```

This statement causes an Employee object to be created in memory and is given the identifier ryan. You now have two strings in memory, an int and a double — all member variables of the ryan object. There are also two member functions for ryan: ComputePay() and PrintCheck().

NOTE: In the ryan object above, the member variables have not been initialized and contain garbage. Before any of its member variables can be used, each one must be initialized, otherwise your program can have unexpected results when executing. I will show you how to avoid this potential problem in the discussion on constructors in a later section.

As I mentioned earlier, you can instantiate as many objects of type Employee as you have memory for. You can also instantiate an Employee object dynamically using a pointer to the object and the new keyword, as the following statement illustrates:

```
Employee * pMegan = new Employee();
```

The pointer pMegan points to a newly allocated Employee object, which will consist of two strings, an int, a double, and the two member functions of the Employee class.

NOTE: Don't forget about potential memory leaks with new. Be sure to delete the pointer pMegan when the object is no longer needed in memory.

In addition, you can create a reference to an Employee object using the following syntax:

```
Employee & refToRyan = ryan;
```

This syntax is identical to how references are created with the built-in data types. Be aware that no new object is instantiated here. Instead, refToRyan is a reference (an alias) to the existing ryan object.

Accessing Members of an Object

Once the object is instantiated, you can access its member variables and functions using either the dot operator or the indirection operator (->) depending on whether the identifier is a pointer or not. The following statements declare an Employee object and a reference to the object, then uses the dot operator to access its members.

```
Employee ryan;
Employee & refToRyan = ryan;
ryan.m_Salary = 1000.00;
refToRyan.PrintCheck();
```

You use the dot operator with the object's identifier and with any references to the object. In the statements above, the salary was assigned to 1000.00 using the identifier, and the PrintCheck() function was invoked using a reference.

If the identifier represents a pointer to the object, there are two ways to access the members:

1. Dereference the pointer and use the dot operator.
2. Use the indirection operator (->).

The following statements declare an Employee object using new — illustrating both of these techniques for accessing its members.

```
Employee * pMegan = new Employee();
(*pMegan).m_Salary = 2000.00;
strcpy(pMegan->m_FirstName, "Megan");
pMegan->PrintCheck();
```

To assign the salary to 2000.00, I dereferenced the pointer and used the dot operator. The parentheses are required due to the order of operations. (The dot operator has a higher precedence, but I wanted to dereference the pointer first.)

The m_FirstName and PrintCheck() members were accessed using the indirection opeator (->). What ever technique you choose is purely a matter of style. However, using the indirection operator is the preferred technique because its syntax is simpler to use.

NOTE: The strcpy function is found in the string header file and is used for copying one string into another.

Controlling Access to Members

One of the features of OOP is the ability to control the accessibility of the members of a class. For example, in the Employee class, the member variables and functions are all declared public, which allows access from anywhere. C++ has two other levels of access: protected and private. Here is what each specifier provides in terms of access:

public — the member can be accessed from anywhere, often referred to as *universal access*.

private — the most restrictive of the three, private members are only accessible from other member functions in the class.

protected — somewhere between public and private, protected members are accessible from within the class and any subclasses. Inheritance and subclassing will be discussed in Chapter 4.

It might seem odd to make a member private because private members are invisible outside of the class. However, I will describe in the next section why hiding the member variables of a class is a common and useful design tool. A protected member is only slightly more accessible than a private member, because protected members are hidden to all other classes except inherited ones.

Encapsulation

One of the important concepts of OOP is encapsulation. Often referred to as data hiding, *encapsulation* is the process of making a member variable private and exposing it through public member functions. This allows the data to be hidden within the object, and allows the object the capability of validating any changes made to its member variables.

To illustrate encapsulation, consider the following class declaration that defines a Date class to represent a day, month, and year.

```
class Date
{
private:
    int m_day, m_month, m_year;
};
```

If this were the entire class, it would not be very useful! For example, the following code would not compile.

```
Date today;
today.m_day = 29;   //invalid statement! day is private
```

The m_day member variable is private and is not accessible from outside the class. I wanted to illustrate the effect that private has on a member variable. The question is: how do we change the day, month, and year of this Date object? The answer is to provide public member functions that act as a buffer between the member variables and the outside world. This is how encapsulation is implemented in C++.

The standard naming convention is to write "set" and "get" functions for each member variable. For example, the m_day member variable could be altered and viewed with a SetDay() and GetDay() function. The following is a Date class with "set" and "get" functions for each member variable.

```
//Filename: Date.h
class Date
{
private:
   int m_day, m_month, m_year;
public:
   void SetDay(int);
   int  GetDay();
   void SetMonth(int);
   int GetMonth();
   void SetYear(int);
   int GetYear();
   void Display();
};
```

The implementation of the "set" function is where the data can be validated, as the following source code for the Date class illustrates. Notice the "get" functions simply return the requested data. They can do anything they want, but returning the value is all I needed my "get" functions to do.

```
//Filename: Date.cpp
#include "Date.h"
#include <string>
#include <windows.h>

void Date::SetDay(int d) {
   if(d >=1 && d <= 31)
      m_day = d;
   else
      MessageBox(NULL, "Invalid day!", "Error", MB_OK);
}
```

```
int Date::GetDay() {
    return m_day;
}

void Date::SetMonth(int m) {
    if(m >= 1 && m <= 12)
        m_month = m;
    else
        MessageBox(NULL, "Invalid month!", "Error", MB_OK);
}

int Date::GetMonth() {
    return m_month;
}

void Date::SetYear(int y) {
    if(y > 0)
        m_year = y;
    else
        MessageBox(NULL,"Year can't be negative","Error",MB_OK);
}

int Date::GetYear() {
    return m_year;
}

void Date::Display() {
    char buffer[11];
    sprintf(buffer,"The date is %d/%d/%d",
            m_month,m_day,m_year);
    MessageBox(NULL,buffer,"Display date", MB_OK);
}
```

When a Date object is instantiated, the member variables are changed using the "set" functions. Any invalid numbers are simply ignored in my Date class, but I could have handled the situation in any number of ways, including throwing an exception or returning a Boolean value to signify success or failure.

NOTE: I could have only provided a "set" function to make a member variable write-only. Similarly, I could have created a read-only member variable by only including a "get" function for the variable.

The following statements create a Date object and initialize its member variables using the various "set" and "get" functions. The attempt to set the day to 40 displays the message box in the SetDay() function. The final output is shown in Figure 3.1.

```
Date newyears;
newyears.SetMonth(1);
newyears.SetDay(40);    //does not change the day
newyears.SetDay(1);     //changes the day to 1
newyears.SetYear(2000);
newyears.Display();     //displays the date in a message box
```

Figure 3.1 The output of the Date::Display() function.

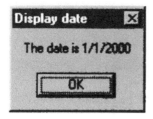

The Interface of a Class

Because the private members of a class are inaccessible outside of the class, programmers using a class rarely concern themselves with how an object stores its data. Instead, they want to know the public members of a class — that is all they have access to. The public member functions of a class are referred to as the *interface* of the class.

Providing this interface to a user of your class allows you to hide the implementation details of the class. For example, you do not need to know how a telephone works to use one. Instead, you only need to know how to use the interface that a telephone provides, i.e., the buttons and the handset. Similarly, if you want to use a class, you only need to know the public member functions (and possibly member variables) of the class.

Member variables are typically private because most classes use encapsulation, so you rarely concern yourself with them. In addition, the way the data is stored is also hidden from the user of the class. I decided to store the day, month, and year of the Date class in the previous section using int's. I did not need to do this, though. The month and day could fit easily into a byte. I can make these members byte's in my Date class, and if I left the interface the same, someone else using my class would not have to alter their code at all. This is one of the important advantages of encapsulation and using public methods to buffer the user from the actual data.

Constructors

When an object is instantiated, a special function called a *constructor* is invoked. The term constructor is used because its purpose is to *construct* the object being built. Member variables will contain garbage in them if they are not initialized properly. The constructor can be used to ensure that each member variable contains valid data.

Another use of constructors is to allow the object to be created with specific data. For example, when instantiating a Date object, it would be nice to be able to determine the day, month, and year without invoking the separate "set" functions individually. This capability is another purpose for constructors.

Every class has a constructor. If you do not write one, the compiler generates a default constructor for you. The *default constructor* is the constructor in a class that does not have any parameters. In most situations, this constructor generated for you is not sufficient because it does not provide any functionality. This following section discusses how to write your own constructors for a class and invoke them when instantiating objects.

Writing Constructors

A constructor is a function that has the same name as the class and does not declare a return value. They do have parameters, though, which allows for the input of data when the object is being constructed. The following shows the Date class, from the previous section, with the addition of a constructor.

```
//Filename: Date.h
class Date
{
private:
    int m_day, m_month, m_year;
public:
    Date(int = 1, int = 1, int = 2000);
    //other member function prototypes
    //left out for brevity
    ...
};
```

Notice the name of the constructor is Date() and does not declare a return value. The definition of the constructor goes in the implementation file, along with the other member function's definitions. The Date() constructor above uses the three int's to initialize the day, month, and year, and its implementation is shown below. Notice in the prototype that each of the parameters will default to a value if necessary.

```
Date::Date(int d, int m, int y) {
    SetDay(d);
    SetMonth(m);
    SetYear(y);
}
```

A common technique is to have the constructor invoke "set" functions to initialize member variables, as I did with the Date() constructor above. This has several advantages, including keeping the validation process of a member variable in one location. The object being created will have incoming data that the constructor needs to validate, and the "set" functions already perform this work for us.

As with any function, constructors can be overloaded. The section "The Copy Constructor" (page 68) demonstrates a class with more than one constructor using overloading. Constructors can also have default arguments, which the Date() uses.

Instantiating Objects Using Constructors

When an object is instantiated, one of the constructors in the class is invoked. A class can have more than one constructor or more than one way to invoke a constructor (if the constructor had default arguments). To determine which constructor is invoked, you need to pass in the appropriate number of parameters when the object is declared.

The following statements create several Date objects, invoking the Date() constructor in various ways.

```
Date newyears;           // 1/1/2000
Date today(20,6,1999);   // 6/20/1999
Date nextyear(20,6);     // 6/20/2000
Date * pChristmas = new Date(25,12,1999);   // 12/25/1999
```

The Date() constructor is invoked for each one of these objects. If no arguments are specified, the default constructor is invoked. Because all of the parameters of the constructor default to some value, that is the default constructor in the Date() class. This creates a Date object representing January 1, 2000, illustrated by the newyears object.

The other three objects invoke the Date() constructor with specific arguments. Notice the syntax for doing this — using parentheses after the identifier. If an object is being created dynamically using new, the arguments for the constructor are placed within the call to new Date(). The pointer pChristmas used this technique to create a pointer to a Date object representing December 25, 1999.

NOTE: Constructors are not the same as member functions of a class. They are unique in that they do not return a value and they cannot be invoked, except initially, when the object is being created in memory.

Constructors and Member Initialization

Classes often contain member variables that are objects of other classes, referred to as *composition*. When a class uses composition, member variables need to be constructed, which involves invoking their appropriate constructor. This process is known as *member initialization*, and this section discusses the syntax used for invoking a member variable's constructor.

Suppose I wanted to add a member variable to the Employee class discussed earlier to represent the date an employee was hired. Because I also wrote a Date class to perform just such a task, I will include a member variable in the Employee class of type Date, as follows:

```
class Employee
{
private:
    char m_FirstName[20];
    char m_LastName[30];
    int m_Number;
    double m_Salary;
    Date m_HireDate;
public:
    Employee(char *,char *, double=0, int=1, int=1, int=1999);
    //necessary "set" and "get" functions
    //and other member functions
    void SetName(char *, char *); //first and last name
    void SetSalary(double);
};
```

When an Employee object is instantiated, a constructor in the Employee class is invoked. Because the Employee's constructor should initialize each of the member variables, a Date constructor needs to be invoked. (Recall the Date constructor has three parameters for the day, month, and year.)

The Employee constructor can invoke the Date constructor using member initialization, which consists of a colon after the constructor's parameter list and a list of all member variables that are to be initialized using their own constructor. The following Employee constructor illustrates how member initialization could be used to invoke the Date constructor for the m_HireDate member variable.

```
Employee::Employee(char * firstName, char * lastName,
                   double salary, int day, int month,
                   int year) : m_HireDate(day, month, year)
{
    SetName(firstName,lastName);
    SetSalary(salary);
}
```

Notice the colon after the parameter list, which signifies member initialization. To demonstrate how this works, consider the following Employee declaration:

```
Employee megan("Megan","Lynn",2000.00,29,6,1999);
```

The m_HireDate object will be instantiated, and its constructor is invoked with the 29, 6, and 1999 values.

NOTE: If a class has several member variables to be initialized using member initialization, commas in the list following the colon separate them.

The Copy Constructor

A class can contain a special constructor known as a *copy constructor*. A copy constructor is a constructor whose parameter is a constant reference to the class it belongs. For example, the following prototypes demonstrate what the copy constructor for the Employee and Date classes would look like:

```
Employee(const Employee &);
Date(const Date &);
```

If you do not provide a copy constructor for a class, the compiler will supply one for you which does a bitwise copy of an object. To provide more control in how objects are copied, you will typically provide your own copy constructor for every class you write. It is also a nice capability to be able to construct a new object from an existing object, which the copy constructor supplies.

A constructor is invoked when an object is instantiated, and the copy constructor can be invoked in this manner as well. The following statements demonstrate the two ways a copy constructor is invoked when instantiating a new object:

```
Date d1(4,7,2000);   //invokes constructor that takes 3 ints
Date d2(d1);         //invokes copy constructor
Date d3 = d1;        //also invokes copy constructor
```

The copy constructor for the Date class is defined as follows:

```
Date::Date(const Date & source) {
    m_Day = source.m_Day;
    m_Month = source.m_Month;
    m_Year = source.m_Year;
}
```

This copy constructor receives a reference to an existing Date object, and I simply assigned each member variable of the source object to the new Date object being constructed. I also could have done any other initialization I needed to do.

Using Objects with Call by Value

Copy constructors are also invoked when one of the following events occurs:
- An object is passed to a function using call by value.
- An object is returned from a function.

Call by value needs to make a copy of the argument, and functions that return data always return a copy. If the argument or return value is an object (as opposed to a built-in data type), the copy constructor is used to create the copy of the object.

The following function called `Tomorrow()` takes in an existing `Date` object and returns a new `Date` object representing the next calendar day. It illustrates exactly when the copy constructor is invoked.

```
Date Tomorrow(Date today) {
    Date tomorrow;
    tomorrow.SetDay(today.GetDay() + 1);
    tomorrow.SetMonth(today.GetMonth());
    tomorrow.SetYear(today.GetYear());
    return tomorrow;
}
```

NOTE: My `Tomorrow()` function obviously needs some work. I only added 1 to the day and did not take into account the end of a month or year. This logic has been left out for brevity.

Suppose this function is invoked with the following statements:

```
Date d1(29,6,1999);
Date d2 = Tomorrow(d1);
```

Let's count how many `Date` objects are created in memory with these two lines of code. The object d1 is instantiated first, then passed to the `Tomorrow()` function. The parameter today gets instantiated, using d1 in the `Date` copy constructor. The local variable tomorrow is instantiated using the default constructor of the `Date` class. Returning the tomorrow object causes a temporary `Date` object to be instantiated, using tomorrow in the `Date` copy constructor. This copy of tomorrow is returned and initialized to the d2 object, which causes a third call to the `Date` copy constructor. That means a total of five objects were instantiated when invoking the `Tomorrow()` function, counting the two calls to the default `Date` constructor.

Using Objects with Call by Reference

The copying of objects in the `Tomorrow()` function in the previous section might seem like a lot of overhead, and it would be if the object being copied consumed a large amount of memory. However, some of the overhead could have been avoided by not using call by value. Now that you have seen when the copy constructor is invoked, sometimes it is important to avoid these situations. One of the most common techniques in C++ to do this is to pass an object by reference, instead of by value. The parameter becomes a reference to the argument, and no copy is made.

For example, the previous `Tomorrow()` function did not need a copy of the `Date` object, and could still accomplish its task with just a reference to the `Date` object. The parameter would declare itself as a reference parameter, as the following prototype illustrates:

```
Date Tomorrow(Date & today)
```

The body of the function would not need to be altered because the syntax for using a reference is the same as when accessing the object directly.

You might ask why I did not return a reference to the tomorrow object, which would have saved yet another call to the copy constructor. Be very careful in this situation! The compiler would not have complained, but at runtime, this would create a serious problem. The tomorrow object goes out of scope immediately after the function executes. The returned reference will not be able to be used because it refers to an object that no longer exists in memory.

I actually needed to return a copy of the tomorrow object in this example, even though the copy involved creating another Date object. When returning an object by reference, you need to make sure that the object being referred to has scope outside of the function.

NOTE: Do not return a reference to a local variable. Only return a reference to an object when the object's scope is beyond the scope of the function.

Destructors

Just as every object has a constructor that is invoked when the object is instantiated, every object has a function called a *destructor* that gets invoked when the object goes out of scope or is deleted. The purpose of the destructor is to allow the object an opportunity to clean itself up properly before being destroyed. This is an important feature in avoiding memory leaks, as the example later in this section will demonstrate. Other tasks a destructor might perform include making sure a file is closed or network connection is disconnected properly.

A destructor shares the same name as the class it belongs to, much like constructors — except the destructor is preceded by the tilde (~). No return value or parameters can be declared, and the destructor cannot be overloaded. The following prototypes declare the destructor for the Employee and Date classes:

```
~Employee();
~Date();
```

To demonstrate the usefulness of destructors, I have included one in the Employee class that frees memory allocated in the constructor. Notice that the member variable for the hire date has been changed to a pointer. I will instantiate the Date object dynamically in the constructor, and free the memory in the Employee destructor.

```
class Employee
{
private:
    char m_FirstName[20];
    char m_LastName[30];
    int m_Number;
    double m_Salary;
    Date * m_HireDate;
```

```
public:
    Employee(char *,char *, double=0, int=1, int=1, int=1999);
    ~Employee();    //destructor
    //necessary "set" and "get" functions
    //and other member functions
};
```

Here is the implementation of the constructor and destructor for this Employee class.

```
Employee::Employee(char * firstName, char * lastName,
                   double salary, int day, int month, int year)
{
    SetName(firstName,lastName);
    SetSalary(salary);
    m_HireDate = new Date(day,month,year); //dynamic memory
}


Employee::~Employee()
{
    delete m_HireDate;
}
```

The following function illustrates when a destructor is invoked. The function declares a local variable of type Employee. When the function is done executing, this variable goes out of scope, causing the destructor to be invoked.

```
void HireTemporaryEmployee() {
    Employee temp("Joe", "Black", 100.00, 25, 12, 1999);
    //do whatever it is you want to do with the Employee object
    ...
    //the function is done now
}
```

The constructor for the temp object allocates memory for a new Date object. When the function HireTemporaryEmployee() is done executing, the variable temp goes out of scope and the destructor for temp is invoked. This is when the memory for the m_HireDate object is freed.

If the destructor did not free this memory, then either the temp object would have had to free it itself (poor programming design), or it would have caused a memory leak. In either case, a memory leak would seem inevitable because someone using this class for the first time might not notice the potential for a memory leak.

This demonstrates the most beneficial purpose of destructors: avoiding memory leaks of dynamically-allocated memory. As I mentioned earlier, you can also use a destructor for any other type of clean-up that an object might need to perform.

Constant Objects

In the section "The Copy Constructor" (page 68), I discussed the overhead of using call by value and the advantages of using call by reference whenever possible. However, passing a reference to a function allows that function to be able to alter the object being passed in. If a function does not actually need to alter the object, then the const keyword can be used to ensure that someone calling the function need not worry about the contents of their object.

You have seen how the const keyword used in a built-in data type makes the contents of the data unchangeable. But what does it mean to not be able to change the contents of an object? In the following section, I will discuss what it means for an object to be "constant" and how to include this functionality in your classes.

Declaring Constant Member Functions

The Tomorrow() function in "Using Objects with Call by Reference" (page 69) took in a Date object and returned a new Date object that represented the next day. I used call by reference to avoid the overhead of call by value, but this gave the Tomorrow() function the option of changing the Date object I gave it. The following prototype shows the Tomorrow() function using a constant reference parameter, which provides me with the security of knowing the Tomorrow() function will not change my Date object.

```
Date Tomorrow(const Date & today)
```

What can the Tomorrow() function do with the today reference? Not much because I did not write my Date class to handle constant Date objects. The only member functions that a constant object can access are those member functions declared with the const keyword. In the Date class I defined previously, none of the member functions were declared const. So the today parameter of the Tomorrow() function would not be able to invoke any of its member functions! Like I said, the Tomorrow() function cannot do much with the constant today reference until I modify the Date class.

To declare a member function as constant, the const keyword is added to the function's prototype. This allows you, as the writer of a class, to determine exactly which member functions can be invoked by a constant object. In other words, you get to define what it means for objects of your class to be constant.

The following is the declaration of the Date class — this time with the appropriate member functions declared as constant.

```
class Date
{
private:
    int m_day, m_month, m_year;
public:
    Date(int=1, int=1, int=2000); //constructor
    Date(const Date &);           //copy constructor
    ~Date();                      //destructor
    void SetDay(int);
```

```
int  GetDay() const;
void SetMonth(int);
int GetMonth() const;
void SetYear(int);
int GetYear() const;
void Display() const;
};
```

Because none of the "get" functions change any of the member variables, I have decided to declare each one as constant. The Display() function does not alter the Date either, so it is also declared constant.

Here is the Tomorrow() function with the constant reference parameter:

```
Date Tomorrow(const Date & today) {
    Date tomorrow;
    tomorrow.SetDay(today.GetDay() + 1);
    tomorrow.SetMonth(today.GetMonth());
    tomorrow.SetYear(today.GetYear());
    return tomorrow;
}
```

Notice the today reference only invokes constant member functions of the Date class. Any attempt to invoke one of the "set" functions using the today reference would result in a compiler error.

Summary

The goal of this chapter was to get you and up and running with the object-oriented side of C++. I discussed the difference between classes and objects, with classes being the blueprints and objects being the instances of a class. A class consists of two components: member variables and member functions. You use encapsulation to hide the member variables of a class and ensure that the objects contain valid data.

Classes are declared in a header file, which contains the prototypes of the member functions. Member functions are implemented in a source file, which is then compiled into object code and linked into the executable.

A constructor is invoked when an object is instantiated. It provides the object an opportunity to initialize its member variables in an efficient manner. The destructor is invoked when the object goes out of scope or is deleted from memory. The destructor can perform any necessary clean up that might need to be done. You also saw when a copy constructor is invoked and how to use call by reference to avoid unnecessarily copying objects when passing them to functions. This led us to a discussion on constant objects and how to write classes that include constant member functions.

Chapter 4

Advanced Object-Oriented Programming Using C++

Object-oriented programming involves a different way of solving a problem. As you saw in Chapter 3, programs are designed in terms of the objects in the problem domain, and a class is written for each object. OOP has four fundamental concepts to assist in this design and creation of classes. They are as follows:

1. Encapsulation   Hiding the member variables of a class, only allowing access to them through an interface.

2. Inheritance   The ability of a class to be defined by deriving itself from an existing class and inheriting the interface of the existing class.

3. Polymorphism   An object taking on many forms as a result of inheritance.

4. Abstraction   The ability of a class to represent an object that is abstract — meaning that no object of the class can be instantiated.

Encapsulation was discussed in Chapter 3, where you saw how to implement encapsulation by making member variables private and creating an interface to these variables using `public` "set" and "get" functions. This gives the object a buffer between its data and the objects using its data — allowing the object to validate any changes and hide how its data is stored.

This chapter will cover the other three fundamental concepts of OOP, which will provide you with the advanced knowledge of C++ necessary to understand and develop MFC applications. Polymorphism and abstraction are directly associated with inheritance, so the details of inheritance will be discussed first. Once you see how to implement inheritance in C++, the details of polymorphism and the concept of a virtual method will be discussed. I will finish the chapter with a discussion on abstract classes in C++ and an example of when to use them.

Inheritance

One of the biggest advantages of OOP is the ability to easily reuse code. For example, in Chapter 3, I used a class called `Date` to represent a calendar day. The class did not rely on any specific situation for it to be used. Instead, it was written to provide the generic attributes and behaviors of a date. This `Date` class can be used in any situation where a date is necessary — a common need in programming.

NOTE: You do not need to create a `Date` class. Because using a calendar date is a common occurrence, MFC has a class called `CDate` that provides this functionality for you.

Another aspect of reusing code is the ability to inherit from an existing class. *Inheritance* is the process of creating a new class from an existing class, where the new class inherits the members of the existing class. The existing class is called the *parent* or *base class*, and the new class is called a *child* or *subclass*. A child class is an extension of its parent, because a child class inherits the functionality of the parent and adds its own functionality.

The "is a" Relationship

The "is a" relationship is a rule-of-thumb when deciding whether or not to use inheritance. Inheritance provides for the reuse of code, but you need to ensure that it is being used properly in the design of your programs.

For example, the `Employee` class in Chapter 3 used a member variable of type `Date` to represent the hire date of the employee. An employee "has a" hire date, so the composition seemed appropriate. The `Employee` class could have inherited from the `Date` class, so that each `Employee` object would have inherited the members of the `Date` class and used these members to store the employee's hire date. For the `Employee` class to inherit from the `Date` class implies that an `Employee` "is a" `Date`, which hardly seems appropriate (see Figure 4.1). This is one of those situations where composition is the preferred solution to giving an employee a hire date.

Figure 4.1   An `Employee` **is not a** `Date`, **so this inheritance is not a good design.**

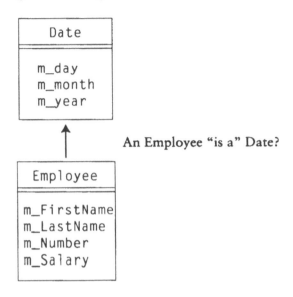

An Employee "is a" Date?

I will now discuss an example where inheriting from the `Employee` class will be used in the design of a payroll administration program, which pays the employees of a company. I want to begin with a discussion as to why the `Employee` class might not be sufficient for the problem I am trying to solve. Consider the following `Employee` class, which is a slight modification from the one in Chapter 3.

```
class Employee
{
private:
    char m_FirstName[20];
    char m_LastName[30];
    double m_Salary;
    char m_Address[100];
public:
    Employee(char *,char *, double, char *);
    void SetName(char *, char *); //first and last name
    char * GetFirstName();
    char * GetLastName();
    void SetSalary(double);
    double GetSalary();
    void SetAddress(char *);
```

```
    char * GetAddress();
    double ComputePay();
    void PrintMailingLabel();
};
```

Notice the Employee class contains a member variable, m_Salary, to represent an employee's salary. This implies that an employee "has a" salary. This may be true for some of the employees of this company, but what about employees who are paid by the hour or are contracted at a daily rate? Then the salary attribute does not apply, and I can no longer correctly state that "an employee has a salary."

What is important to notice in this analysis is that there are different types of employees. Each of these employees has attributes and behaviors in common, such as a name and number. But each employee has unique attributes and behaviors depending on how they are paid. This is a perfect example of when to use inheritance in OOP because each type of employee is going to require a separate class that inherits from Employee.

For example, a SalaryEmployee class can inherit from Employee and add attributes for the annual salary of the employee. An HourlyEmployee class can inherit from Employee and add attributes for the hourly rate and hours worked by an employee. Figure 4.2 shows the inheritance tree for these classes.

Figure 4.2 **The** SalaryEmployee **and** HourlyEmployee **classes extend the** Employee **class and inherit its attributes and behaviors.**

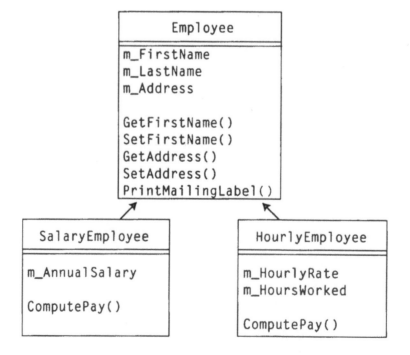

This inheritance is justifiable because a salaried employee "is an" employee and an hourly employee "is an" employee. Each child class of Employee will contain the attributes unique to how the employee is paid, and will also contain a ComputePay() function. Computing the pay of each type of employee requires a different implementation, and you can now see where the difference is coded in your program. The ComputePay() function of the SalaryEmployee class will do the appropriate arithmetic for salaried employees, and the ComputePay() function in the HourlyEmployee class will do the appropriate arithmetic for an employee paid by the hour.

Note that using inheritance enables a new type of Employee to be added to the problem domain without affecting the existing classes. For example, if the company started using contractors paid on a daily rate, a Contractor class could be written that extended Employee and provided its own attributes and ComputePay() function. None of the existing classes would need to be modified.

Multiple Levels of Inheritance

A class can extend another class, and a class itself can be extended as well — making it a child class *and* a parent class. This creates multiple levels of inheritance and allows for a more sophisticated hierarchy of classes when solving problems in terms of objects.

For example, in the payroll administration example, the Employee class was subclassed by SalaryEmployee and HourlyEmployee, as shown in Figure 4.2. For this scenario, let's say there are two types of hourly employees, full-time and part-time, and a separate class is needed for each one. Figure 4.3 shows the HourlyEmployee class being extended by two new classes: FullTimeHourly and PartTimeHourly.

Figure 4.3 The HourlyEmployee **class is a child class *and* a parent class — creating a multiple level of inheritance.**

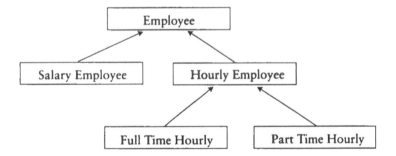

Using the "is a" rule-of-thumb, it seems valid to say that a FullTimeHourly is an HourlyEmployee and is also an Employee. An object of type FullTimeHourly inherits all of the member variables and functions from the HourlyEmployee class and from the Employee class.

Implementing Inheritance

Now that you have seen an example of how inheritance can be used, I will discuss the C++ syntax for implementing inheritance. The last section explained how the Employee class could be modified and extended to create a better object-oriented design for the payroll administration example. This new Employee class will only contain those attributes and behaviors common to all employees.

In particular, I have removed the m_Salary variable and the ComputePay() function. Not every employee has a salary, and the information to compute an employee's pay is going to be placed in the child classes. The new declaration for Employee looks like:

```
class Employee
{
private:
    char m_FirstName[20];
    char m_LastName[30];
    char m_Address[100];
public:
    Employee(char *,char *, char *);
    void SetName(char *, char *); //first and last name
    char * GetFirstName();
    char * GetLastName();
    void SetAddress(char *);
    char * GetAddress();
    void PrintMailingLabel();
};
```

To implement inheritance in C++, a class is declared a child by placing a colon after the class name and stating the name of the parent class. For example, the SalaryEmployee class is declared as:

```
class SalaryEmployee : public Employee
```

The HourlyEmployee class also extends from Employee and its declaration is:

```
class HourlyEmployee : public Employee
```

The public keyword creates *public inheritance*, which means the inherited public attributes and behaviors of the parent will be accessible from objects of the child type. You can also use *private inheritance* by using the private keyword instead of public, but this would mean the inherited attributes and behaviors would not be accessible from the object. Private inheritance somewhat negates the benefits of using inheritance in the first place.

NOTE: Private inheritance is rarely used in C++, because it violates the intended purpose of inheritance.

NOTE: A class can inherit from a structure, which sometimes occurs in MFC. For example, the MFC class, CRect, inherits from the RECT structure. CRect is used frequently in MFC and is discussed in later chapters.

Defining the Child Class

Aside from having a parent, a child class is just like any class. It can contain constructors, a destructor, and member variables and functions. The following lists the declaration of the SalaryEmployee class, which contains a member variable for the salary and a function to compute the pay.

```
class SalaryEmployee : public Employee
{
private:
   double m_Salary;
public:
   SalaryEmployee(char *, char *, char *, double);
   void SetSalary(double);
   double GetSalary();
   double ComputePay();
};
```

The SalaryEmployee class contains a constructor, which has parameters for the parent class constructor. I will discuss the details of parent and child constructors in the section "Invoking a Parent Class Constructor" (page 84). The three strings in the SalaryEmployee constructor will end up as the first and last name and address of the Employee.

Accessing Inherited Members

A child object accesses its inherited members using the same syntax as if they were members of their own class. For example, the following statements instantiate a SalaryEmployee and invoke its ComputePay() function as well as the inherited PrintMailingLabel() function.

```
SalaryEmployee bill("Bill", "Gates",
                 "1 Gates Blvd\nRichmond, WA",12000.00);
bill.ComputePay();    //from the SalaryEmployee class
bill.PrintMailingLabel();    //from the Employee class
```

The object bill initializes its name, address, and salary using the constructor in the SalaryEmployee class. (The next section, "Invoking a Parent Class Constructor," shows the implementation of this constructor.) Once the object bill is constructed, the ComputePay() and PrintMailingLabel() functions are invoked.

Figure 4.4 A `SalaryEmployee` **object inherits the members of the** `Employee` **class.**

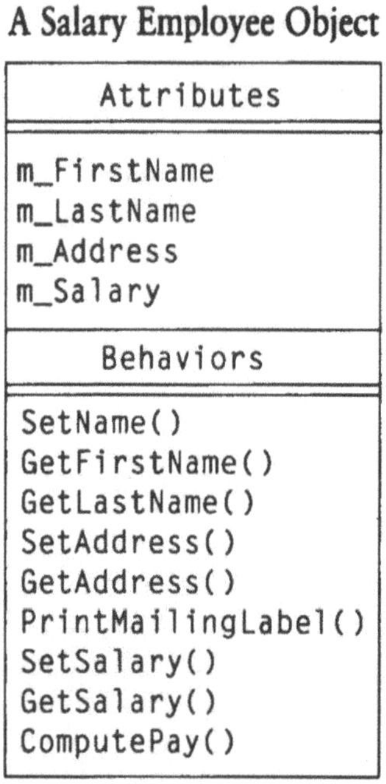

A Salary Employee Object

Attributes
m_FirstName
m_LastName
m_Address
m_Salary

Behaviors
SetName()
GetFirstName()
GetLastName()
SetAddress()
GetAddress()
PrintMailingLabel()
SetSalary()
GetSalary()
ComputePay()

The purpose of this example is to emphasize that invoking `PrintMailingLabel()` is legal and no special syntax is required, even though `PrintMailingLabel()` is not a member function of the `SalaryEmployee` class. The compiler looks up the inheritance tree for a `PrintMailingLabel()` function and finds it in the `Employee` class. More specifically, `PrintMailingLabel()` is a member function of `bill` because `bill` is an `Employee` as well as a `SalaryEmployee` (see Figure 4.4).

Inheriting Private Members

Note that the private members of a class are inherited, but not accessible to the child. The private members are still created in memory, even though the child cannot access them. This is not a surprise with member variables because they are normally encapsulated and can be accessed using public member functions. However, private member functions are not accessible and are hidden from the child.

Consider the following class definitions:

```
class Mammal {
private:
    char m_Name[30];
    int m_Age;
    void Eat();
```

```
public:
   Mammal(char *, int);
   char * GetName();
};

class Cat : public Mammal {
   public:
      void Sleep();
};
```

When a Cat object is instantiated, the string for m_Name, the int for m_Age, and the three member functions Eat(), Sleep(), and GetName() are created for the object in memory. The following statements instantiate a Cat object and attempt to access its members.

```
Cat garfield("Garfield", 5);    //name is "Garfield", age is 5
char * nameOfCat = garfield.GetName(); //valid
garfield.Sleep();    //valid
garfield.Eat();      //invalid! causes a compiler error
```

Not only can garfield not eat, but also the age of the cat is hidden as a member variable in the parent class. The member functions of Mammal have access to the m_Age variable, but the member functions of Cat do not. For example, the following definition for Eat() is valid, but the following Sleep() definition generates a compiler error:

```
void Mammal::Eat() {
   if(m_Age > 0)
      //eat
}

void Cat::Sleep() {
   if(m_Age > 0)    //invalid! causes a compiler error
      //sleep
}
```

The compiler error that Sleep() generates is not because the m_Age variable does not exist; the problem is that the variable is not accessible. For m_Age to be accessible to the Cat class, the access should be either changed to protected, or you could include public "set" and "get" functions to the Mammal class. Recall that protected members are accessible to children of a class.

Invoking a Parent Class Constructor

When a child object is instantiated, its constructor is invoked (just like any object). However, when objects are instantiated, the parent class must be instantiated first. In particular, a constructor in the parent class is executed before the child class constructor. This section discusses the syntax to invoke a particular parent class constructor and demonstrates the order of construction.

In the previous section, you saw how the Employee class was subclassed by SalaryEmployee to provide a class for employees who are paid a salary. The Employee class only has one constructor, which is implemented as follows:

```
Employee::Employee(char * first, char * last,char * address)
{
    SetName(first,last);
    SetAddress(address);
    MessageBox(NULL, "Just created an Employee",
            "Testing", MB_OK | MB_ICONINFORMATION);
}
```

Notice that the only way to instantiate an Employee is to provide three strings. For example, the statement

```
Employee rich;    //does not compile!
```

will not compile because the compiler is looking for a default constructor. The following is a valid Employee declaration:

```
Employee rich("Rich","Raposa","123 Main Street\nSturgis, SD");
```

NOTE: It is a good idea to provide a default constructor in every class, unless it is not feasible for the design of the class. A default constructor is omitted from the Employee class for brevity.

The SalaryEmployee class needed to provide a constructor that invoked the Employee constructor with three strings. The syntax to implement this is similar to member initialization, with a colon following the declaration of the SalaryEmployee constructor. The implementation of the SalaryEmployee constructor follows.

```
SalaryEmployee::SalaryEmployee(char * first, char * last,
                        char * address, double salary)
            : Employee(first, last, address)

{
```

```
    SetSalary(salary);
    MessageBox(NULL, "Just created a SalaryEmployee",
            "Testing", MB_OK | MB_ICONINFORMATION);
}
```

When a SalaryEmployee object is instantiated with three strings and a double, this constructor is invoked. However, before this constructor executes, the Employee constructor is invoked and executes to completion. In the previous section, a SalaryEmployee object was instantiated with the following statement:

```
SalaryEmployee bill("Bill", "Gates",
                "1 Gates Blvd\nRichmond, WA",12000.00);
```

Notice I included a message box in each constructor. Figure 4.5 shows the order in which the constructors execute. The message box from the Employee constructor is displayed first, followed by the message box from the SalaryEmployee constructor.

Figure 4.5   Example of a parent class constructor being executed before a child class constructor.

Overriding Member Functions

In certain situations, it is worthwhile for the child class to contain a method that replaces the functionality of the parent class. For example, when you begin to write MFC applications, you will write classes that inherit from CWnd — an MFC class that represents a window. CWnd has a member function called OnClose() that is invoked when the user closes the window. The default implementation of OnClose() is to destroy the window, which might have drastic side effects if the user had not saved their data. Your child class would override the parent functionality of OnClose() and add any additional tasks to be performed before destroying the window. The process of a child having an identical member function as the parent class is known as *overriding*. For a child to override a parent function, the overriding function must have the same prototype (signature) as the parent function.

NOTE: A common programming error when overriding a function is to change the parameter list or return value. Changing the number or type of parameters is function overloading, discussed in Chapter 3. A child class can overload a parent function, so this is valid. However, this does not result in the desired effect if you wanted to override the parent function. Changing only the return value is not overriding *or* overloading and causes a compiler error.

The following example shows a `SalaryEmployee` class overriding the `ComputePay()` function of its parent class `Employee`.

```
class Employee {
public:
    double ComputePay();
};


class SalaryEmployee : public Employee {
public:
    double m_Salary;
    double ComputePay();
};
```

Notice the `ComputePay()` function in `SalaryEmployee` has the exact same protoype as the one in `Employee`. When a `SalaryEmployee` object invokes `ComputePay()`, the function in the `SalaryEmployee` class is invoked, as the following statements demonstrate.

```
SalaryEmployee rich;
rich.m_Salary = 12000.00;
double pay = rich.ComputePay(); //ComputePay() in
                                //SalaryEmployee is invoked
```

Invoking a Parent's Overridden Function

In certain situations, an overriding function in the child class might only need to add certain functionality to an existing parent function. For example, the `Employee` class in the previous section could contain a member function called `Display()` that displayed the information of the employee. The `SalaryEmployee` child class might override this function to add the information regarding the employee's salary. The `Display()` function in `SalaryEmployee` could invoke the `Display()` function in the `Employee` class, then add whatever additional information is desired.

The scope resolution operator is used by the child class function to invoke an overridden function in the parent class. The following example shows how the `Display()` function is called from `Display()` in the `SalaryEmployee` class.

```
void SalaryEmployee::Display() {
    //display the salary
    char buffer[10];
    sprintf(buffer,"Salary is %f",GetSalary());
    MessageBox(NULL, buffer,
              "Display() in SalaryEmployee", MB_OK);
    //call the overridden parent function
    Employee::Display();
}
```

In this example, the salary of the employee is displayed, and then the `Display()` function in the `Employee` class is invoked. You can invoke an overridden function at any time in the child class function using the scope resolution operator.

Polymorphism

Inheritance allows a new class to be written that extends the functionality of an existing class. *Polymorphism* is a result of inheritance that allows an object to be treated as different types. The term polymorphism comes from the words "poly" meaning "many," and "morph" meaning "form." In other words, an object can take on many forms — a feature of OOP that provides several robust programming capabilities, which are described in this section.

I will begin with a discussion on how an object can take on different forms using parent class pointers to a child object. This will lead to a discussion on virtual functions and heterogeneous collections.

Parent Class Pointers to Child Objects

In polymorphism, a child object can have a parent class pointer. In the example in the previous section "Inheritance," there were two subclasses of `Employee`: `SalaryEmployee` and `HourlyEmployee` (see Figure 4.2, page 78). You can create these objects dynamically using pointers and the new keyword.

To illustrate this, we begin with declarations and assignments with the data types of the left- and right-hand sides being identical, much like you have seen up until now.

```
SalaryEmployee * emp1;
HourlyEmployee * emp2;
emp1 = new SalaryEmployee();
emp2 = new HourlyEmployee();
```

This is not polymorphism, but normal assignments. For example, emp1 is declared as a pointer to a `SalaryEmployee` object, then assigned to point a `SalaryEmployee` object. The emp2 pointer is declared as a pointer to an HourlyEmployee object, then assigned to point to an HourlyEmployee object.

What polymorphism allows you to do is assign a pointer of a parent class to point to an object of a child class. Compare the following statements to the previous declarations.

```
Employee * emp1, * emp2;
emp1 = new SalaryEmployee();
emp2 = new HourlyEmployee();
```

This is an example of polymorphism. Both the emp1 and emp2 pointers were declared to point to Employee objects. However, emp1 actually points to a SalaryEmployee object, and emp2 actually points to an HourlyEmployee object (see Figure 4.6).

Figure 4.6 A parent class pointer pointing to a child class object.

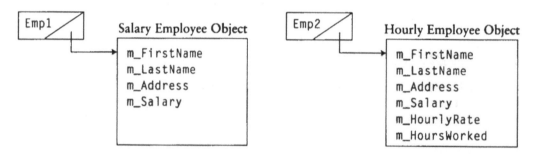

This concept also carries through to multiple levels of inheritance. Figure 4.3 (page 79) shows a FullTimeHourly class derived from HourlyEmployee which is derived from Employee. The following statements illustrate the various forms that a FullTimeHourly object can be represented.

```
FullTimeHourly rich;    //a FullTimeHourly object
FullTimeHourly * f = &rich;
HourlyEmployee * h = &rich;
Employee * e = &rich;
```

The pointers f, h, and e all point to the object rich, yet each is a different data type. The object rich can now take on the form of a FullTimeHourly object, an HourlyEmployee object, or an Employee object.

Parent Class References to a Child Object

As with pointers, a parent class reference can be used to refer to a child class object. For example, the following statements are valid.

```
HourlyEmployee bill;
Employee & refToBill = bill;
```

The object bill is an HourlyEmployee, but refToBill is a reference of type Employee. Polymorphism allows you to do this, as you saw with pointers in the previous section.

Why would you want this capability? Why not just declare the pointers or references to be what they actually refer to? The answer depends on the context in which the objects are being used. The following situations use a parent class pointer or reference to a child object:

- A parameter or return value of a function can be many different types of objects by declaring itself as a common parent.
- Overridden functions can be invoked dynamically at runtime, without knowing at compile time what type the actual object will be.
- A heterogeneous collection of objects can be created, as long as the objects all share a common parent.

Each of these scenarios will be discussed in later sections. First, I need to discuss casting — an issue that arises when using parent class pointers.

Casting Down the Inheritance Hierarchy

C++ allows you to have a parent class pointer that points to a child object. However, there are times when doing this confuses the compiler. For example, consider the following class declarations:

```
class Mammal {
public:
    void Eat();
};

class Cat : public Mammal {
public:
    void Sleep();
};
```

The following statement is valid and will compile.

```
Mammal * garfield = new Cat();
```

Note that the object instantiated in memory is a Cat object, so garfield points to a Cat even though it is declared to point to a Mammal. The Cat object has two member functions: Eat() and Sleep(). However, only the Eat() function can be invoked directly using the garfield pointer. For example, the following statement is valid and compiles:

```
garfield->Eat();
```

The compiler thinks that garfield points to a Mammal, and the Mammal class has a member function called Eat(). The following statement does not compile:

```
garfield->Sleep();   //generates compiler error!
```

The compiler does not find a Sleep() function in the Mammal class, which is expected because the Mammal class does not contain a Sleep() function. To invoke a child class function using a parent class pointer, the pointer needs to be cast down the inheritance hierarchy to the appropriate type of the object.

For example, to invoke the Sleep() function, the garfield pointer needs to be cast to a Cat pointer, which can be accomplished by creating a Cat pointer, as follows:

```
Cat * temp = (Cat *) garfield;
temp->Sleep();
```

Alternatively, you can cast the garfield object and invoke the function in a single statement:

```
((Cat *) garfield)->Sleep();
```

In either situation, you need to be careful when casting down a hierarchy. An illegal cast will cause your program to terminate at runtime. To illustrate, the following declares a Dog class that also inherits from Mammal:

```
class Dog : public Mammal {
public:
    void Sleep();
};
```

The following statements will compile, although the second statement is not valid:

```
Mammal * garfield = new Cat();
((Dog *) garfield)->Sleep();
```

The compiler finds the Sleep() function in the Dog class and assumes the statement is valid. At runtime, when the garfield pointer is cast to a Dog, the result is undefined and the program may crash.

A parent class reference can also be cast down to a child class reference — similar to the technique of casting pointers. This technique is demonstrated in the following statements:

```
Dog lassie;
Mammal & parentRef = lassie;
Dog & childRef = (Dog &) parentRef;
```

The parentRef reference is declared as a reference to a Mammal, but it actually refers to a Dog object. The childRef reference is also a reference to the Dog object, but is initialized by casting the parentRef down to a Dog reference.

Take special care to avoid situations that require casting down a hierarchy. In "Virtual Functions," page 95, I will show you how to use virtual functions to avoid casting in situations like the Sleep() function discussed here.

Polymorphic Parameters

One of the uses of polymorphism is to allow a function to accept a hierarchy of objects, and similarly, return an object belonging to a particular hierarchy. This section illustrates how to implement this with a function that contains an Employee parameter, where the Employee class is the parent of several subclasses.

Suppose you need to write a function that takes in an Employee object and searches the company directory for the employee's phone number. This function needs to be able to search the directory for any type of employee — assuming the classes are arranged in the hierarchy shown in Figure 4.3 (page 79).

You could write a function called FindPhoneNumber() and overload this function for the various types of employees. This would create a group of functions with the following prototypes:

```
//not taking advantage of polymorphism
long FindPhoneNumber(const Employee &);
long FindPhoneNumber(const SalaryEmployee &);
long FindPhoneNumber(const HourlyEmployee &);
long FindPhoneNumber(const FullTimeHourly &);
long FindPhoneNumber(const PartTimeHourly &);
```

You would need a FindPhoneNumber() function for each type of employee. As you can see, this gets tedious and repetitive, and the Employee class only has a few subclasses. In addition, if a new subclass of Employee is added to the program, a new function would need to be written.

To avoid this scenario, take advantage of polymorphism. Each of the overloaded Find-PhoneNumber() functions takes in a different parameter, but the different parameters all have something in common: they are all children of Employee. The following version of Find-PhoneNumber() works for Employee objects and any child objects of Employee:

```
//taking advantage of polymorphism
long FindPhoneNumber(const Employee &);
```

You can invoke this version of FindPhoneNumber() with an Employee object or any object from one of the subclasses of Employee. The following statements illustrate various ways to invoke this function:

```
Employee e1;
SalaryEmployee e2;
HourlyEmployee * h = new HourlyEmployee();
FindPhoneNumber(e1);
FindPhoneNumber(e2);
FindPhoneNumber(*h);
```

Passing the e1 object is valid because it is an Employee object, which the FindPhoneNumber() function is expecting. Passing the e2 and h objects is valid because SalaryEmployee and HourlyEmployee objects are also Employee objects.

Return Values with Polymorphism

Polymorphism can also be used to return a value from a function. For example, the following function declares a return value of type Employee:

```
Employee FindEmployee(char *, char *);
```

Certainly an Employee can be returned from FindEmployee(). However, using polymorphism, any object instantiated from a child class of Employee can also be returned.

Polymorhpism and Overridden Functions

An interesting result occurs when using parent class pointers or references to invoke a member function that is overridden. Which function is invoked at runtime: the parent's or the child's? The answer depends on whether or not the member function in question is virtual or not. This section discusses the effect of invoking overridden functions that are both non-virtual and virtual. I will begin by discussing non-virtual functions because you have been working with them exclusively up until now.

Non-Virtual Functions

A *non-virtual function* is simply a member function of a class that is not virtual. (Virtual functions are discussed in the next section.) To illustrate how non-virtual functions are invoked when using polymorphism, I use the following classes — which contain non-virtual member functions:

```
class Mammal {
public:
    void Eat();
};


class Cat : public Mammal {
public:
    void Eat();
};


class Dog : public Mammal {
public:
    void Eat();
};
```

Notice the Cat and Dog classes override the Eat() function of the parent class Mammal. The Eat() functions simply display a message box stating which type of animal is eating. The implementation for the Mammal class is listed here, and the Cat and Dog implementations are similar.

```
void Mammal::Eat()
{
    MessageBox(NULL,"Mammal is eating","Inside Eat()",
            MB_OK | MB_ICONINFORMATION);
}
```

The following statements do not use polymorphism, and it is no surprise which Eat() function is invoked.

```
Mammal * m = new Mammal();
m->Eat();    //invokes the Eat() function in the Mammal class
Dog * muffy = new Dog();
muffy->Eat();    //invokes Eat() in the Dog class
Cat * garfield = new Cat();
garfield->Eat();    //invokes Eat() in the Cat class
```

Each object invokes its appropriate Eat() function, which is appropriate because cats, dogs, and mammals eat differently. Figure 4.7 shows the output of these statements.

Figure 4.7   Invoking overridden member functions without polymorphism results in the child class function being invoked.

Now consider the following statements that use polymorphism to invoke the Eat() function. Each of these statements is valid and compiles successfully.

```
Mammal * felix = new Cat();
felix->Eat();
Mammal * fido = new Dog();
fido->Eat();
```

Figure 4.8 shows the result of these statements. In both cases, the Eat() function in the Mammal class is executed. What is important to realize in these statements is that the only reason they compile is because the Mammal class contains a member function called Eat(). Equally important is the fact that at runtime, it is this Eat() function in the Mammal class that is executed.

Figure 4.8 Invoking non-virtual, overridden functions using polymorphism results in the parent class function being invoked.

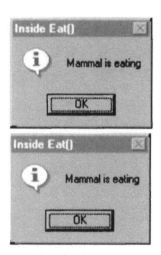

In other words, if an overridden member function is not virtual [like the Eat() function], then the function that is invoked at runtime depends on the reference being used to invoke the function. When invoking a function using a parent class pointer or reference, then the parent function is invoked at runtime.

This may or may not be the desired result. In some design situations, you may want the parent class function to be invoked. However, it is typically more desirable to have the appropriate child class function invoked. For instance, in the Eat() function scenario, it would have been more appropriate if the Eat() function in the Cat and Dog class had been invoked instead of the Eat() function in the Mammal class. The next section shows how virtual functions can be used to accomplish this result.

Virtual Functions

An overridden, virtual function is invoked in a different manner than a non-virtual function. Virtual functions are described as *late-binding*, meaning the compiler does not determine at compile time which function is actually going to be invoked at runtime. Instead, when a virtual function is invoked at runtime, the appropriate child function is determined by the type of class the object is instantiated from.

A virtual member function is created using the virtual keyword. A child class overrides a virtual function just like any other member function, except the child also declares the function as virtual. The following example uses the Mammal, Cat, and Dog classes from the previous section, except the Eat() function is changed to virtual in the Mammal and Cat class to illustrate how virtual functions are invoked when polymorphism is being used.

```
class Mammal {
public:
   virtual void Eat();
};


class Cat : public Mammal {
public:
   virtual void Eat();
};


class Dog : public Mammal {
public:
   virtual void Eat();
};
```

Now that the Eat() function is virtual in each class, the following statements have a different result as compared to the previous section. The output is in Figure 4.9.

```
Mammal * felix = new Cat();
felix->Eat();
Mammal * fido = new Dog();
fido->Eat();
```

Figure 4.9 **Invoking virtual functions using polymorphism results in the child class function being invoked.**

The previous statements compile successfully because the compiler sees the Eat() function in the Mammal class. However, at runtime, because the functions are virtual, invoking Eat() using the felix pointer executes the Eat() function in the Cat class. Similarly, invoking Eat() using fido executes Eat() in the Dog class.

NOTE: A child class can override a parent's virtual function without declaring the overriding function as virtual. This "turns off" the behavior of virtual functions for that particular child class.

Advantages of Virtual Functions

When using non-virtual functions, if you want the child class function to be invoked, then the pointer needs to be cast to the appropriate child class. For example, if the Eat() function in the Dog class is not declared as virtual, then a parent class pointer needs to be cast down to type Dog pointer to invoke the Eat() function of Dog.

```
Mammal * fido = new Dog();
((Dog *) fido)->Eat();
```

This is not always a desired solution because casting a pointer down to a child object means you have to know what type of object to cast the pointer to. In most situations, you do not know what the object actually is, nor do you want to go through the work of discovering this information.

Virtual functions solve this problem for you. If you have a pointer (or a reference) to a Mammal, and you want that Mammal to eat, you can simply invoke the Eat() function using the Mammal pointer. If the Eat() function is virtual, then the Eat() function in the appropriate child class is executed. For example, the following function uses a polymorphic parameter and invokes Eat() on whatever Mammal object is passed to the function.

```
void FeedAnimal(Mammal & animal) {
    animal.Eat();
}
```

Any Mammal object or child object of Mammal can be passed to the FeedAnimal function. The FeedAnimal function does not need to determine what type of Mammal the animal is, and no casting is required to invoke the appropriate Eat() function of the animal.

Heterogeneous Collections

Polymorphism allows you to create a collection of objects that contain different types, as long as the objects share a common parent. A *heterogeneous collection* is a data structure (like an array or linked list) where the objects in the collection are of a different type.

To demonstrate the usefulness of a heterogeneous collection, I will use the payroll administration example discussed throughout the earlier sections of this chapter. Suppose you need to implement the payroll administration program for a company with 200 employees, and you have designed an inheritance hierarchy like the one shown in Figure 4.3 (page 79). In other words, there are three different types of employees: those who are paid a salary and two different types of hourly employees.

Your first task is to find a data structure for storing the employee objects. One solution could be to create three different arrays — one for each type of employee — as the following code demonstrates:

```
SalaryEmployee * salaried[200];
FullTimeHourly * fullhourly[200];
PartTimeHourly * parthourly[200];
```

There are several disadvantages to this approach. First, although you know there are 200 employees at the company, their distribution in terms of how they are paid will vary as employees come and go within in the company. Each array has 200 elements to allow for extreme situations, where each employee is the same type. Another disadvantage is that you need to keep track of three different data structures, instead of one centralized data structure. In addition, if a new type of employee is added to the program later, an array for these other employees will need to be added to the program as well.

You can avoid each of these scenarios by using a heterogeneous collection of Employee objects. Polymorphism allows a parent class pointer to point to a child object. In the payroll administration program, you could put all employees in the same array because the classes involved share a common parent, the Employee class.

The following statements create an array of 200 Employee pointers and show the syntax for initializing some of the elements in the array:

```
Employee * employees[200];
employees[0] = new SalaryEmployee();
employees[1] = new FullTimeHourly();
employees[2] = new SalaryEmployee();
employees[3] = new PartTimeHourly();
//and so forth
```

You do not need to worry about the number of each different type of employee in the array. In addition, if a new type of employee is required later, the employees array will still suffice as long as the new class inherits from Employee.

Abstraction

The topics of inheritance and polymorphism lead to a discussion on abstraction, the last of the four OOP fundamentals discussed at the beginning of this chapter. Abstraction is the process of designing abstract classes that must be subclassed to use the abstract class' functionality. An *abstract class* is a class that cannot be instantiated. In C++, this is implemented by adding a pure virtual function to a class.

This section explains when you might use an abstract class and describes the process of creating and implementing a pure virtual function.

When to Use Abstraction

The best way to determine if a class should be abstract or not is to decide whether the class represents a distinct object, or if the class instead represents a generalization of various different types of objects. For example, I used a class called Mammal in the section "Virtual Functions" as the parent of the Cat and Dog classes. This design is appropriate because a cat "is a" mammal and a dog "is a" mammal. The Mammal class contains all the attributes and behaviors that each mammal has in common.

However, the concept of a mammal is abstract. It does not make sense to instantiate a Mammal object because there is no such thing as an animal that is just a mammal. Does this mean our Mammal class should not be used? Certainly not, and in fact, the opposite is true. There are many animals that are mammals; there aren't any animals that are *just* mammals. This is a perfect scenario of when to use an abstract class.

I will now discuss another example using abstraction from a real-world programming viewpoint. The Employee class in the section "Inheritance" (page 76) is the parent class of several other classes (see Figure 4.3, page 79). It contained the attributes and behaviors common to every employee, such as a name and address. However, I doubt any employee of this company would want to be *just* an Employee object, because all of the information to pay that employee is found in the various child classes. The Employee class in this design is abstract because at no point in the program would you want to instantiate an Employee object.

Taking the argument one step further, you could argue that an Employee object should never be instantiated because Employee objects do not contain any payroll information. The concept of creating abstract parent classes is a common and powerful feature of OOP and C++. The next section discusses how to make a class abstract in C++.

Pure Virtual Functions

A *pure virtual* function is a virtual member function of a class that has no implementation. In other words, the class has a behavior that does not know or want to implement. This section uses the Employee class to illustrate the usage of pure virtual functions and abstract classes.

NOTE: A class in C++ is abstract if one or more of its member functions is a pure virtual function.

Consider the Employee class — which contained "set" and "get" functions and a Print-MailingLabel() function. The behavior that I really want each Employee to be able to perform is computing their pay. However, all of the data needed to compute an employee's pay is in the child classes. I can still add a ComputePay() member function to the Employee class, with the specific implementation being done in the each child class. If I make ComputePay() virtual, then the appropriate function will be invoked at runtime.

The following revised Employee class declares ComputePay() as a pure virtual function. To indicate that a function will *not* have an implementation (thereby making the class abstract), the C++ syntax is to assign the function equal to 0 in its prototype.

```
class Employee
{
private:
    char m_FirstName[20];
    char m_LastName[30];
    double m_Salary;
    char m_Address[100];
public:
    //various constructors and "set" and "get" functions
    ...
    virtual double ComputePay() = 0; //pure virtual
    void PrintMailingLabel();
};
```

C++ does not provide a special syntax to declare a class abstract. (In other words, abstract is not a keyword.) However, the Employee class is now abstract because it contains a pure virtual function, ComputePay(). The Employee class can no longer be instantiated.

In addition, a child class must override any pure virtual functions inherited from a parent or the child class itself will become abstract. For example, if a class inherits from Employee, that class must override ComputePay() or become abstract. This is an important design mechanism in OOP because it ensures that any objects instantiated from a subclass of Employee will have a ComputePay().

This creates a type of agreement between a parent and a child, forcing the child class to implement a function if the child class does not want to be abstract. For example, the following SalaryEmployee class overrides ComputePay() and therefore can be instantiated:

```
class SalaryEmployee : public Employee {
private:
   double m_Salary;
public:
   //various constructors and "set" and "get" functions
   ...
   virtual double ComputePay();
};
The implementation of ComputePay() might look like the following:

double SalaryEmployee::ComputePay() {
   return m_Salary/12.0;
}
```

Similarly, the FullTimeHourly and PartTimeHourly classes would need to include a virtual ComputePay() that overrides the one in Employee. With this implementation, you can now complete the payroll administration program. The following statements create a heterogeneous collection of Employee objects. Taking advantage of the behavior of virtual functions and the fact that each child class object must have a ComputePay() function, the employees of the company are paid using a simple for loop.

```
Employee * employees[200]; //200 pointers
//initialize each pointer
employees[0] = new SalaryEmployee();
employees[1] = new FullTimeHourly();
employees[2] = new PartTimeHourly();
//and so forth
for(int index = 0; index < 200; index++)
   employees[index]->ComputePay();
```

NOTE: You would not initialize the 200 objects in this fashion. The data would probably come from a database or other persistent storage. The code simply illustrates that each Employee pointer from the employees array can point to any child object of Employee.

Notice the for loop is used to invoke ComputePay() on each object in the employees array. Because ComputePay() is virtual, the appropriate child class function is invoked at runtime. For example, the first object in the array is a SalaryEmployee object, so ComputePay() in the SalaryEmployee class is executed when index is 0 at runtime. Similarly, ComputePay() in the

FullTimeHourly class is executed when index is 1, and ComputePay() in the PartTimeHourly class is executed when index is 2.

This design for the payroll administration program takes full advantage of inheritance, polymorphism, and abstraction. The Employee class is an abstract parent of all employees, ensuring that each child object has a ComputePay() function by making ComputePay() a pure virtual function. Polymorphism is used to create a heterogeneous collection of Employee objects, then ComputePay() is invoked on each object in the array without having to worry about which type of employee each object is.

The result is a dynamic and expandable program for paying employees. Suppose, for example, the company starts to hire contractors and a new class needs to be added to the program. A Contractor class will inherit from Employee, implement ComputePay(), and most of the existing code in the program will not even need to be modified.

Summary

The OOP concepts of inheritance, polymorphism, and abstraction allow you to design and implement reusable and functional classes. Inheritance allows a class to be subclassed, with the child class inheriting the members of the parent class. The "is a" relationship is used to determine when inheritance is appropriate.

Polymorphism is the ability of an object to take on many forms, using the fact that a child object "is a" parent object. This allows you to create heterogeneous collections and write virtual functions that link dynamically at runtime.

Abstraction is the process of creating classes that cannot be instantiated, but contain the common functionality of all of its derived classes. A class with a pure virtual function is abstract, and these functions are overridden by the child classes.

You will find that inheritance, polymorphism, and abstraction are found throughout MFC, and a good foundation in understanding these concepts is a necessity in understanding MFC. Now that you are familiar with these fundamental concepts of OOP, you are ready to start writing Windows applications using MFC — the subject of the remainder of this book.

Chapter 5

An Introduction to MFC

Microsoft Foundation Classes (MFC) are a collection of C++ classes used to develop Windows applications using an object-oriented programming language. MFC is often referred to as a collection of wrapper classes because many of the classes act as a wrapper around certain Win32 API functions. *Win32 API* is the 32-bit Windows application programming interface — a collection of C functions that are used to create a Windows application using the procedural language C.

Long before C++ was created, C was the language used to develop the Windows operating system and Windows programs. Thousands of existing programs for Windows are written in C. For this reason, MFC was created on top of the Win32 API, with many of the classes acting as a wrapper around Win32 API functions. For example, there is a collection of Win32 API functions with a handle to a window as a parameter. Because these are behaviors of a window, a CWnd class was created in MFC that contains these API functions as members. In other words, invoking a member function of the CWnd class eventually invokes an appropriate C function in the Win32 API.

Why was MFC created if the Win32 API was already an established and popular API? The following are some of the advantages and goals of MFC:

- MFC is object-oriented, allowing developers to take advantage of OOP concepts like encapsulation, inheritance, polymorphism, and abstraction.
- The amount of code required to develop a Windows application is significantly less with MFC.
- MFC programs are easier to write and understand.

- Execution speed is comparable to that of Win32 apps.
- A Win32 API function can be invoked directly from an MFC app.

These goals are accomplished by the MFC architecture. The term *architecture* refers to the foundation of an MFC program. A Windows application needs a window and a thread of execution for the messages of that window to be processed and dispersed to the appropriate message handlers. Sound like a lot of work? It can be, but the architecture of MFC hides many of these details from you.

For example, a console application has the main() function as its entry point. With a Windows application, the entry point is a function called WinMain(). WinMain() is responsible for starting a message loop to handle and disperse messages for the window. If you write a Windows program in C using the Win32 API, you would need to write a WinMain() function. However, the MFC architecture provides WinMain() for you, allowing you to focus on the details of what your particular application needs to do.

This chapter discusses the architecture of MFC and how it is used to develop Windows applications. You will see a simple MFC application that uses the CWinApp and CFrameWnd classes — two of the fundamental classes in the MFC architecture. Message handling is introduced in this chapter — a fundamental feature of every Windows application. In addition, some of the utility classes of MFC will be discussed, including the CString, CRect, and CArray classes.

The CWinApp **Class**

CWinApp provides member functions for initializing, running, and terminating a Windows application. When writing a Windows program using MFC, you inherit a new class from CWinApp and override its various member functions. You also create one global instance of your CWinApp class, which WinMain() uses to invoke the overridden methods.

There are some specific member functions of the CWinApp class that you should be familiar with because they play an essential role in the MFC architecture. Their prototypes are listed here.

```
virtual BOOL InitInstance();
virtual int Run();
virtual int OnIdle(LONG lCount);
virtual int ExitInstance();
```

Each of these is a virtual member function that is invoked at various times in your program's existence. I will now discuss each of these functions in detail.

InitInstance()

The InitInstance() function is invoked by WinMain() for each instance of your program. Windows allows for multiple instances of the same program to be executing, and InitInstance() is invoked for each of these. You will usually override InitInstance() because this is where you create and display the program's window. If InitInstance() is successful, then the return value is TRUE; otherwise, it returns FALSE.

CWinApp is a child of CWinThread, which provides the main thread of execution for the program. In addition, CWinThread contains a member variable, m_pMainWnd, which is a pointer to the program's main window. When you create the program's main window in InitInstance(), be sure to initialize m_pMainWnd to point to it. This is demonstrated in the upcoming program in "A Minimal MFC Application" (page 107).

Run()

Your CWinApp object runs in its own thread of execution because CWinApp is derived from the CWinThread class. When this thread is started within the MFC architecture, the Run() function is invoked. Here is where your MFC program listens for messages and dispatches them to the appropriate window.

You do not normally need to override this function, unless you want to control how messages are dispersed. The Run() function will continue to listen for messages and disperse them until the WM_QUIT message occurs — usually a result of the user closing the program's window. The return value of Run() is the value returned by WinMain().

OnIdle()

The OnIdle() function allows you to perform small tasks in the background when the program is not busy handling messages. Run() invokes OnIdle() when no messages are in the message queue.

The parameter lCount is the number of times OnIdle() has been invoked since the last message. The return value of OnIdle() determines whether or not Run() should keep invoking OnIdle() while no new messages occur. If the return value is nonzero, Run() will invoke OnIdle() again if no new messages have appeared in the message queue. If OnIdle() returns 0, then the Run() function will no longer call OnIdle() until a new message is received and dispersed.

Be careful not to overdo things in OnIdle(). Your program cannot respond to user input while OnIdle() is executing, so OnIdle() should do tasks that are completed quickly.

ExitInstance()

This function is invoked each time an instance of the program terminates. You do not invoke this function directly. Run() calls ExitInstance() for you when the program is about to terminate. Use ExitInstance() to free up any resources or memory that might have been allocated in the InitInstance() function. The return value is the value that will eventually be returned by WinMain().

The CFrameWnd Class

The CFrameWnd class represents a typical window in a Windows application. Most Windows programs use CFrameWnd for their main window because it provides the standard features most users are familiar with. For example, the CFrameWnd can contain a menu, toolbars, and a status bar. They can also be resized, minimized and maximized, and moved around the screen.

Your `CFrameWnd` is typically created in the `InitInstance()` function of your `CWinApp` object. The memory for a `CFrameWnd` object must be created on the heap using the `new` keyword. You assign the pointer returned from `new` to the `m_pMainWnd` variable. The window then needs to be constructed using one of the following techniques:

- Invoke the `Create()` member function.
- Invoke the `LoadFrame()` member function.
- Indirectly create the window using a `CDocTemplate` object.

The `Create()` and `LoadFrame()` functions are similar, with `LoadFrame()` requiring fewer parameters. The `CDocTemplate` object is part of the Document/View architecture of MFC and is discussed in Chapter 9. I will discuss the `Create()` function in the following section. Using `LoadFrame()` is similar; check the documentation for its prototype.

Create()

The `Create()` function is invoked after the `CFrameWnd` object is instantiated using `new`. The following is its prototype:

```
BOOL Create( LPCTSTR lpszClassName,
             LPCTSTR lpszWindowName,
             DWORD dwStyle = WS_OVERLAPPEDWINDOW,
             const RECT& rect = rectDefault,
             CWnd* pParentWnd = NULL,
             LPCTSTR lpszMenuName = NULL,
             DWORD dwExStyle = 0,
             CCreateContext* pContext = NULL );
```

`Create()` has many parameters, but notice that all but two of them have default arguments.

`lpszClassName` This string refers to the type of window being created. It represents a *class* of window that has been registered with Windows, but do not confuse it with an OOP class. You can register your own class of window using the `AfxRegisterWndClass()` function. An advantage of MFC is that you rarely need to be concerned with creating and registering your own window classes.

`lpszWindowName` This string appears in the title bar of the window. The `dwStyle` parameter defaults to `WS_OVERLAPPEDWINDOW`, which creates a standard frame window with a caption, border, system menu, and minimize and maximize buttons. Use the style parameter to remove some of the styles or add other features like a horizontal and vertical scroll bar. The most commonly used window styles are listed in Table 5.1.

Table 5.1 Window styles.

Style	Result
WS_OVERLAPPED	An overlapped window with a border and caption
WS_MAXIMIZE	Window is initially maximized
WS_MINIMIZE	Window is initially minimized
WS_MAXIMIZEBOX	Includes a maximize button
WS_MINIMIZEBOX	Includes a minimize button
WS_HSCROLL	Includes a horizontal scrollbar
WS_VSCROLL	Includes a vertical scrollbar
WS_VISIBLE	Window is initially visible
WS_THICKFRAME	Creates a thick frame so the window can be resized
WS_CHILD	Window has a parent window
WS_SYSMENU	Includes a system menu

The rect parameter is an object of type RECT, which is a simple structure that contains four integers for the upper-left and lower-right coordinates of a rectangle. The RECT structure is used frequently in Windows programming for determining the size and placement of a window on the desktop. The rect argument passed to Create() represents the initial bounds of the window being created.

Windows can have another window be its parent (not to be confused with inheritance in OOP). For example, a dialog box can be a child of a frame window. Parent windows also play a role in Document/View. If pParentWindow is NULL, then the desktop becomes the window's parent.

The dwExStyle parameter is for any extra styles the window may have. Some of these styles include features like context-sensitive help and various border styles. See the documentation for a complete list of values for dwExStyle.

The final parameter, pContext, is for connecting documents and views. You rarely need to use this value.

A Minimal MFC Application

Now that you have seen some of the features of CWinApp and CFrameWnd, I will show you how easy it is to create a minimal Windows application using these classes and the MFC architecture. You need to create the appropriate workspace in Visual C++ to take advantage of MFC, so be sure to read the sidebar "Creating a Project in Visual C++ that Uses MFC" on page 118.

The following steps create an MFC application that displays the current time in a frame window. I will use the CWinApp and CFrameWnd classes to create the program, which uses event handling to display the time in the window. The details of how the events are handled are explained in detail in "Message Handling" (page 111).

1. Derive a class from CWinApp. To take advantage of the MFC architecture, you need to derive a class from CWinApp and override the appropriate member functions. In this example, I override InitInstance() to create the frame window and initialize the m_pMainWnd member variable.

```
//Filename: TimeDisplayApp.h
#ifndef _TIMEDISPLAYAPP_H
#define _TIMEDISPLAYAPP_H
#include <afxwin.h>


class TimeDisplayApp : public CWinApp {
public:
    virtual BOOL InitInstance();
};
#endif
```

Be sure to declare InitInstance() as virtual so that your child function is executed at runtime.

2. Derive a class from CFrameWnd. The following class inherits from CFrameWnd and includes the necessary declarations for handling the WM_PAINT message, which is generated by the operating system every time the window needs to be repainted.

```
//Filename: TimeDisplayFrameWnd.h
#ifndef _TIMEDISPLAYFRAMEWND_H
#define _TIMEDISPLAYFRAMEWND_H
#include <afxwin.h>


class TimeDisplayFrameWnd : public CFrameWnd {
public:
    TimeDisplayFrameWnd();    //constructor
protected:
    afx_msg void OnPaint();   //WM_PAINT message handler
    DECLARE_MESSAGE_MAP()
};
#endif
```

The Create() function will be invoked in the constructor. The OnPaint() function is invoked from the Run() method when a WM_PAINT message appears. DECLARE_MESSAGE_MAP() is a macro that encapsulates the details of event handling. This must appear at the end of the class declaration.

3. Implement the Application Class. The following shows the implementation file for the `TimeDisplayApp` class.

```
//Filename: TimeDisplayApp.cpp
#include "TimeDisplayApp.h"
#include "TimeDisplayFrameWnd.h"

BOOL TimeDisplayApp::InitInstance() {
    //instantiate the frame object
    m_pMainWnd = new TimeDisplayFrameWnd();
    //show the window, now that it is created
    m_pMainWnd->ShowWindow(m_nCmdShow);
    //send a WM_PAINT message directly to the window
    m_pMainWnd->UpdateWindow();
    return TRUE;
}


    //single global instance of the app class
TimeDisplayApp theApp;
```

The `InitInstance()` function creates a new frame window, then shows the window using the `ShowWindow()` member function. This function must be called to display the window, and the first time it is invoked in an application, you should use the `m_nCmdShow` member variable. This variable displays the window with settings the user might have selected. Subsequent calls to `ShowWindow()` can use one of the values shown in Table 5.2.

Table 5.2 `ShowWindow()` **Styles.**

Style	Result
SW_MINIMIZE	Minimizes the window
SW_MAXIMIZE	Maximizes the window
SW_RESTORE	Restores the window to its previous state
SW_SHOW	Shows the window with its current location and size
SW_SHOWNORMAL	Shows the window and gives it current focus
SW_SHOWNOACTIVE	Shows the window but does not change the focus

The MFC architecture requires a single global instance of your application class, which is instantiated here in the implementation file. The identifier you choose is irrelevant, but App-Wizard uses `theApp`, so I have done the same.

4. Implement the Frame Window Class. The next step is to implement the class you derived from `CFrameWnd`. A typical implementation invokes the `Create()` function in the constructor to create the type of window desired. The event handling is also implemented here, including the message map and each message handler. The following shows the implementation for the `TimeDisplayFrameWnd` class.

```
//Filename: TimeDisplayFrameWnd.cpp
#include "TimeDisplayFrameWnd.h"

TimeDisplayFrameWnd::TimeDisplayFrameWnd() {
    RECT position;
    position.top = 20;
    position.left = 40;
    position.bottom = 170;
    position.right = 340;
    Create(NULL, "My First MFC Application",
        WS_OVERLAPPEDWINDOW, position);
}

BEGIN_MESSAGE_MAP(TimeDisplayFrameWnd, CFrameWnd)
    ON_WM_PAINT()
END_MESSAGE_MAP()

void TimeDisplayFrameWnd::OnPaint() {
    CPaintDC paintDC(this);    //obtain a device context
    //create a string with the current time
    CTime currentTime = CTime::GetCurrentTime();
    CString timeString = currentTime.Format("%#c");
    //draw the string in the window
    paintDC.TextOut(20,20,timeString);
}
```

The constructor creates an overlapped window that will be displayed 40 pixels over and 20 pixels down from the upper-left corner of the window. The width is 300 pixels and the height is 150 pixels, and the string "My First MFC Application" will appear in the window's title bar.

The message map will be discussed in detail in the next section. For now, note that the `OnPaint()` function determines the current time, formats it into a string, and displays the string in the window 20 pixels over and 20 pixels down from the upper-left corner of the window using the `TextOut()` function. Figure 5.1 shows the output of the program.

Figure 5.1   Output of the minimal MFC application.

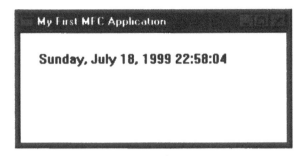

Message Handling

A Windows program is centered around *messages*. A message sent to a Windows application is placed in a queue called the *message queue*. The Run() function in CWinApp() pulls messages out of the queue and invokes a corresponding message handler. A *message handler* is a function that corresponds to a specific message to implement the functionality unique to that message.

Messages can be generated by the operating system, such as the WM_PAINT message. WM_PAINT occurs each time the window needs to redraw itself, which is something the operating system determines. WM_CREATE is sent to an application after a window is created but before it becomes visible. After a window is removed from the screen, a WM_DESTROY message is generated. Many other messages are generated by the operating system during the lifetime of a window.

Messages can also come from user input. For example, clicking the mouse generates events like WM_LBUTTONDOWN and WM_LBUTTONDBLCLK. When a menu item is selected or an accelerator key is pressed, a WM_COMMAND message is generated. A WM_CHAR message is generated from typing a key on the keyboard.

This section discusses how to associate a particular message with a message handler. MFC provides macros for simplifying the process, which encapsulate the details that you do not need to be concerned with. You saw some of the macros in the MFC application in the previous section, and I will now discuss the steps involved to use these macros to handle messages.

1. Determine the Message Handlers.   First, determine which messages you want to handle. Each Windows message has a corresponding message handler that you need to implement in your class. For example, if you want to handle WM_PAINT messages, you need to include a function OnPaint().

You might ask how the message map knows to map the function OnPaint() to the WM_PAINT message. Windows messages that begin with WM_ each have a corresponding, predetermined message handler name. The name of the message handler is the name of the message preceded by On, and it uses mixed-case capitalization. For example, the message handler for a WM_LBUTTONDOWN message is OnLButtonDown(), the message handler for the WM_CREATE message is OnCreate(), and so on. View the documentation for a complete list of Windows messages and their corresponding handlers.

The following declaration demonstrates a class with two message handlers.

```
class MyFrameWnd : public CFrameWnd {
    //member variables and functions...
    afx_msg void OnPaint();
    afx_msg void OnLButtonDown(UINT, CPoint);
    //remainder of the class declaration
};
```

This class can handle WM_PAINT and WM_LBUTTONDOWN messages. The identifier afx_msg simply denotes that the function is a message handler. It has no implementation, and you can omit it if desired. Note that including the message handler in your class does not cause the message to be handled automatically. You need to associate the message with the handler using the message map, discussed next.

2. Declare a Message Map.   The message map is responsible for mapping a message to its corresponding message handler. Any class that inherits from CCmdTarget can contain a message map. The DECLARE_MESSAGE_MAP() macro is placed at the end of the class declaration, as the following class demonstrates.

```
class MyFrameWnd : public CFrameWnd {
    //member variables and function declarations
    afx_msg void OnPaint();
    afx_msg void OnLButtonDown(UINT, CPoint);

    DECLARE_MESSAGE_MAP()
};
```

Notice that a semicolon is not required when using the macro. Behind the scenes, the macro adds an array to your class that contains AFX_MSGMAP_ENTRY structures. Each structure consists of a message and a message handler. The macro also adds an AFX_MSGMAP structure that contains a pointer to the message map array and a pointer to the parent class's message map array. If you want to learn more about the details of DECLARE_MESSAGE_MAP(), you can view the macro in the afxwin.h header file.

3. Implement the Message Map.   In the implementation file of your class that contains the message map, you need to include an implementation of the message map. MFC provides macros to simplify this process. Use the BEGIN_MESSAGE_MAP() and END_MESSAGE_MAP() macros to denote the beginning and end of the message map. You determine which messages this class will handle in between these macros.

For example, the following message map handles the WM_PAINT and WM_LBUTTONDOWN messages.

```
BEGIN_MESSAGE_MAP(MyFrameWnd, CFrameWnd)
    ON_WM_PAINT()
    ON_WM_LBUTTONDOWN()
END_MESSAGE_MAP()
```

The BEGIN_MESSAGE_MAP() macro requires two arguments: the class that is handling the messages and its parent class. (Internally, the macro needs to identify the message map of the parent.) The END_MESSAGE_MAP() macro simply denotes the end of the implementation of this message map.

When implementing a message map, you can use the ON_ macro to include an entry in the message map for a particular Windows message, as the previous statements illustrated with ON_WM_PAINT() and ON_WM_LBUTTONDOWN().

Another common macro is the one for WM_COMMAND messages — generated from many different sources like menu items and toolbars. Each source of a WM_COMMAND message has a unique identifier, and each identifier can have an associated message handler. The following message map has several entries, including an example that maps messages with the ID_LOGON identifier to the LogonToServer() function.

```
BEGIN_MESSAGE_MAP(SomeFrameWnd, CFrameWnd)
    ON_WM_CREATE()    //maps WM_CREATE to OnCreate()
    ON_WM_DESTROY()   //maps WM_DESTROY to OnDestroy()
    ON_WM_CHAR()      //maps WM_CHAR to OnChar()
    ON_COMMAND(ID_LOGON, LogonToServer)
END_MESSAGE_MAP()
```

This particular window is handling WM_CREATE, WM_DESTROY, and WM_CHAR messages. In addition, WM_COMMAND messages that are generated from an item with the ID_LOGON identifier will be handled by the LogonToServer() function.

You can also define your own messages in Windows. The message map macro for creating an entry for user-defined messages is ON_MESSAGE(). The following message map contains an entry for a WM_YOURMESSAGE which declares its message handler as the OnYourMessage() function.

```
BEGIN_MESSAGE_MAP(SomeFrameWnd, CFrameWnd)
    ON_MESSAGE(WM_YOURMESSAGE, OnYourMessage)
    //other message map entries here
END_MESSAGE_MAP()
```

4. Implement the Message Handlers. Each message handler is a member function of a class, so its implementation needs to appear in the implementation file of the class. Once the message map has been declared and implemented, the corresponding message handler of a message is invoked automatically when the message occurs.

The following example shows an implementation of OnPaint() and OnLButtonDown() to demonstrate when the messages occur. The OnPaint() function increments a counter and displays it in the window at the x and y coordinates of where the user clicks the mouse.

```
void MyFrameWnd::OnPaint() {
  m_Counter++;
  CString display;
  display.Format("Painted %d times", m_Counter);
  CPaintDC paintDC(this);
```

```
    paintDC.TextOut(m_X, m_Y, display);
}


void MyFrameWnd::OnLButtonDown(UINT flags, CPoint point) {
    //update x and y
    m_X = point.x;
    m_Y = point.y;
    //repaint the window
    Invalidate();
    UpdateWindow();
}
```

The OnLButtonDown() function needs to generate a WM_PAINT message, which is accomplished by invoking UpdateWindow(). Invoking the Invalidate() function ensures that the entire window is repainted. If Invalidate() is not invoked here, then the call to UpdateWindow() will still create a WM_PAINT message. However, the device context obtained in OnPaint() will think the entire window is valid and nothing will actually be repainted. Device contexts are discussed in detail in Chapter 6, "Device Contexts, GDI Objects, and Common Messages."

Figure 5.2   Clicking the mouse causes the display to appear at the coordinates where the mouse was clicked.

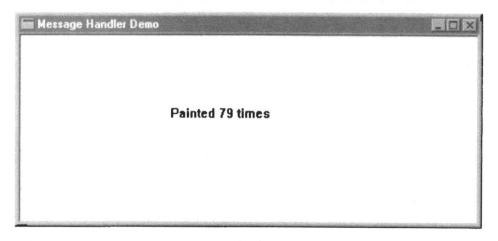

Figure 5.2 shows the window associated with this program. Run the program yourself and manipulate the window to determine when paint events actually occur. For example, you will find that resizing the window can generate hundreds of WM_PAINT messages in a very short time, but moving the window around the screen does not cause WM_PAINT messages to occur. Also, try clicking in the window to see what the OnLButtonDown() message handler does in this example.

MFC Utility Classes

MFC contains various utility classes for data types that appear frequently in programming and for collections. The CString and CTime classes are examples you saw previously in the sample program in "A Minimal MFC Application" (page 107). We will now discuss the CString class in more detail, along with the CRect and CArray utility classes.

The CString **Class**

When using strings, the CString class is simpler to use and has many advantages over using an array of characters. In fact, you no longer need to create arrays of characters because a CString object can be used in any situation that requires a const char * or LPCTSTR.

A string literal can be treated as a CString object, allowing you to create CString objects by simply assigning them to literals or other CString objects.

```
CString name = "Rich";    //assign to a literal
CString sameName = name;  //assign to an existing CString
```

The CString object sameName is actually constructed using the copy constructor, even though I used the assignment operator. The following statements show some of the other constructors in CString.

```
CString empty;            //creates an empty string
CString name("Rich");     //use a string literal
CString sameName(name);   //use an existing CString object
CString fiveX('X', 5);    //creates the string "XXXXX"
```

The CString class contains various member functions for viewing and manipulating CString objects. Some of the more common functions are demonstrated here.

```
int x = name.GetLength();  //x will be 4
empty = name + " Raposa";  //concatenation
name.Compare("RICH")       //evaluates to 1
name == "RICH"             //false, case-sensitive
name.CompareNoCase("RICH")//evaluates to 0
TCHAR c = name.GetAt(2);   //c will be 'c'
name.MakeUpper();          //name is now "RICH"
name.MakeLower();          //name is now "rich"
name.Replace('h','k');     //name is now "rick"
```

The Compare() function performs a case-sensitive comparison and returns 0 if the two strings are equal, a negative value if the first string comes before the second string, and a positive value otherwise. The CompareNoCase() function returns similar values, but the comparison is not case-sensitive.

Notice the comparison operator (==) can be used for a case-sensitive comparison. CString objects can also be compared using the <, <=, >, and >= syntax. In addition, CString objects can be concatenated using the + operator. See the documentation for a complete list of member functions of the CString class and their usage.

The CRect Class

A window on the screen can be represented as a rectangle using the upper-left and lower-right coordinates. The RECT structure in MFC can be used to represent a window's dimensions, and it consists of four LONG member variables: top, left, bottom, and right. However, because structures do not contain any member functions, the CRect class was created to provide some behavior for creating and manipulating rectangles.

The CRect class derives from the RECT structure and inherits its four member variables. Therefore, through polymorphism, a CRect object can be used with function parameters of type RECT, LPRECT (a pointer to a RECT), and LPCRECT (a pointer to a constant RECT). The following statements show various ways that a CRect object can be constructed.

```
CRect rect;                //an uninitialized rectangle
rect.top = rect.left = 10;
rect.bottom = rect.right = 60; //a 50 by 50 square
CRect square(rect);        //copy constructor
CRect big(0,0,1024,768);   //1024 by 768 rectangle
```

The following statements demonstrate some of the member functions of the CRect class. Notice the POINT structure is used throughout the CRect class. The POINT structure consists of two LONG members (x and y) and is the base class of the MFC utility class CPoint.

```
rect.GetWidth();      //returns 50
square.GetHeight();   //returns 50
POINT p = rect.TopLeft(); //p will be (10,10)
rect == square;       //returns true
big.NormalizeRect();  //normalizes big
big.PtInRect(p);      //returns TRUE
```

A rectangle is considered "normal" if its left value is smaller than its right value and its bottom value is larger than its top value. Normalizing a rectangle using NormalizeRect() changes its values, if necessary, to ensure the rectangle is normal. If a rectangle is already normal, then NormalizeRect() has no effect. The PtInRect() function can be useful to determine if a mouse click occurred in a particular window. See the documentation for a complete list of member functions of the CRect class and their usage.

The CArray Class

Arrays in C and C++ cannot change in size. This often results in wasted memory because you do not always know how big an array needs to be when it is created. The CArray class in MFC can be used to avoid this situation. Think of a CArray object as a dynamic array that grows and shrinks as elements are added and removed.

The declaration of CArray is found in the afxtempl.h header file. CArray is actually a template, not a class. The data type that goes in it is determined when the CArray object is declared. The following statements show the syntax for using the template.

```
CArray<int, int> grades;
CArray<CRect, CRect &> windows;
```

The first data type in the angle braces (< >) determines what types of elements the array will consist of. The second data type in the braces determines what data type the template will use for various helper member functions of the CArray class. In the example above, grades will consist of an array of integers, and int will be the data type of the parameters of the various helper functions. The windows CArray object will consist of CRect objects, and the various helper function parameters will use a reference to a CRect object.

Once the CArray object is instantiated, you can add elements to the array using the Add() member function or the InsertAt() function. The following statements demonstrate some of the member functions of CArray.

```
grades.Add(100);        //use Add() function
grades.InsertAt(0, 85); //use InsertAt()
grades.GetSize();       //returns 3
grades.RemoveAt(0);     //all elements shift up one
grades.RemoveAll();     //empties the array
```

The Add() function inserts an element at the end of the array. Use InsertAt() to insert an item at a specific index in the array — which shifts down the other elements in the array. The RemoveAt() function removes an element and shifts up all previous entries in the array. The GetSize() function returns the number of elements in the array, and the RemoveAll() function empties the array.

The following statements demonstrate a CArray that uses SetSize() to initialize the size of the array. They also demonstrate the ElementAt() function and how it compares to using the array syntax to access an element in a CArray object.

```
windows.SetSize(25,5);
windows[0] = rect;   //rect will be the first element
CRect & refToRect = windows.ElementAt(0);
CRect & sameAsRefToRect = windows[0];
windows.GetSize();  //returns 25
CRect different(0,0,200,300);
windows.Add(different);
windows.GetSize();  //returns 26
```

The call above to ElementAt() returns a reference to the first element in the CArray. This reference can also be obtained by using the array syntax windows[0].

The SetSize() function has two parameters: the initial size and an increment size. When the windows array reaches capacity and needs to increase in size, the array will grow by increments of five. When the different CRect object is added to the windows CArray, the size goes up by one, but the CArray object will not need to find new memory until the size goes above 30.

NOTE: When using SetSize(), the increment size parameter defaults to –1. This allows the CArray object to grow in efficient increments that avoid memory fragmentation.

Creating a Project in Visual C++ that Uses MFC

The applications in the book use MFC, and an appropriate project needs to be created in Visual C++. The project workspace for a console application is not easily modified to develop an MFC app. This section steps through the process of creating a project workspace in Visual C++ that uses the MFC architecture.

Assuming you have Visual C++ open, select File/New to display the following New dialog. Select the Projects tab and highlight Win32 Application and give the application a name and directory. See Figure 5.3.

Figure 5.3   Select the Win32 Application project.

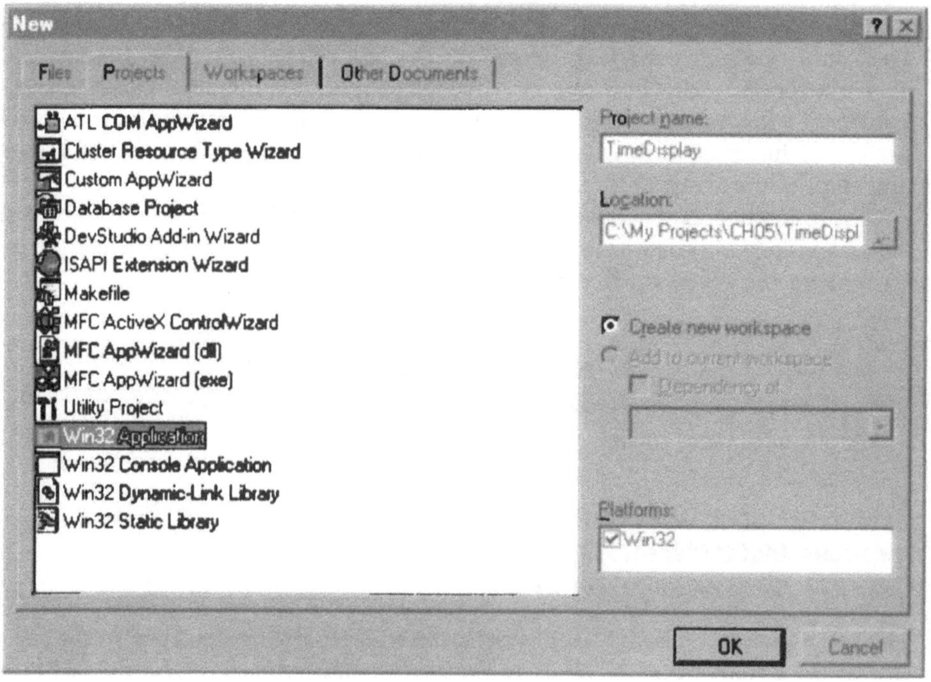

Depending on your version of Visual C++, you will get several options of AppWizard. Select Empty Project and click Finish. The new workspace will be created.

A Win32 Application project does not have the settings for MFC by default, so you will need to turn this feature on. Select Project/Settings from the menu to display the Project Settings dialog. Select the General tab — which contains a choice box for selecting how to use MFC, shown in Figure 5.4.

Figure 5.4   Choose the desired MFC settings.

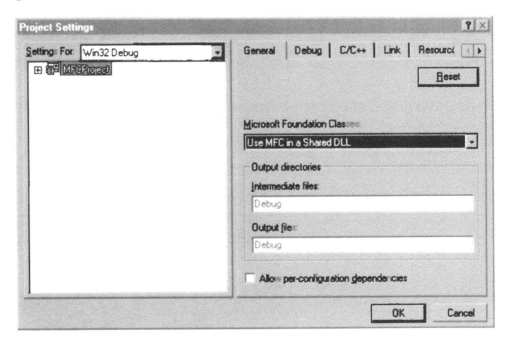

You can choose whether to use MFC in a shared DLL or use it statically. The shared DLL creates a smaller executable, but the DLL needs to be installed during deployment on the client machines. Linking the DLL statically creates a larger executable, but the executable is stand-alone, meaning the MFC DLL does not need to be deployed separately. Choose whichever technique you desire and select OK to close the Project Settings dialog. MFC can now be used for the current project. Be sure to follow these steps for each new MFC project created in this fashion.

Chapter 6

Device Contexts, GDI Objects, and Common Messages

Now that you have seen a simple MFC application, I am going to discuss some common messages in Windows applications — including WM_PAINT, WM_CHAR, and the various mouse messages. You have already seen the WM_PAINT message in Chapter 5 and the OnPaint() message handler. This chapter discusses the details of painting in a window, including device contexts and mapping modes.

Mouse and keyboard input are the two fundamental input devices for the user, so it is no surprise that handling the messages from the mouse and keyboard are a common occurrence in a Windows application. I will discuss the details of handling these messages in the "Mouse Messages" (page 135) and "Keyboard Input" (page 140) sections.

Windows programs also generate messages related to the state of a window. For example, when a window is first created, a WM_CREATE message is generated to allow the window to initialize itself. When a window is destroyed, a WM_DESTROY message is created to allow the window the opportunity to free up any resources. The "Windows Messages" section (page 133) contains a discussion on both of these messages and other common window messages.

I will begin with a discussion on device contexts, which are used to paint inside a window. Once you find out how to obtain a device context, I will discuss how to use them for drawing and painting inside a window — including how to select GDI objects into a device context, such as pens, brushes, and fonts. At the end of the chapter, I tie everything together with a program that simulates a duck hunt game, with an image moving quickly across the window that the user tries to click with the mouse.

Device Contexts

When you want to draw on the screen (or any other output device, such as a printer), you need to obtain what is called a device context. A *device context* represents a physical device where output is displayed. MFC provides a CDC class to represent a device context. A CDC object essentially knows everything there is to know about the device it represents. Whenever your program needs to display something on a device, you use the corresponding CDC object.

For example, in the previous chapter, you saw that the OnPaint() function instantiated a CPaintDC object, which is a device context used for handling WM_PAINT messages. CPaintDC is a child class of CDC and represents the area on the screen that needs to be repainted. When I wanted to display text in the window in response to the WM_PAINT message, I used the TextOut() member function of the CPaintDC object. The paint device context object took care of the details of displaying the text, making sure it stayed within the window's boundary and only repainting the invalidated portion of the window.

When you want to output lines, shapes, or text to a device, you first need to instantiate an appropriate CDC object. There are four different device contexts used in a Windows program — all of which are derived from CDC:

- CPaintDC
- CClientDC
- CWindowDC
- CMetaFileDC

The differences between them and which one you need to use depends on the situation and what you want to draw on. The CPaintDC can only be used in a response to a WM_PAINT message. The CClientDC represents the client area of a window. The *client area* of a window is the window's interior; the area that is left over after the border, status bar, menu, and toolbars are displayed.

The CWindowDC is a device context for the entire window, the client area and the non-client area. The CMetaFileDC allows you to record a sequence of steps to be drawn on a screen, then replay the steps much like a video tape is recorded and played at a later time.

For example, if you wanted to draw shapes or text inside the client area of a window in response to a WM_PAINT message, you could create a CPaintDC object. If it were in response to some other event like WM_LBUTTONDOWN, then you would use a CClientDC object. In either case, if you needed to draw on the non-client area of the window, a CWindowDC is required. The examples in this chapter use the CPaintDC and CClientDC objects, which are the most commonly used device contexts.

The CDC **Class**

The CDC class is the parent class of the four MFC device context classes. If you view the documentation for the child classes, you will notice that the child classes do not add any member functions (with the exception of the CMetaFileDC class, which adds four member functions). In other words, the device context objects that you instantiate only differ by the part of the window they draw on. Their behaviors are all the same and are found in the parent class CDC.

CDC is quite a large class, containing over 150 member functions that allow you to draw various lines, shapes, and text to an output device. For example, the LineTo(), Rectangle(), FillRect(), Pie(), Arc(), Ellipse(), and Polygon() functions draw geometric shapes and lines. The TextOut() and DrawText() functions display text in a window. These are only a few of the many drawing functions of the CDC class.

There are also functions for changing features of the CDC object, such as the color palette and the mapping mode. A *palette* is a table of colors that Windows uses to determine what color to display when your application uses a color that is not available for a particular device. MFC provides the CPalette class for creating user-defined palettes. A *mapping mode* determines the coordinate system of a window. These are discussed in detail in the upcoming section, "Mapping Modes" (page 125).

Selecting GDI Objects into a Device Context

Another function you will find in the CDC class is SelectObject(), which is overloaded to take in five different parameters. Each version of SelectObject() takes in a CGdiObject — an abstract class in MFC that represents a *Graphics Device Interface*, or GDI. The GDI is the interface between your application and the output device, and your program calls the functions of the GDI any time output is displayed.

Your Windows program uses the GDI through a device context, which you have already seen with the CDC classes. Each device context can select a pen, brush, font, bitmap, and region for drawing with on the device. Each of these GDI objects have a corresponding MFC class derived from CGdiObject. The following list shows the type of objects derived from CGdiObject that can be selected into a device context using the SelectObject() function.

CPen   Encapsulates a GDI pen — used to draw lines and boundaries.

CBrush   Encapsulates a GDI brush — used for the fill regions of shapes.

CFont   Encapsulates a GDI font — used when displaying text.

CBitmap   Encapsulates a GDI bitmap — which is an array of 1's and 0's that represents an image.

CRgn   Encapsulates a GDI region — which is an area in the shape of an ellipse of polygon. You can fill a region using a brush.

The CPen, CBrush, and CFont classes are discussed in detail in the section "GDI Objects" (page 126). You can view the documentation to discover the functionality of the CBitmap and CRgn classes.

NOTE: The CPalette class is also derived from CGdiObject, but you do not select palettes into a device context using SelectObject(). The CDC class has a function called SelectPalette().

A device context can select exactly one of each of these GDI objects at a time. For example, the following code illustrates how to draw a rectangle that has a red border 4-pixels wide and filled with a green hatch brush. The rectangle is displayed wherever a left mouse click occurs and is drawn in the WM_LBUTTONDOWN message handler. Figure 6.1 shows what the rectangle looks like.

```
void CDCDemoFrameWnd::OnLButtonDown(UINT flags, CPoint point)
{
    CClientDC clientDC(this);  //create a device context
    //create a pen and brush
    CPen redpen(PS_SOLID, 4, RGB(255,0,0));
    CBrush greenbrush(HS_CROSS, RGB(0,255,0));
    //select the pen and brush into the device context
    clientDC.SelectObject(&redpen);
    clientDC.SelectObject(&greenbrush);
    //draw a rectangle
    clientDC.Rectangle(point.x, point.y,
                       point.x + 200, point.y + 100);
}
```

Figure 6.1   A rectangle drawn with a device context that selected a pen and brush GDI object.

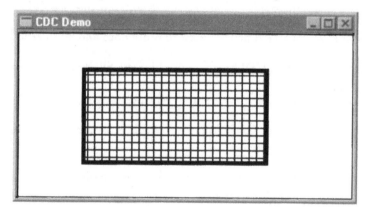

The constructors for CPen and CBrush are discussed in detail in "The CPen Class" on page 126 and "The CBrush Class" on page 128. The point of this example is that the pen and brush are selected into the device context using the SelectObject() function. For example, once the red pen is selected into the `clientDC` object, every line and border drawn after that will be a solid, red line 4-pixels wide. This pen will be used by the device context until a new pen is selected or the device context object goes out of scope.

NOTE: You must ensure that a GDI object does not go out of scope while the device context currently has it selected. An easy way to ensure this is to make the GDI objects' member variables. Alternatively, you can create the GDI objects each time they are needed — as does the `OnLButtonDown()` message handler defined previously.

Mapping Modes

A device context has a characteristic known as a mapping mode. The *mapping mode* is a coordinate system for the window. The default mapping mode of a device context is MM_TEXT, where each coordinate represents a pixel on the screen. In MM_TEXT, the point (0,0) is the upper-left corner of the device context, *x* values increase as you move to the right, and *y* values increase as you move down. The point (0,0) is called the *origin* of the coordinate system.

Table 6.1 shows the other available mapping modes for a device context. Notice that MM_TEXT is the only mapping mode that maps pixels to coordinates, and is also the only one where *y* values increase as you move down. The other mapping modes use exact measurements (either inches or millimeters) as their coordinate system, and their *y* values decrease as you move down. The exceptions are MM_ISOTROPIC and MM_ANISOTROPIC — which allow you to define the logical units as well as the orientation.

Table 6.1 Mapping modes.

Mapping mode	Logical unit	*x* increases	*y* increases
MM_TEXT	1 pixel	right	down
MM_LOENGLISH	0.01 inch	right	up
MM_HIENGLISH	0.001 inch	right	up
MM_LOMETRIC	0.1 mm	right	up
MM_HIMETRIC	0.01 mm	right	up
MM_TWIPS	1/1440 inch	right	up
MM_ISOTROPIC	user-defined	user-defined	user-defined
MM_ANISOTROPIC	user-defined	user-defined	user-defined

The difference between MM_ISOTROPIC mode and MM_ANISOTROPIC mode is that the former uses identical scaling for the *x* and *y* axes, while the latter does not. In other words, a 500×500 rectangle will always look like a square in MM_ISOTROPIC mode. However, in

MM_ANISOTROPIC mode, the square may look like a rectangle if the *x* axis uses a different scale than the *y* axis.

The mapping modes represent how logical coordinates are mapped into device coordinates. *Logical coordinates* are those values relative to the origin of the window, and do not take into account where the window is displayed on the screen. Of course, at some point, Windows needs to know where to display your output relative to the screen, which requires the *device coordinates*.

For example, the following statement draws a 20-pixel square that is 50 pixels over and 200 pixels down (or up, depending on the mapping mode) from the origin:

```
someDeviceContext.Rectangle(50,200,20,20);
```

These values are in terms of the logical coordinates of the device context. The actual device coordinates are determined by the mapping mode and the characteristics of the physical display.

Much more can be said about mapping modes and the details of how they can be used in a Windows program. For example, you can move the origin of the logical coordinates using the SetWindowOrg() function. You can also move the origin using SetViewportOrg(), which maps the origin to a different device coordinate. Depending on the mapping mode, these details can be non-trivial and are beyond the scope of this book. However, for someone new to Windows programming, you need to be familiar with the concept of a mapping mode and understand the differences between the various modes.

GDI Objects

A device context uses the SelectObject() member function of the CDC class to determine which GDI objects to use when displaying output on a device. This section discusses the details of three common GDI objects: pens, brushes, and fonts. MFC encapsulates each of these GDI objects in a corresponding class: CPen, CBrush, and CFont. I will discuss how to construct these GDI objects and some of the functionality of these classes.

The CPen Class

A pen is used for drawing lines and boundaries of geometric shapes. A device context can draw with one pen at a time by selecting a CPen object using SelectObject(). A pen has three characteristics: a style, a width, and a color. These characteristics are determined in the constructor or by using the CreatePen() member function. The constructor with these characteristics looks like:

```
CPen(int nPenStyle, int nWidth, COLORREF crColor);
```

The nWidth parameter is the width in device units of the pen. (In MM_TEXT mode, the device unit is pixels.) The crColor parameter is a COLORREF object. The easiest way to create a COLORREF object is to use the RGB macro, which creates a color from a red, green, and blue value. The nPenStyle parameter is the style of the pen, and can be one of the values shown in Table 6.2.

Table 6.2 Pen styles.

Value	Style
PS_SOLID	A solid pen.
PS_DASH	A dashed pen.
PS_DOT	A dotted pen.
PS_DASHDOT	A sequence of alternating dashes and dots.
PS_DASHDOTDOT	A sequence of dash-dot-dots.
PS_NULL	A null pen (does not draw anything).
PS_INSIDEFRAME	A solid pen that draws inside a specified bounding rectangle.

The PS_NULL pen can be used if you do not want a border around the shapes being drawn. The PS_INSIDEFRAME style affects certain shapes that are drawn with a pen wider than 1 pixel that specify a bounding region. For example, if the PS_INSIDEFRAME is not used and a pen is 5-pixels wide, then the pen will draw on the bounding rectangle, with the pen possibly going outside of the bounding rectangle. Using PS_INSIDEFRAME will not allow the pen to draw outside of the rectangle, but will instead shrink the size of the shape to make everything fit inside the frame. The PS_INSIDEFRAME has no effect on functions like LineTo() that do not specify a bounding rectangle.

NOTE: The pen style PS_DASH, PS_DOT, PS_DASHDOT, and PS_DASHDOTDOT are only valid for pens with a width of 1 or less.

The CreatePen() and CreatePenIndirect() functions can also be used to initialize a pen or alter the characteristics of an existing pen. Their prototypes are declared as:

```
BOOL CreatePen(int nPenStyle, int nWidth, COLORREF crColor);
BOOL CreatePenIndirect(LPLOGPEN lpLogPen);
```

The parameters for CreatePen() are the same as for the CPen constructor above. LOGPEN is a structure that contains the style, color, and width of a pen. The return value for both is TRUE if successful, otherwise FALSE. See the program in "A Sample GDI Program" (page 130) for examples of constructing pens and what the different pen styles look like.

MFC provides three stock GDI pens that can do not need to be created. These pens are selected into a device context using the SelectStockObject() function in the CDC class. The three stock pens are BLACK_PEN, WHITE_PEN, and NULL_PEN — each of which is 1-pixel wide and has the PS_SOLID style.

The following code demonstrates how you can select the WHITE_PEN stock pen into a device context:

```
someDeviceContext.SelectStockObject(WHITE_PEN);
```

The device context will now draw lines and boundaries with a white solid pen 1-pixel wide. The other stock pens are selected in the same manner. You will see in the next two sections that MFC provides stock brushes and stock fonts as well.

The CBrush **Class**

A brush is used for drawing the fill region of a shape. (Those functions of the CDC that do not have a fill region, like LineTo() and Arc(), are not affected by the currently selected brush.) A device context can select a CBrush object using SelectObject(). Brushes fit into three categories: solid brushes, hatch brushes, and pattern brushes. A solid brush fills the region with a solid color. Hatch brushes fill a region with a specified design. A pattern brush uses a bitmap to determine the design of the brush.

These different types of brushes are created by a constructor, or you can use the CBrush member functions CreateSolidBrush(), CreateHatchBrush(), and CreatePatternBrush(). The CBrush class has four constructors:

```
CBrush();//an uninitialized brush
CBrush(COLORREF crColor); //a solid brush
CBrush(int nIndex, COLORREF crColor);  //a hatch brush
CBrush(CBitmap * pBitmap); //a pattern brush
```

The crColor parameter is the color of the brush. The nIndex value is for hatch brushes and is one of the values listed in Table 6.3. The pBitmap parameter points to a CBitmap object to create a pattern brush. The default constructor creates an uninitialized pen that must be created using one of the member functions of CBrush.

Table 6.3 Hatch brush styles.

Value	Style
HS_HORIZONTAL	A horizontal hatch.
HS_VERTICAL	A vertical hatch.
HS_CROSS	A horizontal and vertical crosshatch.
HS_DIAGCROSS	A crosshatch turned 45 degrees.
HS_FDIAGONAL	A left-to-right upward hatch at a 45-degree angle.
HS_BDIAGONAL	A left-to-right downward hatch at a 45-degree angle.

You can create an uninitialized brush using the CBrush default constructor, then initialize the brush using one of the following CBrush member functions:

```
BOOL CreateSolidBrush(COLORREF crColor);
BOOL CreateHatchBrush(int nIndex, COLORREF crColor);
BOOL CreatePatternBrush(CBitmap * pBitmap);
BOOL CreateBrushIndirect(const LOGBRUSH* lpLogBrush);
BOOL CreateSysColorBrush(int nIndex);
```

The parameters are the same as those in the constructors of CBrush discussed earlier. LOGBRUSH is a structure that contains the style, color, and hatch of a brush. The CreateSysColorBrush() creates a hatch brush of the style nIndex whose color is the default system color. Use the SelectObject() function to select any of these brushes into a device context.

MFC provides seven stock GDI brushes that can be selected into a device context using the SelectStockObject() function. The stock brush styles are BLACK_BRUSH, DKGRAY_BRUSH, GRAY_BRUSH, HOLLOW_BRUSH, LTGRAY_BRUSH, NULL_BRUSH, and WHITE_BRUSH. Note that each of the stock brushes is a solid brush.

The CFont Class

The CFont class in MFC is used for creating and manipulating a font. A device context uses a font by selecting it using the SelectObject() function. As opposed to CPen and CBrush, the CFont class has *only* a default constructor. The only way to initialize a CFont object is to instantiate one, then invoke one of the CFont member functions to initialize the font. Create-Font() can be used, and its prototype is:

```
BOOL CreateFont(int nHeight, int nWidth, int nEscapement,
                int nOrientation, int nWeight, BYTE bItalic,
                BYTE bUnderline, BYTE cStrikeOut,
                BYTE nCharSet, BYTE nOutPrecision,
                BYTE nClipPrecision, BYTE nQuality,
                BYTE nPitchAndFamily, LPCTSTR lpszFacename);
```

Look intimidating? It certainly can be. Notice how much control you have over the type of font you want to create. In many common situations, you just want to use a font on the user's computer. The shorter CreatePointFont() function can be used in these situations:

```
BOOL CreatePointFont(int nPointSize, LPCTSTR lpszFaceName,
                     CDC* pDC = NULL);
```

nPointSize is the font height in 1/10 point. For example, to create a 10-point font, the nPointSize would be 100. The lpszFaceName is a string representing the name of the font. The final parameter represents a device context to convert the nPointSize to logical units. The default parameter NULL represents the screen device context. The return value is TRUE if the font was initialized successfully, otherwise the function returns FALSE.

NOTE: You can determine the available fonts on a computer running Windows by invoking the EnumFontFamilies() Win32 API function. See the documentation for details on using this function.

The following statements initialize a CFont object using the CreatePointFont() function. The font is Times New Roman Bold and the point size is 20. The CFont object is selected into a paint device context and the TextOut() function is used to demonstrate the font being used. Figure 6.2 shows the output of the program.

```
void CFontDemoFrameWnd::OnPaint() {
    CPaintDC paintDC(this);
    CFont font;   //an uninitialized font
    //initialize the font using CreatePointFont()
    font.CreatePointFont(200, "Times New Roman Bold");
    //select the font into the device context
    paintDC.SelectObject(&font);
    //use the font
    paintDC.TextOut(20,20,"This is Times New Roman 20 point");
}
```

Figure 6.2 **Use the** CreatePointFont() **function to initialize a** CFont **object.**

MFC provides six font stock objects that can be selected into a device context using SelectStockObject(). The stock font styles are ANSI_FIXED_FONT, ANSI_VAR_FONT, DEVICE_DEFAULT_FONT, OEM_FIXED_FONT, SYSTEM_FONT, and SYSTEM_FIXED_FONT. The fixed fonts represent fixed-width fonts. The SYSTEM_FONT is the default font for menus, dialogs, and text.

A Sample GDI Program

You have seen the syntax for creating the various pens, brushes, and fonts for a device context. Now it is time for a demonstration that illustrates some of the various styles of pens and brushes. Figure 6.3 shows a program that creates various GDI objects and uses them to draw with a paint device context.

Figure 6.3   A program that uses various GDI objects.

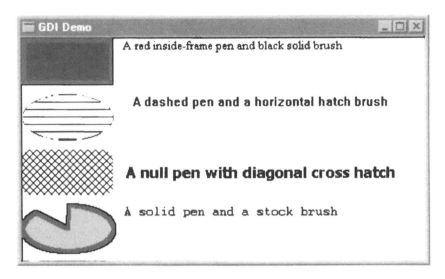

The program does all of its painting in OnPaint(), which invokes two helper functions.

```
void GDIFrameWnd::OnPaint(){
    CPaintDC paintDC(this);
    DisplayPensAndBrushes(&paintDC);
    DisplayFonts(&paintDC);
}
```

The DisplayPensAndBrushes() function demonstrates various ways to create pens and brushes. It also illustrates some of the pen and brush styles by selecting them into the device context and invoking some of the drawing functions of the CDC class.

```
void GDIFrameWnd::DisplayPensAndBrushes(CPaintDC *pDC){
    //a red inside-frame pen and a black solid brush
    CPen pen1(PS_INSIDEFRAME, 5, RGB(255,0,0));
    CBrush brush1(RGB(0,0,0));
    pDC->SelectObject(&pen1);
    pDC->SelectObject(&brush1);
    pDC->Rectangle(0,0,100,50);

    //a green dashed pen and a red horizontal hatch brush
    //created dynamically using "new"
    CPen * pen2 = new CPen(PS_DASH, 1, RGB(0,255,0));
    CBrush * brush2 = new CBrush(HS_HORIZONTAL, RGB(255,0,0));
    pDC->SelectObject(pen2);
    pDC->SelectObject(brush2);
```

```
pDC->Ellipse(0,60,100,110);
//don't delete pen2 and brush2 here!


//a null pen and a diaganol cross hatch brush
CBrush brush3;
brush3.CreateHatchBrush(HS_DIAGCROSS, RGB(0,0,0));
pDC->SelectStockObject(NULL_PEN);
pDC->SelectObject(&brush3);
pDC->RoundRect(0,120, 100, 170,20,20);


//now I can delete pen2 and brush2 since they are
//no longer selected into the device context
delete pen2;
delete brush2;


//a solid pen 10 pixels wide and a stock brush
CPen pen4(PS_SOLID, 5, RGB(0,0,255));
pDC->SelectObject(&pen4);
pDC->SelectStockObject(LTGRAY_BRUSH);
pDC->Pie(0,180,100,230,0,180,50,180);
}
```

Be careful not to delete a GDI object that is currently selected into the device context. Notice I did not delete the pointers pen2 and brush2 until a different pen and brush were selected into the device context. Selecting the old GDI object into the device context is a common way to deselect a GDI object out of a device context.

The DisplayFonts() function uses four fonts: two created using the CreateFont() function and two of the stock fonts.

```
void GDIFrameWnd::DisplayFonts(CPaintDC *pDC) {
    //Times New Roman font
    CFont font1;
    font1.CreatePointFont(100,"Times New Roman");
    pDC->SelectObject(&font1);
        pDC->TextOut(110,0,"A red inside-frame pen and black solid
                             brush");


    //a stock font
    pDC->SelectStockObject(SYSTEM_FONT);
    CRect region1(110,60,410,110);
```

```
pDC->DrawText("A dashed pen and a horizontal hatch brush",
              &region1, DT_CENTER);


//a bold font
CFont font2;
font2.CreatePointFont(120,"Tahoma Bold");
pDC->SelectObject(&font2);
CRect region2(110,120,410,170);
pDC->DrawText("A null pen with diagonal cross hatch",
              &region2,DT_CENTER | DT_VCENTER | DT_SINGLELINE);


//another stock font
pDC->SelectStockObject(ANSI_FIXED_FONT);
CRect region3(110,180,410,230);
pDC->DrawText("A solid pen and a stock brush",&region3,
              DT_BOTTOM | DT_LEFT);
}
```

The DisplayFonts() function uses the DrawText() member function of the CDC class which displays text in a specified rectangle using various settings. For example, DT_CENTER centers the text, DT_LEFT left justifies the text, and DT_BOTTOM aligns the text along the bottom — each within the specified rectangle. View the documentation for the various settings of the Draw-Text() function.

Now that you have seen device contexts and the various GDI objects they can use, I will spend the rest of the chapter discussing some of the common messages that occur in a Windows application and their corresponding message handlers.

Windows Messages

The operating system generates several messages that allow you to initialize a window when it is created and clean up the window when it is destroyed. These messages are handled by the CWnd and CFrameWnd classes, and if necessary, you can override them to add any additional functionality. This section describes the messages associated with the lifetime of a window and their corresponding message handlers.

The WM_CREATE Message

When a window is created using the Create() member function, the first message it receives is a WM_CREATE message. The message is generated and handled before the window becomes visible. This gives you an opportunity to initialize the window before it is displayed to the user.

The message handler for WM_CREATE is the OnCreate() function, declared as:

```
afx_msg int OnCreate(LPCREATESTRUCT lpCreateStruct);
```

The parameter lpCreateStruct is a pointer to a CREATESTRUCT, which contains information you might need to know about the window, such as its position and size, name, parent window, and style. OnCreate() must return 0 if the window is to be displayed. You can return -1 if you want the window to be destroyed — assuming an error occurred in OnCreate() that would cause your program to not display the window.

Use the ON_WM_CREATE() macro in the window's message map to associate the WM_CREATE message with the OnCreate() message handler. Make sure you invoke the parent class's OnCreate() function and check the return value to make sure it was successful. This is important because the OnCreate() function in the parent class performs initialization of its own. The following code illustrates how this might be accomplished:

```
int MyFrameWnd::OnCreate(LPCREATESTRUCT lpCreateStruct) {
    if(CFrameWnd::OnCreate(lpCreateStruct) == -1)
        return -1;
        //perform any initialization unique to your class
        return 0;   //don't forget to return 0
}
```

Be aware that the WM_CREATE message is generated before the window is displayed, so OnCreate() cannot invoke any functions that rely on the window being visible.

The WM_CLOSE **Message**

The WM_CLOSE message is a signal that your window should close. If the WM_CLOSE message is sent to the main window of your application, then it is also a signal that your application should terminate.

The message handler for WM_CLOSE is the OnClose() function, declared as:

```
afx_msg void OnClose();
```

Use the ON_WM_CLOSE() macro in the window's message map to associate the WM_CLOSE message with the OnClose() message handler. Override this function to perform any tasks that need to occur before the window is destroyed. For example, if the user had not saved their recent changes to a document, this would be the time to warn them before continuing. The OnClose() function in the window's parent class invokes the DestroyWindow() member function, so be sure to either invoke the parent's OnClose() or call DestroyWindow() directly.

In either case, it should be the last statement in your OnClose() function. The following example illustrates this:

```
void MyFrameWnd::OnClose() {
    //perform any tasks that should occur before
    //the window is destroyed, then call
    CFrameWnd::OnClose();
    //or alternatively, DestroyWindow();
}
```

The DestroyWindow() function destroys the window created by the CWnd object. (It does not, however, destroy the CWnd object.) DestroyWindow() deactivates the window and destroys its menu and other controls. It then sends a WM_DESTROY and WM_NCDESTROY to the window's message queue.

The WM_DESTROY **Message**

The WM_DESTROY message is received by a window after the window has been closed and is no longer visible on the screen. This is your opportunity to clean up any features of the window that rely on the window still existing. The window has not been destroyed at this point, but is about to be.

The message handler for WM_DESTROY is the OnDestroy() function, declared as:

```
afx_msg void OnDestroy();
```

Use the ON_WM_DESTROY() macro in the window's message map to associate the WM_DESTROY message with the OnDestroy() message handler. As with the other windows messages, be sure to invoke the parent class's OnDestroy() to ensure the window performs a proper clean-up of itself.

The WM_NCDESTROY **Message**

WM_NCDESTROY is the final message your window receives, and it gives you the opportunity to perform any memory freeing or other clean-up. The message refers to the fact that it is generated when the non-client area of the window is being destroyed.

The message handler for WM_NCDESTROY is the OnNcDestroy() function, declared as:

```
afx_msg void OnNcDestroy();
```

The implementation of OnNcDestory() in the parent class is to perform some clean up, then invoke the PostNcDestroy() function. It is recommended that you do not override OnNcDestroy(), but instead override PostNcDestroy() to perform any final clean-up. This ensures the parent class's OnNcDestroy() is invoked as well — which is critical if you want to avoid memory leaks when the window is destroyed. Use the ON_WM_NCDESTROY() macro in the window's message map to associate the WM_NCDESTROY message with the OnNcDestroy() message handler.

Mouse Messages

The mouse plays a key role in a Windows application, generating many messages that your application needs to handle. Many of these mouse messages are associated with visual controls such as menus, text fields, buttons, and list boxes. These types of mouse messages are handled by the control itself; you rarely handle these messages yourself.

However, there are many situations where you will want to handle messages generated from pressing and clicking the mouse buttons. This section discusses the various messages generated from mouse input and their corresponding message handlers.

Mouse Up and Mouse Down Messages

Clicking a mouse button generates two messages: a mouse down message and a mouse up message. The actual message generated depends on the mouse button that was clicked. Windows uses separate messages for the left, right, and middle mouse buttons. These messages and their corresponding message handlers are listed in Table 6.4.

Table 6.4 Mouse up and mouse down messages and message handlers.

Message	Message Handler
WM_LBUTTONDOWN	void OnLButtonDown(UINT nFlags, CPoint point);
WM_LBUTTONUP	void OnLButtonUp(UINT nFlags, CPoint point);
WM_MBUTTONDOWN	void OnMButtonDown(UINT nFlags, CPoint point);
WM_MBUTTONUP	void OnMButtonUp(UINT nFlags, CPoint point);
WM_RBUTTONDOWN	void OnRButtonDown(UINT nFlags, CPoint point);
WM_RBUTTONUP	void OnRButtonUp(UINT nFlags, CPoint point);

The parameter point in each handler is a CPoint object representing the x and y coordinates of the cursor where the mouse was clicked. This point is relative to the upper-left corner of the window.

The nFlags parameter represents the state of the Shift and Ctrl keys when the mouse event occurred. You can also determine if one of the other mouse buttons is pressed, even though this functionality is rarely used in a Windows program. The value of nFlags is a combination of the values listed in Table 6.5.

Table 6.5 Possible values for the nFlags parameter.

Value	Result
MK_CONTROL	The Ctrl key is down.
MK_SHIFT	The Shift key is down.
MK_LBUTTON	The left button is down.
MK_RBUTTON	The right button is down.
MK_MBUTTON	The middle button is down.

The mouse messages in Table 6.4 are only generated when the mouse is over the client area of the window. Be aware that mouse messages are not automatically sent to the window that has focus. By default, a mouse message is sent to the window directly underneath the cursor. In other words, you cannot assume that if your window receives a WM_LBUTTONDOWN message, it will be followed by a WM_LBUTTONUP message because the user could have dragged the mouse out of the client area of your window.

If you want a window to receive mouse input even if the cursor is over a different window, then the window needs to capture the mouse. To capture the mouse, a window invokes the SetCapture() member function of the CWnd class. Note that only one window can capture the mouse at a time. The window with the captured mouse will receive all mouse input until the window invokes the ReleaseCapture() function, or until a mouse button click (press and release) occurs in another window. If another window captures the mouse, your window will lose capture and receive a WM_CAPTURECHANGED message.

Each of the messages in Table 6.4 has a macro for adding it to the entries in the message map. The macro is the name of the message with ON_ preceding it. For example, the ON_WM_LBUTTONDOWN() macro associates the message WM_LBUTTONDOWN with the OnLButton-Down() handler.

Double-Clicks

Any of the three mouse buttons can generate a double-click message. For this to occur, the user must press and release the mouse twice within a given time interval. The three double-click messages and their handlers appear in Table 6.6.

Table 6.6 Mouse double-click messages and message handlers.

Message	Message Handler
WM_LBUTTONDBLCLK	void OnLButtonDblClk(UINT nFlags, CPoint point);
WM_RBUTTONDBLCLK	void OnRButtonDblClk(UINT nFlags, CPoint point);
WM_MBUTTONDBLCLK	void OnMButtonDblClk(UINT nFlags, CPoint point);

The values of point are the x and y coordinates of where the mouse event occurred, and the values of nFlags are shown in Table 6.5. The macros for the message map are also of the same form for other mouse messages. For example, the ON_WM_LBUTTONDBLCLK() macro associates WM_LBUTTONDBLCLK messages with the OnLButtonDblClk() message handler.

Double-clicking a mouse button actually generates four messages. For example, double-clicking the left mouse button generates WM_LBUTTONDOWN, WM_LBUTTONUP, WM_LBUTTONDBLCLK, and WM_LBUTTONUP — generated in that order. For this reason, the behavior of double-clicking the mouse should add functionality to a single click because the message for a single click will have already been handled. A common occurrence in a Windows application is to have a single click select an item and have a double-click perform an action associated with that item. You are familiar with this behavior with program icons on your Windows desktop.

The WM_MOUSEACTIVATE **Message**

The WM_MOUSEACTIVATE message is generated when the user presses a mouse button in a window that is not active. This message is sent before the mouse click message, which gives you control as to what should be done with the incoming mouse message. You specify the reaction to the incoming mouse message by the return value of the OnMouseActivate() message handler, declared as:

```
afx_msg int OnMouseActivate(CWnd* pDesktopWnd, UINT nHitTest,
                            UINT message);
```

The pDesktopWnd parameter points to the window's parent. The nHitTest parameter is a hit-test code that determines the location of the cursor. Its value will be HTCLIENT for client-area messages. The message parameter is the incoming mouse message that was the cause of this WM_MOUSEACTIVATE message. The return value must be one of the following values:

MA_ACTIVATE   Activates the window and handles the incoming mouse message.

MA_ACTIVATEANDEAT   Activates the window but "eats" the incoming mouse message.

MA_NOACTIVATE   Handles the incoming mouse message but does not activate the window.

MA_NOACTIVATEANDEAT   Does not activate the window or "eat" the incoming mouse message.

The implementation of OnMouseActivate() in the CWnd class passes the message to the parent window, which will be the desktop for your program's main window. Use the ON_WM_MOUSEACTIVATE() macro to add this message to your message map and override the default behavior of OnMouseActivate().

The WM_MOUSEMOVE **Message**

This message is generated when the user moves the mouse over your window. Your window can also receive WM_MOUSEMOVE messages when the cursor is over a different window if your window has captured the mouse. (Refer back to "Mouse Up and Mouse Down Messages," page 136, for more on capturing the mouse.) The message handler is OnMouseMove(), declared as:

```
afx_msg void OnMouseMove(UINT nFlags, CPoint point);
```

The point parameter represents the coordinates of the mouse location relative to the upper-lefthand corner of the window. The possible values of nFlags are shown in Table 6.5.

Use the ON_MOUSEMOVE() macro for the window's message map to handle WM_MOUSEMOVE messages. Keep in mind that your message handler for WM_MOUESMOVE should not be very time-intensive because it is very easy for the user to generate hundreds of WM_MOUSEMOVE messages in a relatively short amount of time.

The WM_MOUSEWHEEL **Message**

Newer styles of a mouse contain a wheel between the left and right buttons. Moving the wheel generates a WM_MOUSEWHEEL message. Use the ON_WM_MOUSEWHEEL() macro to associate WM_MOUSEWHEEL messages with the OnMouseWheel() message handler, declared as:

```
afx_msg BOOL OnMouseWheel(UINT nFlags, short zDelta,
                          CPoint pt);
```

The possible values of nFlags are shown in Table 6.5, and pt is the x and y coordinates of where the mouse is located in the window.

The zDelta parameter indicates the distance the wheel was rotated. The value is in multiples of 120 — a predetermined value found in the WHEEL_DELTA constant. (The WHEEL_DELTA constant was established to allow for future mouse wheels that may have a finer resolution.) The value of zDelta is negative if the wheel was rotated toward the user and positive if the wheel was rotated away from the user.

Most implementations of the wheel on a mouse involve scrolling up and down in a window. However, because the wheel generates events just like other mouse input, you are free to provide any behavior you desire for the wheel. Keep in mind that it is a relatively new input device, and your program should not provide behavior that is only available to users with a wheel on their mouse.

Timers

The CWnd class has the ability to set a timer for a window. A timer generates a WM_TIMER message after the specified time interval elapses. Use the SetTimer() member function of the CWnd class to start a timer. The timer will continue to generate WM_TIMER messages after each time interval until the KillTimer() member function is invoked.

Why would you want a timer in the background generating a WM_TIMER message at a given time interval? There are actually many useful scenarios in a Windows application where a timer can be used to avoid having to create separate threads. For example, a window could use a timer event to update the status of a progress bar, or a timer can be used to read input from a file or other source without blocking the program. Timers are also useful in animation. I used a timer to simulate an object flying across the window in the program in the "A Duck Hunt Game" section (page 142).

Creating a Timer

The SetTimer() function creates a timer with a specified interval, and its prototype is declared as:

```
UINT SetTimer(UINT nIDEvent, UINT nElapse,
    void(CALLBACK EXPORT* lpfnTimer)(HWND,UINT,UINT,DWORD));
```

Every timer has an ID, which is specified by the nIDEvent parameter. (This value cannot be zero.) The nElapse parameter specifies the interval, in milliseconds, between WM_TIMER messages.

The last parameter is a callback function to handle the message. Typcially you will use NULL for this parameter and have the OnTimer() message handler handle your WM_TIMER messages. Use the ON_WM_TIMER() macro in your window's message map to make this association. The OnTimer() function is declared as:

```
afx_msg void OnTimer(UINT nIDEvent);
```

The parameter nIDEvent is the ID of the timer that generated the WM_TIMER event. This allows your message handler to handle timer messages from more than one timer.

Once the timer is started, WM_TIMER messages will be placed in the window's message queue after the specified time interval has elapsed. Note that WM_TIMER messages are a low-priority message — meaning most other messages will be processed ahead of the timer message.

To stop a timer, use the KillTimer() member function of the CWnd class, declared as:

```
BOOL KillTimer(int nIDEvent);
```

The parameter nIDEvent is the ID of the timer. The return value will be TRUE if the timer was successfully stopped. If the ID could not be found, the function returns FALSE. If successful, any pending WM_TIMER messages for this particular timer will be removed from the message queue.

Keyboard Input

Another common source of input messages is the keyboard. The input from the keyboard is divided into two categories: system keys and non-system keys. There are two system keys: Alt and F10. The default message handlers for the system keys are usually sufficient. The Alt key often represents an accelerator key, which are discussed in detail in Chapter 7, "Windows Resources."

If a non-system key is pressed, then a WM_KEYDOWN message is generated. In most situations, you want to know which character was pressed, which is why the WM_KEYDOWN messages are translated into WM_CHAR messages. When the key is released, a WM_KEYUP is generated. This section discusses these three messages and their message handlers.

The WM_KEYDOWN Message

A non-system keystroke generates a WM_KEYDOWN message. Use the ON_WM_KEYDOWN() macro in your window's message map to associate WM_KEYDOWN messages with the OnKeyDown() message handler, declared as:

```
afx_msg void OnKeyDown(UINT nChar, UINT nRepCnt, UINT nFlags);
```

The nChar parameter is the code for the character that was pressed. This will be either the character's ASCII value, or a virtual key code if the key represents a non-ASCII key. Table 6.7 shows the virtual key codes for some of the common keys. The nRepCnt parameter is the number of times the key-down event was generated if the user has held the key down long enough to repeat. The nFlags parameter contains various state settings.

Table 6.7 Common virtual key codes.

Key Code	Key
VK_RETURN	Enter
VK_BACK	Backspace
VK_ESCAPE	Escape
VK_INSERT	Ins
VK_DELETE	Del
VK_PRIOR	PgUp
VK_NEXT	PgDn
VK_SPACE	Spacebar
VK_UP	Up arrow
VK_DOWN	Down arrow
VK_LEFT	Left arrow
VK_RIGHT	Right arrow
VK_END	End
VK_HOME	Home
VK_CTRL	Ctrl
VK_ALT	Alt
VK_F#	F# key, # is 1 through 12

The WM_CHAR **Message**

Your window handles and disperses messages in the Run() function from your CWinApp object. The Run() function pulls messages out of the queue using the GetMessage() function. Each message is then sent to the PreTranslateMessage() member function of your CWinApp object. This function is responsible for determining whether the key pressed was a virtual key or not, and disperses it appropriately. PreTranslateMessage() accomplishes this by invoking the Win32 API TranslateMessage() function. TranslateMessage() determines if a printable ASCII character was pressed on the keyboard and generates a corresponding WM_CHAR message if the key was an ASCII character.

NOTE: You can override the PreTranslateMessage() function in your CWinApp class to filter out unwanted messages. If you do this, be sure your overridden version calls PreTranslateMessage() in the parent class to ensure proper handling of system and non-system keyboard messages.

Knowing that the key pressed is an ASCII character can be very helpful in handling keyboard input, because it can be quite difficult to determine the character that was pressed using only WM_KEYDOWN and WM_KEYUP messages. For example, to determine if the character was capitalized or not, you would have to test to see if the Shift or Caps Lock key is pressed down but not released yet. Thankfully, TranslateMessage() determines these scenarios for you.

Use the ON_WM_CHAR() macro in your window's message map to associate WM_CHAR messages with the OnChar() message handler, declared as:

```
afx_msg void OnChar(UINT nChar, UINT nRepCnt, UINT nFlags);
```

The nChar parameter is the character pressed, nRepCnt is the repeat count. nFlags contains information like the state of the Alt and Ctrl keys, the repeat count, and the previous state of the key. Due to repetition of keystroke, the nFlags parameter is often not useful in an application because it only applies to the WM_CHAR message immediately after the WM_KEYDOWN message.

The nChar parameter is the most useful because it represents the character pressed on the keyboard. The value of nChar in the OnChar() function will be an ASCII value for the letters or digit that was pressed.

The WM_KEYUP Message

Letting go of a key generates a WM_KEYUP message. You have seen that WM_KEYDOWN messages generate WM_CHAR messages via the TranslateMessage() function. Note that the sequence of messages for a character keystroke is not always WM_KEYDOWN, WM_CHAR, then WM_KEYUP. If the key is held down, a sequence of WM_KEYDOWN messages will be generated. Also, it is possible for a window to lose focus between a WM_KEYDOWN and WM_KEYUP message, causing the WM_KEYUP message to be sent to a different window.

The OnKeyUp() function is the message handler for WM_KEYUP, and the association is made in the message map using the ON_WM_KEYUP() macro. The prototype of OnKeyUp() is:

```
afx_msg void OnKeyUp(UINT nChar, UINT nRepCnt, UINT nFlags);
```

The parameters contain the same information as you have seen in the WM_KEYDOWN and WM_CHAR messages.

A Duck Hunt Game

In this chapter, you have seen how to draw in a window using device contexts and GDI objects. You have also seen how to handle many of the basic messages in a Windows application. I have written a (somewhat rudimentary) duck hunt game to demonstrate drawing in a window and message handling. The game displays a duck (which is nothing more than a small yellow square) flying across the screen. The user has to click the duck with the mouse, which increments the user's score displayed in the upper-left corner of the window. It sounds simple, but with a small moving target, you will find it takes a certain skill with the mouse. Figure 6.4 shows what the game looks like.

Figure 6.4 The duck hunt game.

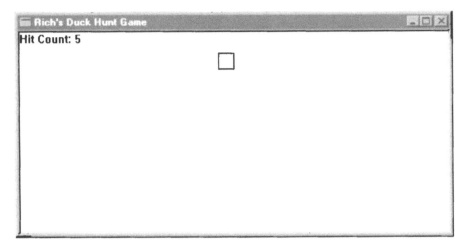

I used a timer to simulate the duck flying across the screen. Without the timer, I would have needed to create a separate thread, which is beyond the scope of this book. I also needed to handle WM_LBUTTONDOWN messages to determine if the user hit the duck (clicked inside the rectangle). To demonstrate character messages, I added the functionality of changing the speed of the duck using the up and down arrow keys (for faster or slower), and also for changing the size of the duck. The remainder of this section discusses the three classes I used to create the program.

The Duck Class

To emphasize an object-oriented design, I wrote a class called Duck that provided the functionality of the duck which moves across the screen and has various attributes such as size, color, and speed. The Duck class is declared as follows:

```
class Duck {
private:
    CPoint m_Location;
    int m_Size;
    COLORREF m_Color;
    int m_HitCount;
    double m_Slope;
    int m_YIntercept;
    int m_Delay;
```

```
public:
    //constructor
    Duck();
    //behaviors
    void MoveRandom(CRect);
    void Hit();
    //set and get functions
    CPoint GetLocation();
    void SetLocation(CPoint);
    int GetSize();
    void SetSize(int);
    COLORREF GetColor();
    void SetColor(COLORREF);
    void SetDelay(int);
    int GetDelay();
    int GetHitCount();
};
```

The duck flies in a straight line across the screen. When the duck flies out of view, a new slope and y-intercept are randomly generated and the duck sets off on its new path. The "set" and "get" functions of the Duck class are straightforward and can be found on the accompanying CD-ROM. I will show you the definition of the MoveRandom( ) function because that is most of the functionality of the Duck class.

```
void Duck::MoveRandom(CRect boundary) {
    //if it's at the end of the window, I need to change the
    //values of slope and y-intercept
    if(m_Location.x > boundary.right - m_Size
        || m_Location.y > boundary.bottom - m_Size
        || m_Location.y <= 0) {
        m_YIntercept = rand(); //y-intercept is random
        //make sure y-intercept is within the window
        if(m_YIntercept > boundary.Height())
            m_YIntercept %= boundary.Height();
        //slope is a random number between -1 and 1
        m_Slope = ((double) rand()/ (double) RAND_MAX * 2 - 1);
        //update the location
        m_Location.y = m_YIntercept;
        m_Location.x = 0;
    }
}
```

```
else {   //move the duck to the next location
   m_Location.x += 15;   //x is increased by 15
   //y is calculated using y = mx + b
   m_Location.y = (int)(m_Slope*m_Location.x+m_YIntercept);
}
}
```

The boundary parameter contains the size of the window. Because the window can be resized, I want to make sure the duck stays in view. If the duck is still in view, then it moves horizontally 15 pixels and the vertical movement is computed using the m_Slope attribute.

The Duck Hunt Application Class

Every MFC program needs to derive a class from CWinApp. The application class for the duck hunt game simply overrides InitInstance() to create a window for the program. The declaration and implementation are shown here:

```
//class declaration in DuckHuntApp.h
class DuckHuntApp : public CWinApp {
public:
   virtual BOOL InitInstance();
};


//class implementation in DuckHuntApp.cpp
BOOL DuckHuntApp::InitInstance() {
   m_pMainWnd = new DuckHuntFrameWnd();
   m_pMainWnd->ShowWindow(m_nCmdShow);
   m_pMainWnd->UpdateWindow();

   return TRUE;
}


//global instance of app object
DuckHuntApp theApp;
```

Don't forget that a global instance of the CWinApp object needs to be instantiated in an MFC application. The DuckHuntFrameWnd() object instantiated in InitInstance() is discussed in the next section.

The Duck Hunt Window Class

The main window for the duck hunt game is a CFrameWnd. The window object is responsible for handling all of the messages for the game. The name of the class is DuckHuntFrameWnd and its declaration is listed here:

```
class DuckHuntFrameWnd : public CFrameWnd {
private:
   Duck m_Duck;
   CString m_HitCountMessage;
   public:
      //constructor
   DuckHuntFrameWnd();
   //behaviors
      void ChangeTimer(int);
   void HitTarget();
protected:
   //message handlers
   afx_msg void OnPaint();
   afx_msg void OnLButtonDown(UINT, CPoint);
   afx_msg void OnCreate(LPCREATESTRUCT);
   afx_msg void OnDestroy();
   afx_msg void OnTimer(UINT);
   afx_msg void OnKeyDown(UINT, UINT, UINT);
   afx_msg void OnChar(UINT,UINT,UINT);
   DECLARE_MESSAGE_MAP()
};
```

You can determine from the class declaration that the window is handling WM_PAINT, WM_LBUTTONDOWN, WM_CREATE, WM_DESTROY, WM_TIMER, WM_KEYDOWN, and WM_CHAR messages. The message map makes all of the associations with the corresponding handlers, and is defined as follows:

```
BEGIN_MESSAGE_MAP(DuckHuntFrameWnd, CFrameWnd)
   ON_WM_TIMER()
   ON_WM_PAINT()
   ON_WM_CREATE()
   ON_WM_DESTROY()
   ON_WM_LBUTTONDOWN()
   ON_WM_KEYDOWN()
   ON_WM_CHAR()
END_MESSAGE_MAP()
```

The constructor for DuckHuntFrameWnd creates the window by invoking Create() and using all of the default parameters.

```
DuckHuntFrameWnd::DuckHuntFrameWnd(){
    Create(NULL,"Rich's Duck Hunt Game");
}
```

The Create() function generates a WM_CREATE message, which in turn, causes OnCreate() to be invoked. The OnCreate() message handler starts the timer that will be used to animate the duck flying across the window. Notice the timer interval is an attribute of the Duck object.

```
int DuckHuntFrameWnd::OnCreate(LPCREATESTRUCT createStruct){
    if(CFrameWnd::OnCreate(createStruct) == -1)
        return -1;
    SetTimer(1, m_Duck.GetDelay(), NULL);
    return 0;
}
```

After the window is closed, a WM_DESTROY message is generated. The OnDestroy() message handler stops the timer using the KillTimer() function and passing in the ID of the timer.

```
void DuckHuntFrameWnd::OnDestroy(){
    KillTimer(1);
    CFrameWnd::OnDestroy();
}
```

The timer generates WM_TIMER messages which are handled by the OnTimer() function. In the duck hunt game, OnTimer() moves the duck within the window by invoking MoveRandom() on the duck object. The window is then invalidated and a WM_PAINT event is generated by invoking UpdateWindow().

```
void DuckHuntFrameWnd::OnTimer(UINT id){
    if(id == 1) { //verify WM_TIMER message was from timer 1
        //move the duck randomly
        CRect windowSize;
        GetClientRect(&windowSize);
        m_Duck.MoveRandom(windowSize);
        //repaint the entire window
        Invalidate();
        UpdateWindow();
    }
}
```

Notice that MoveRandom() requires a bounding rectangle. The OnTimer() function uses the current client area of the window as the bounding rectangle, calculated by the GetClientRect() member function.

The timer causes the window to be repainted frequently, which is how the animation is performed. The `OnPaint()` message handler paints the duck (which is really a square). A running total of the number of hits is displayed in the upper-left corner of the window.

```
void DuckHuntFrameWnd::OnPaint(){
    //create a device context
    CPaintDC paintDC(this);
    //select a solid brush of the appropriate color
    CBrush brush(m_Duck.GetColor());
    paintDC.SelectObject(&brush);
    //draw the duck with the appropriate location & size
    CPoint location = m_Duck.GetLocation();
    int size = m_Duck.GetSize();
    paintDC.Rectangle(location.x, location.y,
                      location.x + size, location.y + size);
    //display the score
    paintDC.TextOut(0,0, m_HitCountMessage);
}
```

With these message handlers in place, the duck will now fly across the window. The goal of the game is to click the duck with the mouse before it leaves the window. The mouse clicks will generate `WM_LBUTTONDOWN` messages, which are handled in `OnLButtonDown()`. This function uses the `PtInRect()` function of the `CRect` class to determine if the mouse click occurred within the duck. If it has, then the `HitTarget()` function is invoked to deal with the duck being hit. If it's a miss, then the duck keeps flying. The code is shown here:

```
void DuckHuntFrameWnd::OnLButtonDown(UINT flags, CPoint point) {
    //determine the square where the duck is now
    CPoint upperLeft = m_Duck.GetLocation();
    int size = m_Duck.GetSize();
    CRect duck(upperLeft.x, upperLeft.y,
               upperLeft.x + size, upperLeft.y + size);

    //determine if the user clicked the duck
    if(duck.PtInRect(point)){
        HitTarget();
    }
}
```

The `HitTarget()` function is listed next and simulates the duck falling out of the sky by moving the duck vertically down until it drops out of the window. The hit counter is incremented and a new duck starts flying across the window. The timer is stopped momentarily because I do not want any `WM_TIMER` messages being generated while the duck is falling.

```
void DuckHuntFrameWnd::HitTarget(){
    //stop the timer momentarily
    KillTimer(1);
    //increment the hit count
    m_Duck.Hit();
    //update the message
    m_HitCountMessage.Format("Hit Count: %d",
                            m_Duck.GetHitCount());
    //change the color of the duck to red
    m_Duck.SetColor(RGB(255,0,0));
    //make the duck fall out of the sky
    CRect windowSize;
    GetClientRect(&windowSize);
    int x = m_Duck.GetLocation().x;
    int y = m_Duck.GetLocation().y;
    while(y < windowSize.Height()) {
        y += 10;   //move the duck vertically down
        CPoint newLocation(x,y);
        m_Duck.SetLocation(newLocation);
        //cause the window to repaint
        Invalidate();
        UpdateWindow();
    }
    //start the timer again to continue the game
    m_Duck.SetColor(RGB(255,255,0));
    SetTimer(1,m_Duck.GetDelay(),NULL);
}
```

The game is now functional. The duck flies across the screen and, if it is clicked by the mouse, drops out of the sky. A running total of the number of hits is displayed.

Once I got a feel for the game, I thought it would be nice if the user could control the size and speed of the duck. To change the speed of the duck, I added handlers for the up and down arrows. These are virtual keys and do not generate WM_CHAR messages, so I needed to handle WM_KEYDOWN messages. The OnKeyDown() function is defined as follows:

```
void DuckHuntFrameWnd::OnKeyDown(UINT nChar, UINT nRepCnt,
                                 UINT nFlags) {
  switch(nChar) {
  case VK_UP :
    //increase the speed by lowering the delay
    ChangeTimer(-10);
    break;
  case VK_DOWN :
    //decrease the speed by increasing the delay
    ChangeTimer(10);
    break;
  }
}
```

Changing the time interval is not a capability of a timer, so I wrote a small function called ChangeTimer() to accomplish this.

```
void DuckHuntFrameWnd::ChangeTimer(int change){
  //change the delay on the duck
  m_Duck.SetDelay(m_Duck.GetDelay() + change);
  //reset the delay of the timer (recall the ID is 1)
  SetTimer(1, m_Duck.GetDelay(), NULL);
}
```

To make the duck bigger, the user presses the 'B' key. To make the duck smaller, the user presses the 'S' key. These generate WM_CHAR messages, and the OnChar() handler simply invokes SetSize() on the duck to increase or decrease the size by 5 pixels each time the message occurs.

```
void DuckHuntFrameWnd::OnChar(UINT nChar, UINT nRepCnt,
                              UINT nFlags){
  switch(nChar) {
  case 'b' :
  case 'B' :
    //increase the target size
    m_Duck.SetSize(m_Duck.GetSize() + 5);
    break;
```

```
   case 's' :
   case 'S' :
      //decrease the target size
      m_Duck.SetSize(m_Duck.GetSize() - 5);
      break;
   }
   }
```

The user can now make the duck quite small (5 pixels square) or quite large. The user can also slow the duck down or speed it up. Try playing the game and generating some of these messages. You should notice some interesting results. For example, if you hold down a key on the keyboard, the duck stops moving. This is because WM_TIMER and WM_PAINT messages have a lower priority, so the WM_CHAR and WM_KEYDOWN messages are being handled and the duck stops flying. You will also notice that you may have to "lead" the duck a little to hit it. Sometimes clicking directly on the duck does not produce a hit, because by the time the WM_LBUTTONDOWN message is handled, the duck has moved. Of course, this is true in real duck hunting. If you aim directly at the duck, you are likely to shoot behind it!

Chapter 7

Windows Resources

A *resource* is a binary data object that is defined outside of your program's source code. Resources are an essential component of a Windows program, and this chapter will introduce you to creating resources and accessing them from your source code. The following is a list of resources that can be created using the resource editor in Visual C++:

- Menus
- Keyboard accelerators
- Bitmaps, including icons and cursors
- Toolbars
- Dialog windows
- String tables
- Version information

A Visual C++ project typically contains a single resource file, which is named with an rc extension. The resource file is actually a text file, but you do not have to edit it yourself. It is generated for you by Visual C++ from the resource editor. Each resource has a WYSIWYG tool for creating and editing the resource.

The resource file is not C++ code, but a scripting language that is compiled using a resource compiler. The resource compiler generates a res file, which is linked with your executable during the build process. Your application has access to a resource in the res file through an identifier — which every resource has.

This chapter discusses the details of creating a resource using the Visual C++ resource editor, assigning an identifier to the resource, and using it in your application. The "Menus" section describes how to create a menu, add it to a frame window, and handle the messages it generates. Keyboard accelerators are often associated with menu items, so those will be discussed next, followed by a discussion on toolbars and status bars.

This chapter also describes how to use a string table to avoid hard-coding text in an application. You will also see how to create an icon and associate it with your executable file. The dialog resources are discussed in detail in Chapter 8. A discussion on version information is omitted. (Version information is seldom a concern for a beginning MFC developer.)

ResourceView

Before I begin discussing how to create resources, I want to show you how to manage and navigate through your resources using the ResourceView window. The ResourceView window is found in the Workspace window and is displayed by selecting the ResourceView tab.

NOTE: The ResourceView tab and window are not available if your project does not contain any resources. Once a resource is added to a project, the ResourceView tab and window will become visible.

Figure 7.1 shows a ResourceView window with an accelerator table, an icon, two menus, a string table, and two toolbars. The ID is shown for each resource, and you can open up a resource in the resource editor by double-clicking on its ID.

Figure 7.1   A ResoureView window.

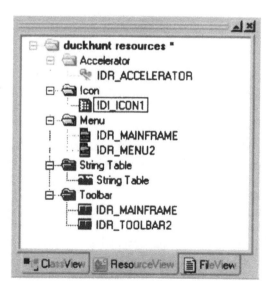

A resource can be removed from a project by selecting it in the ResourceView window and pressing the Del key. The next section discusses the various ways to add a resource.

Adding a Resource to a Project

You can add a resource to a project using one of the following techniques.

- Selecting Insert/Resource from the menu to display the Insert Resource dialog.
- Using the accelerator key Ctrl-R, which also displays the Insert Resource dialog.
- Right-click on a folder in the ResourceView window and select the appropriate menu item in the pop-up menu.

The Insert Resource dialog is shown in Figure 7.2. You select the type of resource you want to add and click the New button. The resource will be created and opened in the resource editor.

Figure 7.2 The Insert Resource dialog.

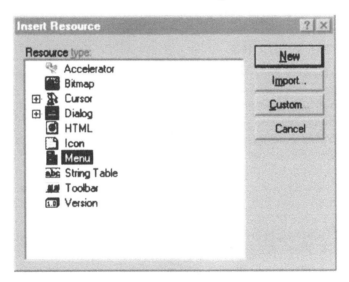

Each type of resource appears in a folder in the tree view of ResourceView. You can right-click on one of these folders to add the appropriate resource. For example, you can add a new menu by right-clicking on the Menu folder. Figure 7.3 shows the pop-up menu that appears. Selecting Insert Menu adds a new menu. Notice you can also save the resource file or select Insert to display the Insert Resource dialog.

Figure 7.3 Adding a resource using the pop-up menu in ResourceView.

As I mentioned earlier, if your project does not contain resources, the ResourceView tab will not appear. Once you insert a resource, the ResourceView tab should become visible. If it does not, then you might need to save the resources in an rc file.

The resource.h File

Each time you edit a resource and save your changes, a new rc text file is created by Visual C++. In addition, a new resource.h file is created which contains define directives for each identifier. Every resource is denoted by an identifier. In addition, an identifier is used for every menu item, toolbar button, string table entry, and so forth.

Each identifier is an integer value. You include the resource.h file into your source code so the identifiers can be used in your program. The resource.h file can have many entries in it, but you do not need to worry about assigning each identifier a unique value. The resource editor does this for you.

As with the rc text file, you should not edit the resource.h file. Let Visual C++ do it for you. If for some reason you want to change the value of an identifier in resource.h, you can view and edit the values using the Resource Symbols dialog, shown in Figure 7.4. To open this dialog, select View/Resource Symbols from the Visual C++ menu. Don't forget to include the resource.h file into any source code files that use a resource identifier.

Menus

A *menu* is a resource found in almost every Windows application that displays a frame window. The term "menu" refers to various components. The bar displayed at the top of a window is referred to as a *top-level menu*. A top-level menu contains *drop-down menus* which drop down when they are selected by the user. A drop-down menu contains *menu items*, which create a message to be handled by your application. Since Windows 95 was introduced, users have become quite familiar with *pop-up menus* — floating menus that typically appear at the location of a right mouse click.

Figure 7.4   The Resource Symbols dialog.

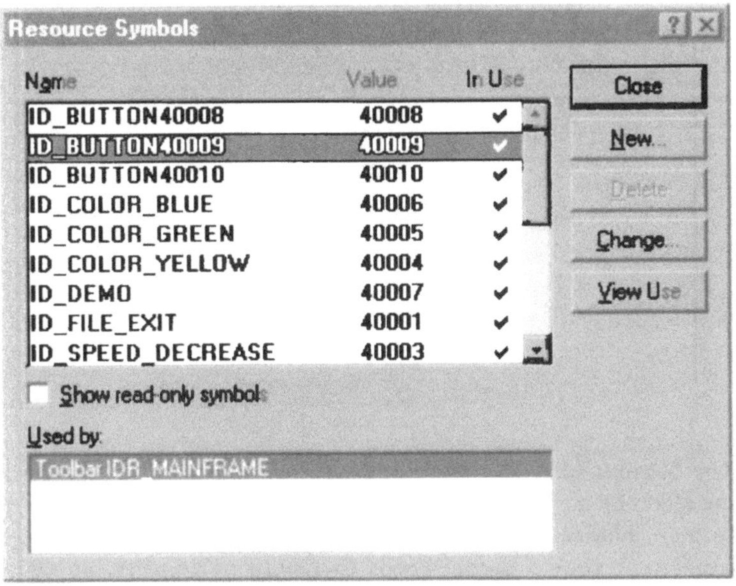

Creating a Menu

To add a menu to a project, select Menu and press the New button in the Insert Resource dialog. The new menu will appear in the resource editor, which will display an empty, top-level menu. You add drop-down menus by typing the names of the menus directly onto the top-level menu.

Every resource has an ID to be used by the source code. The ID of the menu is displayed in the ResourceView window. The resource editor will give you a default ID of ID_MENU1 (or something similar). You can change the ID of a menu or any resource by using its Properties window. The Properties window is displayed by right-clicking on the resource and selecting Properties from the pop-up menu. The main application menu typically has an ID of IDR_MAINFRAME.

Menus can be accessed using accelerator keys by pressing Alt and a letter. For example, Alt-F selects the File menu on most applications, then selecting X exits the application. This is a built-in feature of a menu. You can determine which accelerator key a menu or menu item uses by placing an ampersand (&) in front of the desired letter when you create the menu. For example, the File menu would be entered as "&File." The menu will underline the accelerator key of a menu or menu item. Figure 7.5 shows a top-level menu with two entries: File and Color. Alt-F will display the File drop-down menu and Alt-C will display the Color menu.

Figure 7.5 Use the ampersand (&) in front of the letter that corresponds to the accelerator key.

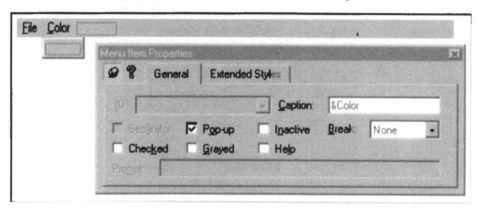

The Menu Item Properties window shown in Figure 7.5 can be opened by double-clicking on the menu or menu item. Use this window to change the ID and the various settings of the menu item. Notice that drop-down menus do not have an ID because they do not generate messages that your program needs to handle. The behavior of displaying the drop-down menu is done for you.

NOTE: Every resource item has a corresponding Properties window that can be displayed by double-clicking the particular resource item. The window has a stick-pin button in the upper-lefthand corner that can be selected to keep the window on the screen. Otherwise, the Properties window will be removed when you click outside of the window.

Adding Menu Items

Each drop-down menu contains menu items which are added in the resource editor by typing directly on the drop-down menu. Alternatively, you can double-click on the entry and type the name in the Menu Item Properties window. Each menu item can also have an accelerator key shortcut using the ampersand in front of the letter to represent the shortcut key.

When the user selects a menu item, a WM_COMMAND message is generated. The message has a corresponding ID associated with it. For this reason, each menu item needs a unique ID — denoted in the Menu Item Properties window. The resource editor will generate an ID for you based on the menu item's name, but you can choose any ID you want. Figure 7.6 shows a Green menu item on the Color drop-down menu with an ID of ID_COLOR_GREEN.

Figure 7.6 Each menu item has a corresponding ID.

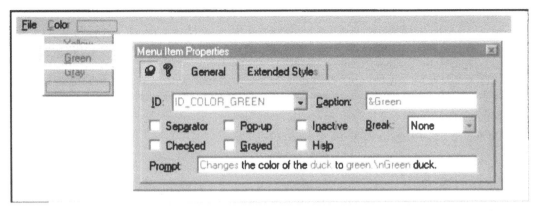

Notice the Prompt edit box in the Menu Item Properties in Figure 7.6 has a description typed in it. The text before the "\n" will be displayed in the windows status bar when the user highlights the menu item. The text after the "\n" will appear as a tool tip if the menu item has a corresponding button on a toolbar. Toolbars are discussed later in this chapter (see page 164).

A menu item can be a drop-down menu, which results in a cascading menu. Select Pop-up in the Menu Item Properties window to make a menu item a cascading menu. Figure 7.7 shows a cascade menu that also contains a separator. A separator menu item is created by selecting the Separator property in the Menu Item Properties window.

Figure 7.7 A cascade menu and a separator menu item.

Once your menu is created in the editor, save your changes by saving the resource file. Select File/Save from the Visual C++ menu.

Adding a Menu to a Window

A top-level menu is added to a window when the window is created. The Create() member function of the CFrameWnd class has a parameter for the ID of a menu. The parameter takes in a string, but the ID of a menu is an integer value. However, MFC provides the MAKEINTRESOURCE macro to convert an integer into a string.

The following constructor creates a frame window with a menu attached whose ID is IDR_MAINFRAME. When the window is displayed, the menu will appear at the top of the window.

```
DuckHuntFrameWnd::DuckHuntFrameWnd() {
    Create(NULL, "Duck Hunt Game", WS_OVERLAPPEDWINDOW,
        rectDefault, NULL,
        MAKEINTRESOURCE(IDR_MAINFRAME));
}
```

The rectDefault parameter is a member variable of the CFrameWnd class that lets Windows determine the initial size and location of the window. The fifth parameter is a pointer to the parent window, which defaults to NULL. The sixth parameter is the menu name as a string — created from the MAKEINTRESOURCE macro.

You will notice something interesting if this window is displayed. The menu items are all "grayed out." This is because message handlers have not been added for the menu items. The next section discusses the WM_COMMAND message and how it is used to handle messages from a menu item.

The ON_COMMAND() Macro

When a menu item is selected by the user, a WM_COMMAND message is generated. Command messages are handled slightly differently than a typical Windows message. The handler that is invoked depends on the ID of the source of the message. Use the ON_COMMAND() macro in the window's message map to associate an ID with a particular handler.

For example, suppose that when the user selected the Color/Yellow menu item, your program changed the color of an object to yellow. If the menu item ID is ID_COLOR_YELLOW and the function you want invoked is OnYellow(), the following entry would be added to the appropriate message map:

```
ON_COMMAND(ID_COLOR_YELLOW, OnYellow)
```

The OnYellow() message handler should be declared as:

```
afx_msg void OnYellow();
```

When the user selects the menu item Color/Yellow, the OnYellow() function will be invoked.

Each identifier needs to have an ON_COMMAND() entry in the message map. More precisely, each identifier can have one ON_COMMAND() entry in the message map at most, i.e., an identifier cannot be mapped to two different message handlers.

In the previous example with the ID_COLOR_YELLOW identifier, the ON_COMMAND() macro mapped the corresponding WM_COMMAND message to the OnYellow() function. Notice I did not specify that ID_COLOR_YELLOW was associated with a menu item. In other words, ON_COMMAND() associates a resource ID with a message handler, independent of the source of the event. This allows you to use the ID_COLOR_YELLOW for other resources and not have to make a repetitive entry in the message map. For example, a toolbar button can be given the identifier ID_COLOR_YELLOW as well. This means the OnYellow() function will be invoked when the toolbar button is pressed or when the menu item is selected. This is a common occurrence in a Windows application where there are several different ways to perform the same task.

As I mentioned earlier, a menu item is disabled (appears grayed) if a corresponding ON_COMMAND() message handler cannot be found. This is an attribute of the CFrameWnd class that can be overridden by changing the member variable m_bAutoMenuEnable to FALSE.

Command Ranges

Adding a message handler for each menu item can result in repeating code unnecessarily. For example, selecting a color from a menu results in essentially the same code being executed. You can use a command range to write a message handler that handles messages from a range of consecutive ID's. The ON_COMMAND_RANGE() macro makes the association in the appropriate message map.

For example, in the menu in Figure 7.7 (page 159), the Color menu had five menu items representing different colors. Instead of writing five message handlers and making five ON_COMMAND() entries in the message map, you can associate all five ID's with one message handler. This only works if the ID values are consecutive. For example, if ID_COLOR_YELLOW = 40001, ID_COLOR_GREEN = 40002, and so forth up to ID_COLOR_BLUE, then the following message map entry will map each ID to the OnChangeColor() handler.:

```
ON_COMMAND_RANGE(ID_COLOR_YELLOW,ID_COLOR_BLUE,
                 OnChangeColor)
```

The OnChangeColor() function receives an argument containing the ID of the actual menu item selected. It should be declared as:

```
afx_msg void OnChangeColor(UINT);
```

The implementation might look like the following:

```
void DuckHuntFrameWnd::OnChangeColor(UINT id) {
    switch(id) {
    case ID_COLOR_YELLOW :
        m_Duck.SetColor(RGB(255,255,0));
        break;
    case ID_COLOR_GREEN :
        m_Duck.SetColor(RGB(0,255,0));
        break;
    //and so forth
    }
    Invalidate();
    UpdateWindow();
}
```

A switch statement can be used because each of the identifiers is a constant integer. In this example, the color of the duck is changed to the corresponding value and the window is repainted to reflect the changes.

Keyboard Accelerators

The previous section on menus discussed how the Alt key can be used to navigate through a menu using the keyboard. This allows for an alternate way of selecting menu items — without requiring the use of a mouse. You can also create a shortcut key linked directly to a menu item that does not navigate through the menu, but instead has the same effect as selecting the menu item. This shortcut key is called a *keyboard accelerator*. The keyboard accelerators are defined in an *accelerator table* — a resource of your Windows application.

You are probably already familiar with accelerator keys. For example, in many applications that use cut, copy, and paste, Ctrl-X is the accelerator key for cut, Ctrl-C is copy, and Ctrl-V is paste. Pressing these accelerator keys has the same result as selecting the items from a menu; a WM_COMMAND message is generated containing the ID of the source of the event. The corresponding message handler for this ID is invoked.

The previous section discussed how to associate a message handler with a resource ID. This section describes how to associate a keyboard accelerator with a menu item by assigning an accelerator to a resource ID.

The Accelerator Table

A Windows resource file can contain multiple accelerator tables. As with all resources, each accelerator table has an ID. Use the Insert Resource dialog to add an accelerator table to a project. You can open an accelerator table in the resource editor by double-clicking on its ID in the ResoureView window. Figure 7.8 shows an accelerator table opened in the resource editor.

Figure 7.8   Use the resource editor to view and edit the entries in an accelerator table.

ID	Key	Type
ID_COLOR_BLUE	Ctrl + B	VIRTKEY
ID_COLOR_GREEN	Ctrl + G	VIRTKEY
ID_COLOR_GRAY	Ctrl + R	VIRTKEY
ID_COLOR_RED	Alt + R	VIRTKEY
ID_COLOR_YELLOW	Ctrl + Y	VIRTKEY

An accelerator table is simply a list of keyboard accelerators. Each entry in the table consists of three items: the accelerator key, the ID, and the type of accelerator key. The type of the key is either virtual or ASCII. The ASCII type is used in rare situations where the accelerator key is an ASCII character. In most situations, an accelerator key uses some type of virtual key like Ctrl, Alt, or Shift.

Adding Items to an Accelerator Table

The resource editor provides a simple dialog for adding an entry in an accelerator table. Assuming you have the accelerator table opened in the resource editor, you will notice that the last entry is a blank line. Double-click on this blank line to display the dialog shown in Figure 7.9.

Figure 7.9   The Accel Properties dialog.

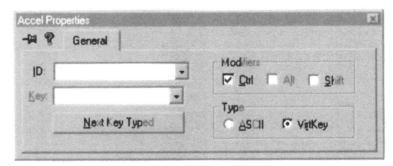

The Accel Properties dialog shows the ID of the accelerator, the key that is to be pressed (including its modifiers like Ctrl or Alt), and the type of key (either ASCII or VirtKey). The easiest way to assign the key to be pressed is to press the Next Key Typed button and type in the accelerator key. The Accel Properties dialog will then display the button you just typed.

You can select the ID for the accelerator key from the drop-down list in the Accel Properties dialog. The list contains all IDs previously defined. Alternatively, you can simply type in the ID of the accelerator key — which you may have to do if the ID you want is not previously defined.

Figure 7.10   Select an ID from the drop-down list or type in the accelerator's ID.

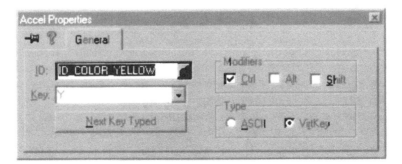

Figure 7.10 shows an entry that associates Ctrl-Y with the ID_COLOR_YELLOW identifier. If your program already handles WM_COMMAND messages with this ID, then no additional message handling is required for the keyboard accelerator to have the same behavior as the menu item. If the ID for a keyboard accelerator is unique to the accelerator, than you handle the message

as with any other resource ID, using the ON_COMMAND() macro in a message map to associate the ID with a message handler.

Be sure to save the resource file once you have added the entries or made all of your changes to an accelerator table. As with all resources, the resource editor will make the necessary changes in the rc file and resource.h.

Loading an Accelerator Table

Once an accelerator table is created, it needs to be loaded by the frame window for the keyboard accelerators to become functional. The CFrameWnd class uses its LoadAccelTable() member function, which is declared as:

```
BOOL LoadAccelTable(LPCTSTR lpszResourceName);
```

The lpszResourceName parameter is the name of the resource. Use the MAKEINTRESOURCE macro to convert an integer ID to a string. The function returns TRUE if successful; otherwise FALSE.

An accelerator table is typically loaded in the OnCreate() message handler of the frame window, as the following example illustrates.

```
int DuckHuntFrameWnd::OnCreate(LPCREATESTRUCT createStruct){
    if(CFrameWnd::OnCreate(createStruct) == -1)
        return -1;
    //load the accelerator table
    if(!LoadAccelTable(MAKEINTRESOURCE(IDR_ACCELERATOR1))
        return -1;
}
```

The main accelerator table of a window typically uses the IDR_MAINFRAME identifier — just like the window's main menu. (You will see this identifier with other resources as well.) The example above loads the IDR_MAINFRAME accelerator table, and the keyboard accelerators in that table will now become functional.

Toolbars

A *toolbar* is a collection of buttons that provides a visual interface for various features of a program, much like menus. Toolbars are typically displayed just below the window's menu. However, most toolbars are dockable, i.e., they can be dragged around the window and docked to other sides of the window. They can also float in their own window.

This section discusses how to create a toolbar using the resource editor in Visual C++. The CToolBar class is also discussed, which is used to create a toolbar object from a resource and to associate the toolbar with a window. As with menus and keyboard accelerators, toolbars create WM_COMMAND messages, so the event handling will be identical to what you have seen in the previous sections.

Creating a Toolbar Using the Resource Editor

A toolbar appears to be a collection of buttons. However, the entire toolbar is a single bitmap consisting of tiles 16 pixels wide and 15 pixels high. The resource editor provides a WYSI-WYG tool for creating the tiles on a bitmap and assigning an ID to each tile.

To insert a toolbar into a project, select Toolbar from the Insert Resource dialog and press the New button. A new toolbar will be displayed in the resource editor, as shown in Figure 7.11.

Figure 7.11 The resource editor provides a WYSIWYG tool for creating the tiles of a bitmap.

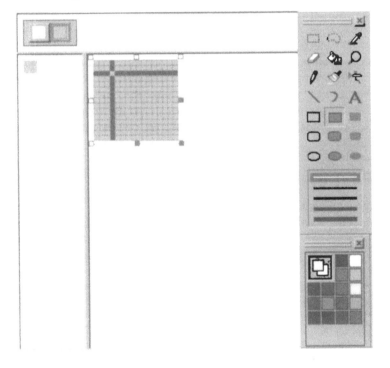

The top portion of the window shows the toolbar. The left side of the window shows what the toolbar button will look like, and the large window is where you draw the tile. The resource editor allows you to draw the bitmap of each tile using various pens, brushes, colors, and shapes — similar to the Paint program in Windows. Select the various drawing tools from the Graphics and Colors toolbar.

As with other resource items, each toolbar button has an ID. To assign an ID to a button while within the resource editor, double-click on the button the toolbar in the top portion of the window. Figure 7.12 shows the Toolbar Button Properties window, which will appear for the particular tile that was double-clicked.

Figure 7.12 The Toolbar Button Properties window.

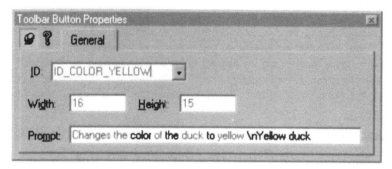

Many toolbar buttons are often a shortcut for a menu item. If the ID of a toolbar button corresponds to an existing menu item ID, then you can select the ID from the drop-down list. Figure 7.12 selected ID_COLOR_YELLOW, which corresponded to a Color/Yellow menu item. Notice the Prompt edit displays the same prompt that was created for the menu item. For toolbars, the prompt does two things: the first portion of the prompt will be displayed in the status bar, and the portion of the prompt after the "\n" will appear as a tooltip.

If the toolbar button does not represent an existing ID, you can enter a new ID and prompt. Notice the width and height of the tile can be changed in the Toolbar Button Properties window.

Displaying a Toolbar

Once the toolbar resource is created, a CToolBar object is used to embed the toolbar into a window. The CToolBar class is a child of CControlBar and uses much of the functionality from CControlBar. The CControlBar class inherits from CWnd, so a toolbar is also a window. This means any of the styles and behaviors of CWnd can be applied to a toolbar.

NOTE: The CToolBar and CControlBar classes are declared in the afxext.h header file. Be sure to include this into the necessary source files.

There are four steps involved in creating and displaying a toolbar in a window.

1. Instantiate a CToolBar object.
2. Invoke the Create() member function of the CToolBar object to create the toolbar and associate it with a window.
3. Invoke the LoadToolBar() function of the CToolBar object to load a toolbar resource for the toolbar.
4. Dock the toolbar to the frame window using the DockControlBar() function of the CFrameWnd class.

The Create() function determines the parent window of the toolbar. You also determine the various styles of your toolbar. The function is declared as:

```
BOOL Create(CWnd* pParentWnd,
            DWORD dwStyle=WS_CHILD|WS_VISIBLE|CBRS_TOP,
            UINT nID = AFX_IDW_TOOLBAR);
```

The pParentWnd parameter is the window with which the toolbar is associated. The dwStyle represents the styles of the toolbar. The possible values of dwStyle include any window styles — like WS_CHILD and WS_VISIBLE — and any combination of the toolbar styles. Some of the common styles are listed in Table 7.1. View the documentation for a complete listing. The nID parameter is an ID that the parent window can use to identify the child window toolbar.

Table 7.1 Common toolbar styles.

Value	Style
CBRS_TOP	Toolbar appears at the top of the window.
CBRS_BOTTOM	Toolbar appears at the bottom of the window.
CBRS_ALIGN_LEFT	Toolbar appears at the left edge of the window.
CBRS_ALIGN_RIGHT	Toolbar appears at the right edge of the window.
CBRS_ALIGN_ANY	Toolbar can be docked to any edge of the window.
CBRS_TOOLTIPS	Allows tool tips to be displayed.
CBRS_FLOATING	Toolbar is not docked to the window.
CBRS_FLYBY	Prompt is displayed in the status bar.
CBRS_GRIPPER	Causes a gripper to appear at the left or top edge of the toolbar.

The docking feature of a toolbar can be changed using the EnableDocking() member function of CControlBar. A CFrameWnd object can also determine its docking styles using its own EnableDocking() member function. You can also change the styles of a toolbar using the SetBarStyle() member function found in CControlBar.

Once the toolbar is created in memory, the toolbar resource needs to be loaded using the LoadToolBar() member function of the CToolBar class. The function is overloaded to take in either an integer or a string value to represent the resource.

```
BOOL LoadToolBar(LPCTSTR lpszResourceName);
BOOL LoadToolBar(UINT nIDResource);
```

The toolbar is now ready to be docked to the window. The toolbar needs to enable docking, as does the frame window. The CControlBar and CFrameWnd classes each contain an EnableDocking() function, each with the same prototype:

```
void CFrameWnd::EnableDocking(DWORD dwDockStyle);
void CControlBar::EnableDocking(DWORD dwDockStyle);
```

The dwDockStyle parameter is of the form CBRS_ALIGN_*location*, where *location* is TOP, BOTTOM, LEFT, RIGHT, or ANY. The styles allow you to determine which edges of the window the toolbar can dock to.

Once docking is enabled, the final step is to dock the toolbar using the DockControlBar() member function of the CFrameWnd class. You can also float the toolbar using the FloatControlBar() member function. DockControlBar() is declared as:

```
void DockControlBar(CControlBar* pBar,
                    UINT nDockBarID = 0,
                    LPCRECT lpRect = NULL);
```

The pBar parameter points to the toolbar to be docked. The nDockBarID parameter is where to dock the toolbar initially. Its values can be AFX_IDW_DOCKBAR_*location*, where *location* is TOP, BOTTOM, LEFT, or RIGHT. The lpRect parameter determines where to dock the toolbar in the nonclient area of the window.

The FloatControlBar() function is declared as:

```
CFrameWnd* FloatControlBar(CControlBar * pBar,
                           CPoint point,
                           DWORD dwStyle=CBRS_ALIGN_TOP);
```

The pBar parameter points to the toolbar, which is initially displayed at the point parameter. The point value is in screen coordinates, not window coordinates. The dwStyle parameter allows you to display the toolbar either vertically or horizontally. It defaults to horizontal, but it can be changed to vertical using the CBRS_ALIGN_LEFT or CBRS_ALIGN_RIGHT style.

Invoking DockControlBar() or FloatControlBar() will display the toolbar when the window is visible. The behavior of a toolbar is now handled by the framework. For example, the user can slide the toolbar or dock it on other sides of the window. Your application only needs to handles the WM_COMMAND messages generated from clicking the buttons. This message handling is the same as it is for menus, using the ON_COMMAND() macro in a message map to associate a resource identifier with a message handler.

An Example Using a Toolbar

A typical technique for adding a toolbar to a frame window is to add a CToolBar member variable to your CFrameWnd class, then invoke the Create(), LoadToolBar(), and docking functions in the OnCreate() message handler. Using this technique allows you to handle any creation problems before the window is displayed.

The following code illustrates this technique by adding a toolbar to a DuckHuntFrameWnd object.

```
//add a CToolBar member variable
class DuckHuntFrameWnd : public CFrameWnd {
private:
   CToolBar m_ColorsToolbar;
   //remainder of class definition
}


int DuckHuntFrameWnd::OnCreate(LPCREATESTRUCT createStruct){
   if(CFrameWnd::OnCreate(createStruct) == -1)
      return -1;

   //create the toolbar
   if(!m_ColorsToolbar.Create(this, WS_CHILD | WS_VISIBLE |
CBRS_GRIPPER|CBRS_TOOLTIPS|CBRS_FLYBY|CBRS_SIZE_DYNAMIC))
      return -1;

   //load the toolbar resource
   if(!m_ColorsToolbar.LoadToolBar(IDR_MAINFRAME))
      return -1;

   //the toolbar cannot be docked
   m_ColorsToolbar.EnableDocking(0);

   //the frame window allows docking on any side
   EnableDocking(CBRS_ALIGN_ANY);

   //locate the upper-left corner of the window
   CRect rect;
   GetWindowRect(&rect);
   CPoint offest(200,50);
   FloatControlBar(&m_ColorsToolbar, rect.TopLeft()+offset);

   return 0;
}
```

This particular example uses a floating toolbar. The EnableDocking() call on the toolbar means this toolbar can never dock, even though the frame window allows docking on all of its sides because it used the CBRS_ALIGN_ANY style. The output of the new duck hunt game is shown in Figure 7.13.

Figure 7.13 The duck hunt game with a floating toolbar.

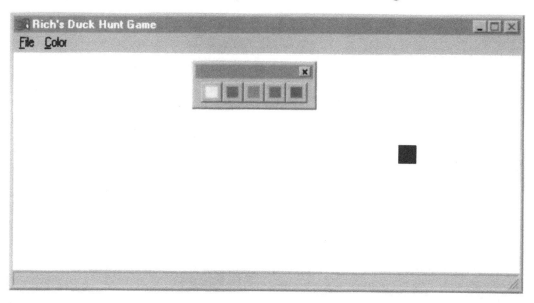

Toolbars require a lot of additional code to be displayed properly in a frame window that does not also contain a view. Views are discussed in Chapter 9, "The Document/View Architecture." For this reason, the example above floated the toolbar instead of docking it to the frame. If the toolbar were docked, the frame would repaint the toolbar frequently and it would flicker and barely be visible at times. The details to fix this problem are omitted because most of the applications that use toolbars will also have a view.

Update Handlers

Menu items and toolbars often change state during the lifetime of a Windows application. For example, when using a text editor, it does not make sense to copy or cut text when none is selected. Most text editors will disable the menu items and toolbars associated with copy and cut until the user has selected text. Determining the status of a resource is handled in MFC using *update handlers*. An update handler is invoked during idle-time processing and right before a drop-down menu is about to be displayed.

The idle-time messages can be used to update the status of a continually visible resource like a toolbar or status bar. The status of a menu item can be determined just before the drop-down menu appears. This section discusses how to handle these update messages using the ON_UPDATE_COMMAND_UI() macro and the CCmdUI class.

The ON_UPDATE_COMMAND_UI() Macro

You use the ON_COMMAND() macro to associate a resource ID with a message handler. Similarly, you use the ON_UPDATE_COMMAND_UI() to associate a resource ID with an update handler. The macro appears in the message map of the appropriate class. The following message map contains entries for the resource identifier ID_COLOR_YELLOW — both a message handler and an update handler:

```
BEGIN_MESSAGE_MAP(DuckHuntFrameWnd, CFrameWnd)
    ON_COMMAND(ID_COLOR_YELLOW, OnYellow)
    ON_UPDATE_COMMAND_UI(ID_COLOR_YELLOW, OnYellowUI)
END_MESSAGE_MAP()
```

The update handlers receive a single parameter: a pointer to a CCmdUI object. For example, the prototype of OnYellowUI() should look like:

```
void OnYellow(CCmdUI *);
```

The CCmdUI object represents the user interface resource being displayed. This object contains a member variable (m_nID) that will contain the identifier of the resource being updated. There are also four member functions of CCmdUI that can be used to determine the state of the resource: Enable(), SetCheck(), SetRadio(), and SetText(). These functions are discussed in the next section.

As with the ON_COMMAND_RANGE() macro, you can use the ON_UPDATE_COMMAND_UI_RANGE() macro to associate a range of resource identifiers with a single update handler.

The CCmdUI **Class**

The CCmdUI class has no parent class and is used only in update handlers. The Enable() function enables or disables the item and is declared as:

```
virtual void Enable(BOOL bOn = TRUE);
```

A menu item that is disabled is "grayed out" and cannot be selected. A disabled toolbar button is grayed out and cannot be pressed. A disabled status bar entry is made invisible. Invoke Enable() with a FALSE argument to disable the item.

The SetCheck() function is used to set the state of checked menu items and radio button toolbars. The function is declared as:

```
virtual void SetCheck(int nCheck = 1);
```

If the value of nCheck is 1, the menu item will be checked or the toolbar button will be pressed. The value 0 deselects these items, and a value of 2 is used if the state is indeterminate.

The SetRadio() function is declared as:

```
virtual void SetRadio(BOOL bOn = TRUE);
```

SetRadio() has the same behavior as SetCheck() for toolbar buttons and status bar items. When used with a menu item, a dot is placed by the menu item if TRUE is the argument.

The SetText() function is used for changing the text of a menu item or status bar item. It is declared as:

```
virtual void SetText(LPCTSTR lpszText);
```

The SetText() function has no effect on toolbar items.

An Example Using Update Handlers

To demonstrate update handlers, I added them to the menu items and toolbar for changing the color of the target in the duck hunt game. The following macro was added to the message map:

```
ON_UPDATE_COMMAND_UI_RANGE(ID_COLOR_YELLOW,ID_COLOR_BLUE,
                    OnChangeColorUI)
```

The OnChangeColorUI() is the update handler for all of the colors. Its implementation uses the SetRadio() function of the CCmdUI class to check the menu item and toolbar corresponding to the color.

```
void DuckHuntFrameWnd::OnChangeColorUI(CCmdUI * pCmdUI) {
    pCmdUI->SetRadio(m_ColorID == pCmdUI->m_nID);
}
```

In order to avoid having a separate update handler for each color, I used a m_ColorID member variable of the DuckHuntFrameWnd class to keep track of the current color. Notice the use of the m_nID attribute to determine which resource is being updated. If the ID of the resource being updated is equal to the current color, then the resource item will be selected. The menu item will have a dot, and the toolbar button will be pressed. If the m_nID value is *not* the ID of the current color, the item will not be selected. Figure 7.14 shows the resources when the color green is selected.

Figure 7.14 The menu items and toolbars using an update handler to display the current color.

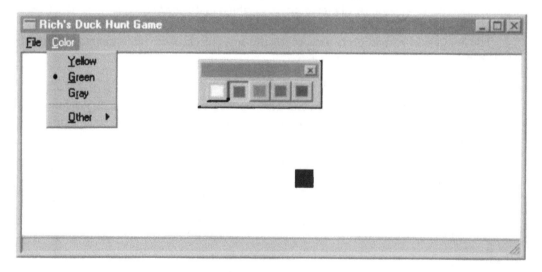

Status Bars

A *status bar* is a window displayed at the bottom of a frame window that can be used to display information. The information is displayed in panes, which are determined by an array of integers called *indicators*.

A status bar is not actually a resource, but its use is similar to toolbars, and the information in a status bar is often linked to a resource. This section discusses how to create an array of indicators and use the SetIndicators() function to associate your indicators with the status bar.

Creating a Status Bar

The panes on a status bar are indexed left to right, starting at 0. For example, the leftmost pane is index 0, the next pane is 1, and so forth. Each pane is associated with a corresponding entry in a static array of UINT's called *indicators*. An indicator is an identifier — much like an identifier for a resource. You use the ID of an indicator for update handlers, which is typically how a status bar is updated.

The following is the array of indicators that AppWizard generates for a standard MFC application:

```
static UINT indicators[] = {
    ID_SEPARATOR,      // status line indicator
    ID_INDICATOR_CAPS,
    ID_INDICATOR_NUM,
    ID_INDICATOR_SCRL,
};
```

These four indicators represent unique identifiers that are handled internally. The ID_SEPARATOR indicator is unique in that the text displayed in its pane is the prompt information for other resources like menu items and toolbars. The ID_INDICATOR_CAPS is the text CAPS, which is toggled on and off with the Caps Lock key. Similarly, the ID_INDICATOR_NUM indicator is the status of the Num Lock key, and ID_INDICATOR_SCRL is the status of the Scroll Lock key.

Creating User-Defined Indicators

You can create your own panes on the status bar by creating your own array of indicators. For example, the following array of indicators creates a status bar for the duck hunt game that displays the prompt messages and the *x* and *y* coordinates of where the last shot occurred. Figure 7.15 shows the resulting status bar.

```
static UINT indicators [] = {
    ID_SHOT_X,      //x coordinate of shot
    ID_SHOT_Y,      //y coordinate of shot
    ID_SEPARATOR    //status message
};
```

Figure 7.15 The duck hunt status bar consists of two user-defined indicators and the ID_SEPARATOR indicator.

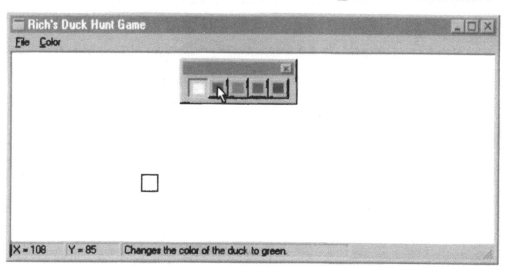

The ID_SEPARATOR pane is updated internally. The ID_SHOT_X and ID_SHOT_Y values need to be defined somewhere. When defining your own indicators, the string table can be used to define the identifier, its value, and also the width of the pane on the status bar. The next section, "String Tables," discusses how to add an entry to a string table. For example, the ID_SHOT_X and ID_SHOT_Y indicators are defined in the string table in Figure 7.16 as a string of X's. The actual string is not relevant, but the width of the string determines the width of the pane on the status bar.

Figure 7.16 Use the string table to define an indicator and determine the width of its pane.

ID	Value	Caption
ID_COLOR_GREEN	40003	Changes the color of the duck to green.\nGreen duck
ID_COLOR_GRAY	40004	Changes the color of the duck to gray\nGray duck
ID_COLOR_YELLOW	40005	Changes the color of the duck to yellow.\r Yellow duck
ID_COLOR_RED	40007	Changes the color of the duck to red.\nRed Duck
ID_COLOR_BLUE	40008	Changes the color of the duck to blue.\nBlue Duck
ID_SHOT_X	40018	XXXXXXXX
ID_SHOT_Y	40019	XXXXXXXX

Displaying the Status Bar

A status bar is created in your application using the CStatusBar class. CStatusBar is a child of CControlBar — just like the CToolBar class. There are three steps to creating a status bar for a frame window:

1. Instantiate a CStatusBar object. This is typically a member variable of the frame window class.
2. Invoke the Create() function of the CStatusBar object — which associates the status bar with a window.
3. Invoke the SetIndicators() function of the CStatusBar object.

The Create() and SetIndicators() functions are both members of CStatusBar and are declared as:

```
BOOL Create(CWnd* pParent,
            DWORD dwStyle=WS_CHILD|WS_VISIBLE|CBRS_BOTTOM,
            UINT nID=AFX_IDW_STATUS_BAR);


BOOL SetIndicators(const UINT* lpIDArray, int nIDCount);
```

In the Create() function, the pParent parameter is the window that owns the status bar. The dwStyle parameter can be the window styles combined with either CBRS_BOTTOM or CBRS_TOP. The nID parameter is a child ID for the parent window. The lpIDArray parameter in SetIndicators() is the array of indicators, and nIDCount is the number of elements in the array.

The following statements illustrate displaying a status bar by adding one to the DuckHunt-FrameWnd object. As with toolbars, the code to display a status bar is placed in the OnCreate() handler, so error checking can be done if the status bar cannot be created properly.

```
int DuckHuntFrameWnd::OnCreate(LPCREATESTRUCT createStruct){
    if(CFrameWnd::OnCreate(createStruct) == -1)
        return -1;


    //create a status bar
    if(!m_StatusBar.Create(this))
        return -1;
    //load the indicators
    m_StatusBar.SetIndicators(indicators,
                        sizeof(indicators)/sizeof(UINT));
    //create other window resources ...
}
```

Figure 7.15 (page 174) shows the status bar in the duck hunt game. The next section discusses how to change the text in the status bar panes.

Updating the Status Bar

If the information changes frequently, which is most often the case, then an update handler is the preferred technique for updating a status bar. You can use the CCmdUI member functions SetText() and Enable() to change the text of a pane and disable the pane.

The following message map associates an update handler for the status bar panes. The update handlers display the x and y coordinates of the latest shot — contained in a CPoint member variable m_Shot and updated in the OnLButtonDown() handler.

```
BEGIN_MESSAGE_MAP(DuckHuntFrameWnd, CFrameWnd)
    ON_UPDATE_COMMAND_UI(ID_SHOT_X, OnUpdateX)
    ON_UPDATE_COMMAND_UI(ID_SHOT_Y, OnUpdateY)
    //other message map entries ...
END_MESSAGE_MAP()


void DuckHuntFrameWnd::OnUpdateX(CCmdUI * pCmdUI) {
    CString location;
    location.Format("X = %d",m_Shot.x);
    pCmdUI->SetText(location);
}


void DuckHuntFrameWnd::OnUpdateY(CCmdUI * pCmdUI) {
    CString location;
    location.Format("Y = %d", m_Shot.y);
    pCmdUI->SetText(location);
}
```

The x and y coordinates are displayed in the status bar at each click of the mouse. Notice the prompt for the menu items and toolbars is displayed in the third pane of the status bar.

String Tables

A *string table* is a resource that contains a list of strings. Each string is denoted by a resource identifier. A string table is useful because it allows you to develop an application without using string literals. This can be useful for translating a program to other languages or for managing the various string literals of a program.

Figure 7.16 (page 174) shows the string table for the duck hunt game. Notice that an entry is automatically made for menu item and toolbar prompts. You can add an entry to a string table by double-clicking on the blank line in the string table resource editor. A String Properties window will appear, as shown in Figure 7.17.

Figure 7.17 Add strings to the string table by double-clicking on the blank line.

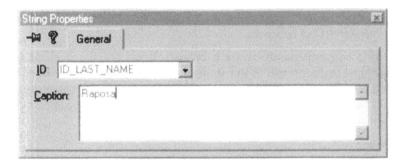

Type in the ID of the string, or select an ID from the drop-down list. Type the string literal in the caption. The resource editor will then create a value for the ID if one does not already exist. The IDs are defined in the resource.h file, and you can use the strings in your source code using the LoadString() function of the CString class.

```
BOOL LoadString(UINT nID);
```

The nID parameter is the resource ID of the string in the string table. The function returns TRUE if the string is loaded successfully, otherwise FALSE. For example, the following statements create a CString object from a resource identifier ID_LAST_NAME:

```
CString name;
BOOL success = name.LoadString(ID_LAST_NAME);
```

Bitmaps

A *bitmap* is an image stored as a sequence of 0's and 1's. Bitmaps in Visual C++ are resources compiled with the other resources and linked through the res file. You can use the resource editor to create a bitmap and assign it a resource identifier. You'll use the CBitmap class to employ the bitmap in your application.

Drawing a bitmap is part artistic ability and part mouse skills. I will not discuss the details of drawing a bitmap, but you will find that the bitmap resource editor in Visual C++ is straightforward to use. Instead, I will focus on the steps involved in displaying a bitmap.

Displaying a Bitmap

As you saw in Chapter 6, a CBitmap object is a GDI object. However, you do not simply select a bitmap into a device context to display it in a window. Instead, the image is first loaded into memory using a memory device context, then blitted to the screen using the BitBlit() function. Here are the steps involved:

1. Create a CBitmap object and load the resource into the object using LoadBitmap().
2. Create the desired window device context — either a CClientDC, CPaintDC, or CWindowDC object.

3. Create a compatible memory device context using a `CDC` object and the `CreateCompatibleBitmap()` function.
4. Select the bitmap into the memory device context.
5. Copy the bitmap from the memory device context to the window device context using the `BitBlt()` function.

The following statements create a bitmap object for the duck hunt game. When the user misses the target, a small splat is displayed on the window. The bitmap only needs to be loaded from the resource file once, so that is done in the `OnCreate()` message handler. The `m_Splat` variable is a `CBitmap` object and a member of the `DuckHuntFrameWnd` class. The identifier of the bitmap is IDB_SPLAT.

```
CBitmap m_Splat;  //declared in the header file
m_Splat.LoadBitmap(IDB_SPLAT); //in OnCreate()function
```

The image is displayed in a function called `DisplaySplat()`, which follows the steps listed previously for displaying a bitmap.

```
void DuckHuntFrameWnd::DisplaySplat() {
    //create the desired window device context
    CClientDC clientDC(this);

    //create a compatible memory device context
    CDC memoryDC;
    memoryDC.CreateCompatibleDC(&clientDC);

    //select the bitmap into the memory device context
    memoryDC.SelectObject(&m_Splat);

    //copy the bitmap into the window
    clientDC.BitBlt(m_SplatLocation.x, m_SplatLocation.y,
                20, 20, &memoryDC, 0, 0, SRCCOPY);
}
```

The `CreateCompatibleBitmap()` function creates a memory device context compatible with the given window device context. Just like any device context, you can select GDI objects into the memory device context and draw on it using the `CDC` functions. The bitmap is selected into the memory device context using the `SelectObject()` function.

NOTE: Bitmaps cannot be selected into non-memory device contexts.

The bitmap is now ready to be blitted to the screen — the process of transferring pixels from one device context to another. The CDC contains two functions for blitting a bitmap: `BitBlt()` and `StretchBlt()`. `BitBlt()` preserves the size of the region, while `StretchBlt()`

allows the image to be shrunk or expanded. Both functions are similar to use. The BitBlt() function is declared as:

```
BOOL BitBlt(int x, int y, int nWidth, int nHeight,
            CDC* pSrcDC, int xSrc, int ySrc, DWORD dwRop);
```

The first four int's represent the rectangle in the destination to be copied onto. The pSrcDC parameter points to the source device context. (The destination device context is the one that invokes this function.) The xSrc and ySrc int's represent the upper-left point in the source device context. The final parameter determines the raster operation used to blit the pixels. The SRCCOPY raster operation does not changes the pixels as they are copied. There are many raster operations available. View the documentation for a complete list of available dwRop values.

In the DisplaySplat() function above, a 20×20 pixel region of the memoryDC object is copied into the clientDC at the location of the m_SplatLocation point. Figure 7.18 shows the IDB_SPLAT bitmap displayed when the user misses the target.

Figure 7.18 This bitmap is displayed at the *x* and *y* coordinates of any mouse clicks that miss the target.

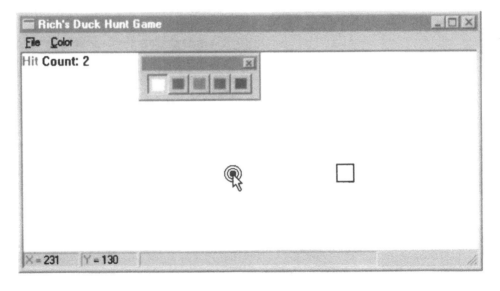

Icons

A Windows application has an icon associated with it that is used in various situations. For example, Windows Explorer uses the icon for the executable file. The icon is also displayed in the upper-left corner of the title bar of the window and on the taskbar when the program is running.

An icon is a resource that is saved in a *.ico file and compiled with the other resources in Visual C++. An application can have as many as three icons, which differ only by size. A small 16×16 pixel icon is used for the upper-left corner of the window and the taskbar. A

32×32 pixel icon is used for the desktop and Windows Explorer views. A 48×48 pixel icon is also used in certain Explorer views.

NOTE: If an application contains only a 32×32 icon, it will be scaled up or down for the other sizes when necessary.

An icon is a bitmap, and the resource editor for creating icons is the same as the bitmap resource editor. This section discusses how to assign an icon that you have created to your application. There are several techniques for doing this, and I will discuss two of the simpler techniques.

Assigning an Icon to an Application

The simplest way to add an icon to your application is to assign it the AFX_IDI_STDFRAME resource identifier. This value is looked for by the CFrameWnd class, so you do not need to add any code to your application. Use the Icon Properties dialog in the resource editor to select this ID from the drop-down list.

Figure 7.19 Change the icon's resource identifier to
AFX_IDI_STDFRAME using the Icon Properties dialog.

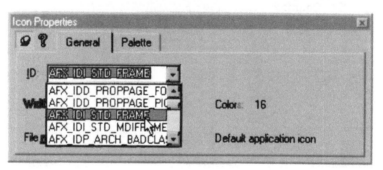

Using the AFX_IDI_STDFRAME identifier only works for CFrameWnd objects. An alternate method is to use the LoadIcon() and SetIcon() functions. LoadIcon() is a member of the CWinApp class and loads an icon using its resource identifier. SetIcon() is a member of the CWnd class. These functions are declared as:

```
HICON LoadIcon(UINT nIDResource) const;
HICON SetIcon(HICON hIcon, BOOL bBigIcon);
```

Notice the first parameter of SetIcon() is of type HICON, a handle to an icon. Use the return value of LoadIcon() for this parameter. The bBigIcon parameter is TRUE if the icon is 32×32 pixels; FALSE if its 16×16 pixels.

Because LoadIcon() is a member of the CWinApp class, you need to either invoke it from within your CWinApp class, or you can get a pointer to your CWinApp object using the

AfxGetApp() global function. You would probably use the latter technique because you typically want to call LoadIcon() from your frame window class. The following code illustrates this by loading an icon whose resource identifier is IDI_DUCK.

```
int DuckHuntFrameWnd::OnCreate(LPCREATESTRUCT createStruct) {
    if(CFrameWnd::OnCreate(createStruct) == -1)
        return -1;

    //assign an icon for the window
    HICON duck = AfxGetApp()->LoadIcon(IDI_DUCK);
    SetIcon(duck, TRUE);
    //remainder of OnCreate() ...
}
```

Notice the call to LoadIcon() takes place in OnCreate(), which is a member of the frame window class. The previous example uses AfxGetApp() to retrieve a necessary pointer to the application's global CWinApp object, which is then used to invoke LoadIcon().

Cursors

Similar to icons, you can create a custom cursor for your window. *Cursors* are resources created with the resource editor. As with icons, they are merely bitmaps that you draw using the bitmap resource editor. A cursor is 32×32 pixels, and using the icon resource editor, you can draw the cursor and determine its hot spot. The *hot spot* is the point of the cursor where the mouse click occurs. For example, the hot spot on the arrow cursor is the tip of the arrow. The hot spot on the cross cursor is the center.

Windows Standard Cursors

Windows has several pre-defined cursors that your application can use. The CWinApp class contains a LoadStandardCursor() function declared as:

```
HCURSOR LoadStandardCursor(LPCTSTR lpszCursorName) const;
```

The value of lpszCursorName is the standard cursor you want to load. Table 7.2 shows the standard cursors predefined in Windows.

Table 7.2 Windows standard cursors.

Value	Cursor
IDC_ARROW	Standard arrow cursor
IDC_IBEAM	Cursor used when typing text
IDC_WAIT	Hourglass cursor used to signify waiting
IDC_CROSS	Cross-hair cursor
IDC_UPARROW	Arrow pointing straight up
IDC_NO	Circle with a line through it
IDC_APPSTARTING	Hourglass and arrow next to each other
IDC_HELP	Question mark and arrow next to each other
IDC_SIZEALL	Four arrows: pointing up, down, left, and right

The IDC_SIZEALL cursor is used for resizing a window. Not listed in Table 7.2 are four other cursors used when resizing a window. They are IDC_SIZEWE and IDC_SIZENS for west–east and north–south arrows, and IDC_SIZENWSE and IDC_SIZENESW for two-sided arrows that point in a 45-degree angle. You rarely have to worry about loading these cursors because the behavior of a frame window does that for you.

MFC provides for a simple mechanism to change to the hourglass cursor. The CCmdTarget class (the parent class of CWnd) contains the member functions BeginWaitCursor() and End-WaitCursor(), which display the hourglass and restore the cursor, respectively. The return value of LoadStandardCursor() is used for displaying the cursor, discussed next.

Displaying a Cursor

If you draw your own cursor in the resource editor, you can use it in your application using the LoadCursor() member function of the CWinApp class. The function is prototyped as:

```
HCURSOR LoadCursor(UINT nIDResource) const;
```

The nIDResource parameter is the ID of your cursor assigned in the resource editor. The return value is a handle to the cursor, if the function is successful.

Whether you use LoadCursor() or LoadStandardCursor() to load a cursor, this does not *display* the cursor. Menus, icons, toolbars, and other resources can be loaded into your window or application using various functions to display them. However, displaying a cursor involves registering your own window class. The function used to register your own window class is `AfxRegisterWndClass()`, declared as:

```
LPCTSTR AFXAPI AfxRegisterWndClass(UINT nClassStyle,
                HCURSOR hCursor = 0,
                HBRUSH hbrBackground = 0,
                HICON hIcon = 0);
```

As you can see, registering your own window class allows you to determine the cursor, icon, and background brush. The default values give you the arrow cursor, a NULL brush, and the Windows logo icon. The `nClassStyle` parameter is the style of the window, which can be various values. View the documentation for a complete list of class styles. The MFC applications you have written up until now all use the default class style, where `nClassStyle` is 0. The return value is the name of your new window class. Use the return value as the first parameter in the `Create()` function of your window.

The following statements show how to display a cursor by registering a window class. The code appears in the constructor of the window object because the window class needs to be registered before the `Create()` function is invoked.

```
DuckHuntFrameWnd::DuckHuntFrameWnd() {
    //want a custom cursor, so create a custom window class
    CBrush whitebrush;
    whitebrush.CreateStockObject(WHITE_BRUSH);
    CString className = AfxRegisterWndClass(0,
                AfxGetApp()->LoadCursor(IDC_BULLSEYE),
                whitebrush,
                AfxGetApp()->LoadIcon(IDI_DUCK));
    //use the registered window class when creating the window
    Create(className,"Rich's Duck Hunt Game",
            WS_OVERLAPPEDWINDOW,rectDefault, NULL,
            MAKEINTRESOURCE(IDR_MAINFRAME));
    //remainder of constructor ...
}
```

Notice a white stock brush was created for the background because the default NULL brush would not have been appropriate for this window. The IDI_DUCK icon is also loaded and registered with the window class, so invoking `LoadIcon()` and `SetIcon()` later in the program is not necessary. When the program executes, the cursor in the client area of the duck hunt window will now be IDC_BULLSEYE — a circle with a cross in it to look like the view through a scope. Figure 7.20 shows the window with the custom cursor displayed.

Figure 7.20 A window with a custom cursor.

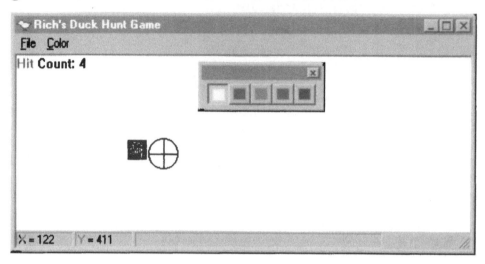

Chapter 8

Dialog Boxes and Common Controls

Dialog boxes are common occurrences in most Windows applications. They are how input is obtained from the user and messages are shown to the user, thus the term "dialog." A dialog box is actually a window, but they are created using a WYSIWYG editor much like the resource editors discussed in Chapter 7.

Dialog boxes have a client area like a frame window, but the typical contents of a dialog box are controls. A *control* is a child window of a dialog that provides a certain behavior. Examples of the common controls include edit boxes, list boxes, buttons, check boxes, combo boxes, and static text. The visual aspect of dialog boxes and controls are created in your application resource file, and MFC provides classes that allow you to link your C++ code to the dialogs and controls in the resource.

This chapter discusses how to add dialog boxes to your resource file using the dialog editor provided with Visual C++. The MFC classes used to display and work with dialogs and controls will be discussed — including the classes for a button, edit box, list box, combo box, and for displaying static text.

Dialog Boxes

A dialog box is used to communicate with the person running your program. You have seen a simple type of dialog box with message boxes. A *message box* is an example of a modal dialog box. There are two types of dialog boxes: *modal* and *modeless*. Most dialogs are modal which force the user to respond before the program resumes execution. An example of a modal dialog is the Open File dialog that requires you to select a file or press the Cancel button. Modeless dialogs do not stop execution of the program, but they remain visible until the user closes them. The Find dialog in Visual Studio is an example of a modeless dialog.

This section discusses how to create a dialog box using the editor in Visual C++. Once you know how to create them, the section "The CDialog Class" (page 188) will show how to create the dialogs in your application.

The Dialog Editor

Dialogs are resources. You create them visually using the dialog editor. Visual C++ takes care of the details of generating the corresponding resource script which is compiled when you build your application. You add a dialog in the same manner other resources are added, using the Insert Resource dialog.

You can select various dialogs to insert. The only difference between them is the initial size and controls that are created for you. If you select Dialog in the Insert Resource dialog and press the New button, the editor will create a dialog like the one in Figure 8.1.

Figure 8.1 The dialog editor in Visual C++.

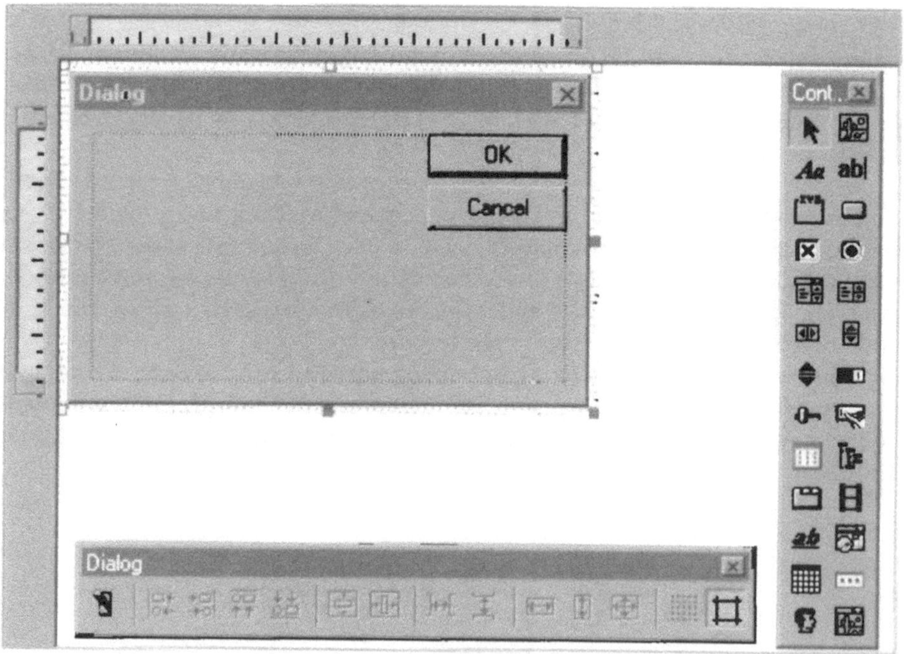

The dialog editor is a WYSIWYG environment. There are two toolbars in the editor. The toolbar on the right-hand side of Figure 8.1 shows the common controls available. To add a control to your dialog, click on the control on the toolbar, then click in the dialog window where you want the control. The controls can be moved and resized using the mouse.

The other toolbar is the Dialog toolbar, displayed at the bottom of Figure 8.1. These features are for sizing and aligning the controls in the dialog. For example, you can select two edit boxes, make them the same size, and then align them horizontally on the screen. Similarly, you can select two buttons, make them the same size, align them vertically, and center them horizontally in the window.

Figure 8.2 shows a dialog with two static text fields — Username and Password — and two edit boxes. The edit boxes are the same size, as are the static text windows. The OK and Cancel buttons are centered horizontally along the bottom of the dialog.

Figure 8.2 A sample dialog created in the dialog editor using the Controls and Dialog toolbars.

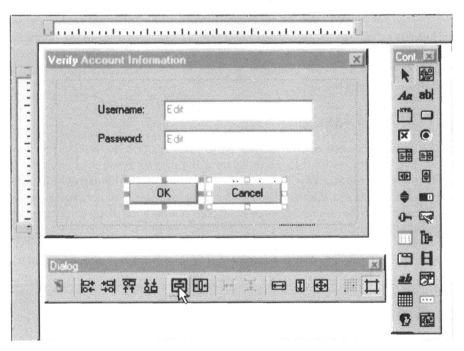

Each control has a corresponding property window for changing the various settings of the control. The property window is displayed by right-clicking on the control and selecting Properties. Each control has a corresponding identifier, much like the identifiers used for menu items and other resources. Similarly, the controls generate WM_COMMAND events which are mapped to handlers using the ON_COMMAND() macro. The message handling of the controls is unique for each control and is discussed in the corresponding sections later in this chapter.

Figure 8.3 shows the property window for the password edit box in Figure 8.2. The identifier IDC_EDIT_PASSWORD is added to resource.h and will be used in the source code to map messages from this edit box to a specified handler.

Figure 8.3 The Properties window for an edit box control.

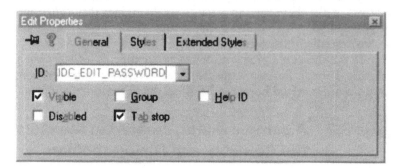

Be sure to give each control an identifier, except for controls that do not generate messages, like the static text control. The dialog resource also needs an ID to be accessed by your source code. You can also use the Properties window to select and change the various styles of a control. As you will discover, the dialog editor in Visual C++ is a simple yet powerful tool for creating dialog boxes.

The CDialog Class

Once the dialog is created in the resource editor, it is ready to be used in your program. The CDialog class in MFC is used to encapsulate a dialog box resource and use it in your program. CDialog inherits from the CWnd class, and you will typically derive your own class from CDialog to represent the dialog window. Your dialog class will contain a member variable for each control in the dialog window that receives data or displays data to the user. The data stored in the member variables is transferred to and from these member variables in the DoDataExchange() member function of CDialog.

The next sections discuss how to create modal and modeless dialogs in your application. There is also a section discussing the DoDataExchange() function.

Modal Dialog Boxes

There are two ways to create a CDialog object. The technique you use depends on the type of the dialog you want. Modal dialog boxes are created using the following constructor:

```
CDialog(UINT nIDTemplate, CWnd* pParentWnd = NULL);
```

The nIDTemplate parameter is the resource identifier of the dialog box. The pParentWnd parameter is the parent window. The parent window of a modal dialog is the window that is blocked until the modal dialog is closed.

To display a modal dialog box, you invoke its `DoModal()` member function. `DoModal()` is declared as:

```
virtual int DoModal();
```

This function does not return a value until the user closes the dialog. More precisely, it does not return until your program invokes the `EndDialog()` function. So how does `EndDialog()` get invoked? Typically, a modal dialog has OK and Cancel buttons which have identifiers, `IDOK` and `IDCANCEL`, respectively. You can write message handlers for these that invoke `EndDialog()`, or you can use the message handlers for `IDOK` and `IDCANCEL` inherited from `CDialog`: `OnOK()` and `OnCancel()`.

For modal dialogs, the default behavior of `OnOK()` and `OnCancel()` is sufficient. The return value of `DoModal()` is the argument passed to `EndDialog()` which is declared as:

```
void EndDialog(int nResult);
```

The default `OnOK()` function calls `EndDialog()` with `IDOK`. The `OnCancel()` function in `CDialog` calls `EndDialog()` with `IDCANCEL`. These values are subsequently returned by `DoModal()`.

The important thing to understand about `OnOK()` is that the data from the controls in the dialog are transferred to the member variables of your dialog class. If the user presses Cancel and `OnCancel()` is invoked, the data from the controls is not transferred. `OnOK()` performs this transfer by invoking `UpdateData()`, discussed in "The DoDataExchange() Function" (page 195).

A Dialog-Based Application

Some Windows applications use a dialog box as their main window. (A common dialog-based program is the Windows Internet Dial-up Connection.) If you have a program that does not require frame-window features like a menu, toolbars, a status bar, and so forth, then a dialog-based application may be sufficient.

The following program demonstrates the structure of a dialog-based application, and illustrates the steps involved in creating and displaying a modal dialog box. The `MainDlgWnd` class is a user-defined class inherited from `CDialog`. It is instantiated and displayed in the `CWinApp`'s `InitInstance()` function. The `CWinApp` class is declared and defined as:

```
class ModalDemoApp : public CWinApp {
public:
    virtual BOOL InitInstance();
};


BOOL ModalDemoApp::InitInstance() {
    //instantiate the dialog object
    MainDlgWnd mainWnd(IDD_MODAL_DEMO);
    //assign the main window to m_pMainWnd
    m_pMainWnd = &mainWnd;
```

```
   //display the modal dialog
   int response = mainWnd.DoModal();
   if(response == IDOK) {
      //user selected OK button
   } else if (response == IDCANCEL) {
      //user selected Cancel button
   }
   //the function returns FALSE since the
   //program is done executing
   return FALSE;
}


//single global instance of the app class
ModalDemoApp theApp;
```

The InitInstance() function does not show and update the window in a dialog-based application. Instead, the dialog is displayed by invoking its DoModal() function. This function does not return until the user dismisses the dialog. This particular dialog has an OK and Cancel button, so the value of response will be either IDOK or IDCANCEL.

The declaration of MainDlgWnd is listed here. The class inherits from CDialog and handles WM_PAINT messages.

```
class MainDlgWnd : public CDialog {
public:
   MainDlgWnd(UINT);   //constructor
protected:
   afx_msg void OnPaint();  //WM_PAINT message handler
   DECLARE_MESSAGE_MAP()
};
```

The constructor has an UINT parameter that represents the resource identifier of the dialog box. The constructor passes this information to the CDialog constructor. Recall that modal dialogs are created using this particular constructor of the CDialog class.

```
MainDlgWnd::MainDlgWnd(UINT nIDResource)
         : CDialog(nIDResource) {
}
```

The OnPaint() function displays the current time on the screen. You do not typically need to handle WM_PAINT messages in a dialog because its view is determined by the resource. Later in this chapter you will see how to add controls to the resource, which are typically member variables of your CDialog class. Figure 8.4 shows the display of the modal dialog box.

Figure 8.4   A dialog-based Windows application.

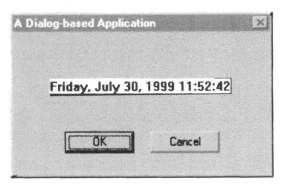

Modeless Dialog Boxes

A modeless dialog box is created differently than a modal dialog. Modeless dialogs are created similarly to frame windows. In your program logic, you need to include destroying the dialog window when the user dismisses it. The following steps create and destroy a modeless dialog box.

1. Write a class that inherits from CDialog. Override the OnOK() and OnCancel() functions, if the dialog contains them.
2. Create an instance of your class that invokes the default constructor of the parent class CDialog.
3. Invoke the Create() function of the CDialog object to associate the dialog with a resource.
4. Invoke DestroyWindow() to close the modeless dialog. This is typically done in the OnOK() and OnCancel() message handlers.

The default constructor of CDialog has protected access. This forces you to write a class that inherits from CDialog before this default constructor can be invoked. In addition, you must ensure that neither OnOK() nor OnCancel() in CDialog are invoked. These functions are virtual, so your child class can simply override them. If your modeless dialog does not contain an OK or Cancel button, then you must provide some mechanism for the dialog to be closed and DestroyWindow() to be invoked.

To illustrate how to create a modeless dialog box, I added one to the time display program from Chapter 5. The dialog is an About dialog — a common feature of most Windows programs. Most About dialogs are modal, but I made this one modeless to illustrate how a modeless dialog is is created and destroyed. The class that inherits from CDialog is declared as:

```
class ModelessDemo : public CDialog {
public:
    ModelessDemo();  //constructor
protected:
    virtual void OnOK();
};
```

```
ModelessDemo::ModelessDemo() {
    //nothing to initialize, but this emphasizes
    //that the default CDialog constructor is invoked
}
void ModelessDemo::OnOK() {
    //user selected OK to dismiss dialog
    DestroyWindow();
}
```

The dialog in this example does not contain a Cancel button, so OnCancel() did not need to be overridden. The OnOK() handler closes the modeless dialog by invoking DestroyWindow(). Notice that the ModelessDemo class did not need to declare and define a message map to handle the WM_COMMAND generated from clicking the OK button. This is because the CDialog class handles that message with OnOK(), but OnOK() is a virtual function. Through polymorphism, OnOK() in the child class is invoked — which destroys the modeless dialog in the previous example.

A modeless dialog is displayed by invoking its Create() function. If the dialog is from a resource, then the version of Create() that you use is declared as:

```
BOOL Create(UINT nIDResource, CWnd* pParentWnd = NULL);
```

The nIDResource parameter is the dialog's resource identifier. The pParentWnd parameter represents the parent window. A modeless dialog box will always appear on top of its parent window, even when it loses focus to the parent.

Be sure that your modeless dialog has the WS_VISIBLE window style when you create the dialog in the resource editor. Otherwise, the call to Create() will create the dialog in memory, but it will not be visible and a call to ShowWindow() will be necessary. To add the WS_VISIBLE style, select Visible from the More Styles tab of the Dialog Properties window, as shown in Figure 8.5.

Figure 8.5   Make sure your modeless dialog has the Visible style selected. Otherwise the dialog will not appear when Create() is invoked.

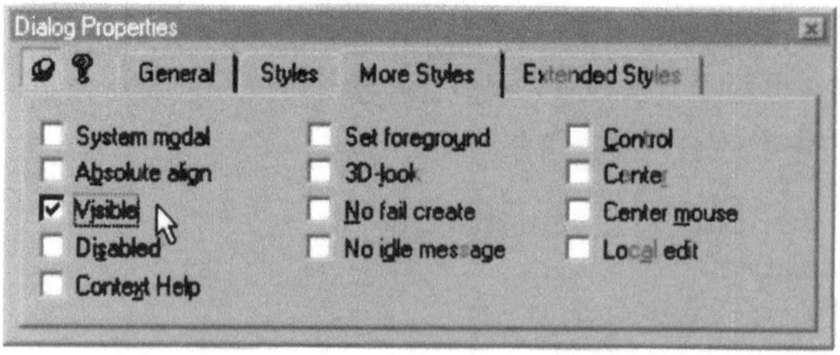

To display the ModelessDemo dialog declared previously, I added a Help/About menu item to the frame window. The resource identifier for this menu item is ID_ABOUT, and the message handler is the OnAbout() function, defined as:

```
void TimeDisplayFrameWnd::OnAbout(){
    if(!m_Dialog) {
        m_Dialog.Create(IDD_ABOUT, this);
    }
    else {
        m_Dialog.SetFocus();
    }
}
```

The variable m_Dialog is a member variable of the TimeDisplayFrameWnd class of type ModelessDemo. Why didn't I simply declare a local variable? Be careful in this situation. The Create() function returns immediately. If the variable were declared locally, the object would go out of scope while the dialog was visible on the screen, which results in undefined behavior. Make sure your modeless dialog object stays within the current scope for the lifetime of the dialog. It should either be a global variable, a static variable, or as we see here, a member variable.

Notice that I checked to see if the m_Dialog value was not NULL. If the value is NULL, then the dialog needs to be created using the Create() function. If the value is not NULL, then the dialog is already created. In this case, I gave the dialog the current focus. This is another situation where care needs to be taken to ensure that Create() is not invoked on a dialog box that is already created.

The modeless dialog box generated from the previous code is shown in Figure 8.6. When the OK button is pressed, the OnOK() message handler is invoked, which in turn, calls DestroyWindow() to close the modeless dialog.

Figure 8.6   An About dialog box that is modeless.

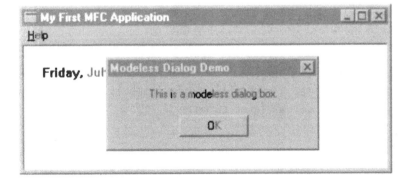

Common Dialogs

Windows provides a collection of dialog boxes that are used frequently by many Windows programs. These dialog boxes are referred to as "common dialogs" and are a built-in feature of the operating system. Each of these classes is encapsulated in an MFC class derived from CDialog. Table 8.1 lists the child classes of CDialog and the type of dialog they represent.

Table 8.1 Windows common dialogs.

Class	Dialog
CColorDialog	A color selection dialog box.
CFileDialog	Open or save a file dialog box.
CFindReplaceDialog	Find and replace text dialog box.
CFontDialog	A font selection dialog box.
CPrintDialog	A printer selection dialog box.

Most users of Windows are familiar with the CFileDialog, which allows you to either open or save a file. The following statement creates a CFileDialog that looks for a *.cpp file to be opened.

```
CFileDialog openFile(TRUE, "cpp","*.cpp",
                OFN_FILEMUSTEXIST);
```

The first argument specifies a File Open dialog. If the argument is FALSE, a File Save dialog is created. The second argument is the default filename extension. The third argument is the initial filename, which in this example, shows all files with the cpp extension. The final argument specifies that the file to be opened must exist.

The CFileDialog class represents a modal dialog, so the DoModal() function needs to be invoked before the dialog appears. The following statements illustrate how to retrieve the name of the file selected in a File Open dialog:

```
int result = openFile.DoModal();
if(result == IDOK) {
   CString fileName = openFile.GetFileName();
   //use file for whatever purpose
}
```

View the documentation for more information on CFileDialog and the other common dialog classes in Table 8.1.

The DoDataExchange() **Function**

As you saw in the previous sections, using dialogs in an application involves writing a class for each dialog box. The class you write inherits from CDialog, which provides default behavior for features like displaying the dialog and the OnOK() and OnCancel() message handlers.

Another important behavior inherited from the CDialog class is its ability to transfer data between your code and the various controls in the dialog box. The function responsible for this is the DoDataExchange() member function of the CWnd class. This section discusses how and when DoDataExchange() is invoked, and also the various functions that perform the data exchange.

The UpdateData() **Function**

When you derive a class from CDialog, the typical design in an MFC application is to provide a member variable in the derived class for each control in the dialog box that contains data. For example, if you have an edit box for entering a string and a combo box of integers in a dialog, then the class you derive from CDialog will probably contain a CString and int member variable. The following class demonstrates what the class might look like:

```
class SomeDialog : public CDialog {
private :
    CString m_NameOfItem;
    int m_StyleOfItem;
    //remainder of class definition
};
```

The objective here is have the m_NameOfItem be the value of the string in the edit box, and m_StyleOfItem be the value of the integer selected from the combo box. Perhaps these member variables have an initial value you want displayed in the dialog box when it first appears. When the user is done making changes in the edit box and combo box, you want these member variables to be updated to the new values if the user selects OK or Apply. If the user selects Cancel, then the updating should be skipped.

The CWnd class contains a member function UpdateData() that performs this exchange of data for you. The function is declared as:

```
BOOL UpdateData(BOOL bSaveAndValidate = TRUE);
```

If the bSaveAndValidate parameter is FALSE, then the values stored in the member variables are transferred into the corresponding dialog controls. The MFC framework invokes Update-Data() with a FALSE argument when the dialog is initially displayed. If the bSaveAndValidate parameter is TRUE, then the data is transferred from the controls into the corresponding member variables. This is done, for example, in the default OnOK() message handler.

How does this work behind the scenes? The UpdateData() function determines which direction the data is being transferred, then it invokes the DoDataExchange() function of the CWnd class. DoDataExchange() is a series of data exchange and validation function calls, discussed in the next section. The DoDataExchange() function is declared as:

```
virtual void DoDataExchange(CDataExchange * pDX);
```

The pDX parameter points to a CDataExchange object needed for the data exchange and validation functions.

You do not invoke DoDataExchange() directly in your source code. Instead, if you want data to be transferred between member variables and dialog controls, use the UpdateData() function, which subsequently invokes DoDataExchange().

The DDX and DDV Functions

MFC contains a collection of dialog data exchange and dialog data validation functions referred to as DDX and DDV functions. These functions are invoked within DoDataExchange(). The DDX functions are used to exchange data back and forth from the member variables and the dialog controls. The DDV functions are used to validate data entered into a control. They display warning messages if invalid data is entered, and they can be used to cause the dialog to remain active until valid data is entered into a particular control.

The DDX and DDV functions you use depend on the control and the type of data the control is storing. When I discuss the controls later in this chapter, I will describe the DDX and DDV functions corresponding to that control. Table 8.2 lists some of the common DDX and DDV functions, so that you can get a feel for how they work and the type of validation they can perform.

Table 8.2 Some common DDX and DDV functions.

Function	Description
DDX_Text	Transfers data of type int, UINT, long, DWORD, CString, float, and double between an edit control and a CString member variable.
DDX_Check	Transfers an int between a check box and an int member variable, which contains information about the state of the check box.
DDX_LBIndex	Transfers an int between a list box and an int member variable, which will be the index of the item currently selected.
DDX_LBString	Transfers a CString between a list box and a CString member variable, which will be the value of the item currently selected.
DDX_Radio	Transfers an int between a radio button and an int member variable, which contains information about the state of the radio button.
DDX_Scroll	Transfers an int between a scroll bar and an int member variable, which is the value of the current position of the scroll bar.
DDV_MaxChars	Verifies that the length of a string does not exceed a specified number of characters.
DDV_MinMaxInt	Verifies that an int value falls within a specified range.

Table 8.2 lists two DDV functions. The others are similar to DDV_MinMaxInt() — except they verify a range for the other numeric data types. For example, there is a DDV_MinMaxByte() function and a DDV_MinMaxDouble() function. The details of the functions in Table 8.2 will be discussed in the upcoming sections for the corresponding control. For example, DDX_Text() and DDV_MaxChars() are discussed in the section "The Edit Control" (page 203).

Common Controls

Now that you have seen how to create and display dialog boxes, the next step is to discuss how to use the controls in a dialog and link those controls to your source code. The dialog resource editor allows you to arrange the controls in the dialog to create the look that you want. The resource editor is also where you assign each control an ID, which are declared in the resource.h file and allow you to interact with a control in your code.

There are many controls available for you to add to a dialog box. For example, you may be familiar with the term *ActiveX control*. An ActiveX control can be placed in your dialog box just like one of the common controls. What is unique about an ActiveX control is that they are not necessarily written in C++. You can take an ActiveX control written in Visual Basic and plug it into your C++ program — the primary advantage to using and creating ActiveX controls. This opens the door to a world of controls at your disposal because developers have been writing ActiveX controls for many years.

Because there are so many different controls available, it is not feasible to discuss the usage of each one. The remainder of this chapter discusses how to use some of the common controls in Visual C++, like buttons, edit boxes, list boxes, and combo boxes. Once you become familiar with adding these common controls to your dialog box resource and linking them to your C++ code, you will discover that using other controls is similar.

The Button Control

The most common control in dialog boxes is the button control. There are three types of buttons: a standard push button, a check box, and a radio button. This section discusses how to create these types of buttons and handle their messages in your program.

Push Buttons

The OK and Cancel buttons in a dialog box are examples of push buttons. Push buttons generate WM_COMMAND messages when they are pressed, so you use the ON_COMMAND() macro to associate the identifier of a button with a message handler. The CDialog class maps IDOK to the OnOK() handler and IDCANCEL to the OnCancel() handler.

Use the Push Button Properties dialog to assign an appropriate identifier to the button. Figure 8.7 shows a button whose label is New. Its identifier has been assigned the value IDC_NEW_ENTRY. There are two ways a message handler can be assigned to the button click.

1. Use the ON_COMMAND() macro.
2. Use the ON_BN_CLICKED() macro.

Figure 8.7   The Push Button Properties dialog is used to change the ID and styles of a button.

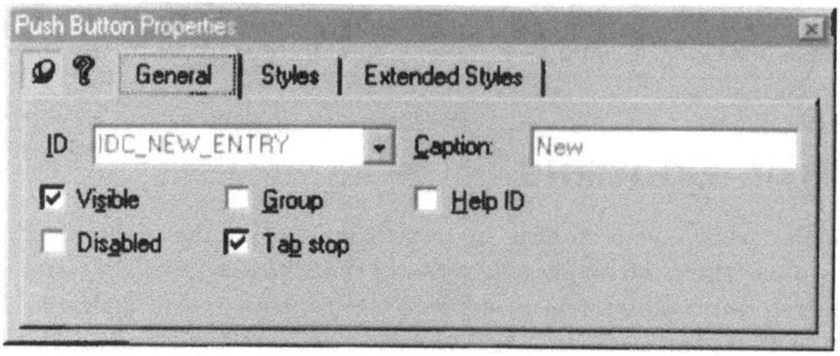

The button click generates a WM_COMMAND message associated with its ID. For example, the following message map entry maps this message to the OnNewEntry() function:

```
ON_COMMAND(IDC_NEW_ENTRY, OnNewEntry)
```

Using this technique, handling messages from a push button is identical to menu items from other resources. The advantage to this technique is if your application has a menu item with the identifier IDC_NEW_ENTRY, then selecting that menu item would have the same effect as clicking the New button with this same identifier.

When a button is pressed, it also generates a BN_CLICKED message. You can use the ON_BN_CLICKED() macro in the corresponding message map. For example, the following message map entry associates the New button with the OnNewEntry() function, similar to the ON_COMMAND() entry above.

```
ON_BN_CLICKED(IDC_NEW_ENTRY, OnNewEntry)
```

Using the ON_BN_CLICKED() macro may make your message map more readable because it is clear from the name of the macro that the message comes from a button click. The ClassWizard in Visual C++, discussed in Chapter 10, uses the ON_BN_CLICKED() macro when generating message map entries for you.

Check Boxes

A *check box* consists of a label and a box that is either checked or unchecked. A checked box contains a small check mark. Check boxes do not look like buttons, but their behavior is similar to a button that is either pressed or not. Figure 8.8 shows a dialog box with three check boxes that prompt to user to input some of their hobbies.

Figure 8.8   A check box consists of the box and a label. Clicking the box toggles the check mark.

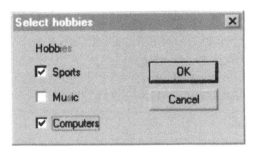

Check boxes are assigned a label and identifier using the Check Box Properties window. A check box is a button, so the ON_COMMAND() or ON_BN_CLICKED() macro can be used to respond to the user checking the box.

When a push button is pressed, an action typically occurs that involves either a new window appearing or a change in execution. With check boxes, the only action the user expects is for the check mark to visually appear or disappear in the box. In other words, you do not need to respond to the messages generated from a check box. Instead, when the user dismisses the dialog or accepts their selections, you want to know which check boxes were selected and which ones were not.

To accomplish this, you associate a member variable in your dialog class for each check box control in the dialog, then use the DDX_Check() function to transfer the data from the check box to the corresponding member variable. To illustrate this, the following class contains member variables for the three check boxes in Figure 8.8:

```
class HobbyDialog : public CDialog {
private:
    BOOL m_ckSports;     //Sports check box
    BOOL m_ckMusic;      //Music check box
    BOOL m_ckComputers;  //Computers check box
protected:
    virtual void DoDataExchange(CDataExchange*);
//remainder of class declaration
};
```

A check box uses a BOOL member variable, with TRUE representing a checked box and FALSE for an unchecked box. The DoDataExchange() function is invoked initially when the dialog is displayed, which transfers the BOOL values to the control. If the user dismisses the dialog by pressing the OK button, the OnOK() message handler will invoke UpdateData(), which subsequently calls DoDataExchange() again. This time the state of the check boxes will be transferred to the BOOL member variables.

To accomplish the transfer of data, you need to add the appropriate DDX function calls in the DoDataExchange() function. The DDX_Check() function is used for check boxes, which the following code illustrates:

```
void HobbyDialog::DoDataExchange(CDataExchange* pDX){
    CDialog::DoDataExchange(pDX); //invoke parent's
    DDX_Check(pDX, IDC_SPORTS, m_ckSports);
    DDX_Check(pDX, IDC_MUSIC, m_ckMusic);
    DDX_Check(pDX, IDC_COMPUTERS, m_ckComputers);
}
```

The DDX_Check() function is invoked for each of the three check boxes. The first argument is the pointer to the CDataExchange object. This object determines which direction to transfer the data. The second and third arguments associate the member variable with the ID of the check box.

The following OnOK() function displays which hobbies the user selected. The OnOK() function in CDialog is invoked first, which causes the data exchange to occur. Figure 8.9 shows the output of OnOK() if the user selects the check boxes in Figure 8.8.

```
void HobbyDialog::OnOK() {
    //the parent's OnOK() invokes UpdateData()
    CDialog::OnOK();

    CString message("You like ");
    if(m_ckSports)
        message += "sports ";
    if(m_ckMusic)
        message += "music ";
    if(m_ckComputers)
        message += "computers";
    MessageBox(message, "Hobbies");
}
```

Figure 8.9 **The OnOK() function in the parent causes DoDataExchange() to execute, which updates the corresponding BOOL member variables.**

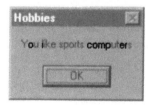

Radio Buttons

A radio button is a special type of check box that is associated with other radio buttons in its group. In a group of radio buttons, only one of them can be selected at a time. Figure 8.10 shows a group of radio buttons in a dialog box. The term "radio button" refers to older car radios that used to have buttons to change the radio station. When one of the buttons was pressed, the other buttons would pop out, so that only one could be selected at a time.

Figure 8.10 Radios buttons are a group of check boxes, and only one can be selected at a time.

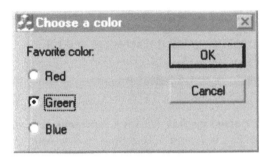

A group of radio buttons can be thought of as a single entity. You do not need to know the state of each button, only which button is selected. Therefore, you only need to add one member variable to your dialog class for a radio button group. The variable used is an int — the index of the selected radio button, relative to where it resides to the group. In other words, the first radio button has an index 0, the next has an index 1, and so forth. The DDX_Radio() function is used to transfer the int back and forth from the dialog.

To create a radio button group, you need to select the Group style for the first button in the button. The following radio buttons will be in the same group. The radio button group in Figure 8.10 was created by selecting the Group style for the Red radio button, as shown in Figure 8.11. Make sure the Green and Blue radio buttons do not have this style selected.

Figure 8.11 Create a radio button group by selecting the Group style of the first radio button in the group.

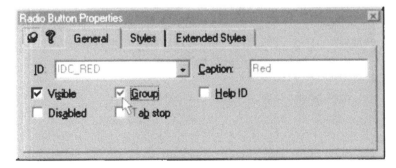

The following class contains a member variable for the radio button group in Figure 8.10. The implementation of its DoDataExchange() function demonstrates the DDX_Radio() function.

```
class ColorDialog : public CDialog {
private:
   int m_SelectColor;  //index of radio button group
protected:
   virtual void DoDataExchange(CDataExchange*);
//remainder of class definition
};


void ColorDialog::DoDataExchange(CDataExchange* pDX) {
   CDialog::DoDataExchange(pDX);
   DDX_Radio(pDX, IDC_RED, m_SelectedColor);
}
```

The IDC_RED argument passed to DDX_Radio() represents the first radio button in the group. Its index is 0, IDC_GREEN is 1, and IDC_BLUE is 2. The following OnOK() function displays a message box with the selected color. Figure 8.12 shows the result of this function if the user selects the Green radio button.

```
void CRadioButtonsDlg::OnOK() {
   CDialog::OnOK();
   CString message("Your favorite color is ");
   switch(m_SelectedColor) {
   case 0:
     message += "red";
     break;
   case 1:
     message += "green";
     break;
   case 2:
     message += "blue";
     break;
   default:
     message = "You did not select a color";
   }
   MessageBox(message, "Favorite color");
}
```

Figure 8.12 The DDX_Radio() **function transfers the index of the selected radio button to the member variable of the dialog class.**

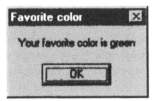

Static Controls

A *static control* is a control that provides a visual display but does not involve any user interaction. Two common static controls are the text control and the group box control. The text control displays text, and the group box control displays a visual border around a collection of radio buttons.

For example, the text "Hobbies" in Figure 8.8 and "Favorite color:" in Figure 8.10 are static text controls. Figure 8.13 shows a group box control around a group of radio buttons. Keep in mind that the group box control is strictly visual and is not used for creating a group of radio buttons.

Figure 8.13 An example of a static group box control.

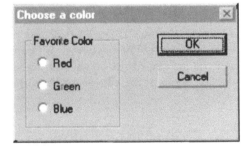

Static controls all share the same identifier: IDC_STATIC. There is no reason to give a static control a unique ID because they do not generate messages.

The Edit Control

The edit control provides a mechanism for obtaining text from the user. The edit control window provides a single line of text for the user to type in. If the text goes beyond the width of the control, the right and left arrows are used to scroll back and forth within the line of text. An edit control typically uses a static text control as a description for the type of input desired. Figure 8.2 (page 187) shows a dialog box with two edit controls for inputting a username and password.

Data is transferred between an edit control and a member variable of your dialog class using the DDX_Text() function. The CString class is used for transferring text, but an edit control is not limited to inputing strings. DDX_Text() is overloaded to transfer data to the numeric types byte, short, int, long, float, double, DWORD, and UINT.

No matter the data type of the input, you can use the DDV functions to validate the data. The DDV_MaxChars() function can be used to limit the number of characters in the string. There is also a DDV function for each of the numeric types for specifying a range of values. For example, there is a DDV_MinMaxInt() function for specifying a range of int's.

The messages an edit control generates mostly deal with the display of the edit box — useful if you are not using a dialog resource. Because you will most likely use a dialog resource, you typically do not need to handle the edit control messages. Instead, you want to know what is typed in the edit box when the user is done typing. Because the DoDataExchange() validates and exchanges the data using the DDX and DDV functions, you can use edit controls without any special message handling.

The dialog box in Figure 8.2 has two edit boxes. The input for both is text, so the corresponding member variables are CString objects, as shown in the following class declaration:

```
class LogonDialog : public CDialog {
private:
   CString m_Username;
   CString m_Password;
protected:
   virtual void DoDataExchange(CDataExchange*);
//remainder of class declaration
};
```

The corresponding ID's for the edit controls are IDC_USERNAME and IDC_PASSWORD. These values are used in the DDX and DDV function calls. The password edit control also uses the "Password" style, which displays asterisks instead of the actual characters typed by the user. The "Password" style is found on the Styles tab of the edit control's properties window, shown in Figure 8.14.

Figure 8.14 Use the Edit Properties window to select an ID and styles for an edit control.

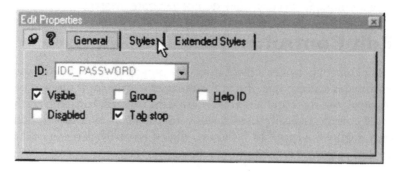

For the dialog in Figure 8.2, I wanted to limit the size of the username to 10 characters. This is accomplished by invoking the DDV_MaxChars() function in the DoDataExchange() function:

```
void LogonDialog::DoDataExchange(CDataExchange* pDX) {
    CDialog::DoDataExchange(pDX);
    DDX_Text(pDX, IDC_PASSWORD, m_Password);
    DDX_Text(pDX, IDC_USERNAME, m_Username);
    DDV_MaxChars(pDX, m_Username, 10);
}
```

The DDX_Text() function transfers the string back and forth between the control and the m_Password and m_Username member variables. The DDV_MaxChars() limits the number of characters of m_Username to 10. The cursor in the IDC_USERNAME edit control will not move after 10 characters are entered. If the user selects the OK button, then DoDataExchange() transfers the data into m_Password and m_Username, which the following OnOK() message handler uses to verify the user's account information.

```
void LogonDialog::OnOK() {
    CDialog::OnOK();

    if(m_Username == "raposa" && m_Password == "password")
        MessageBox("Successfully logged in!", "Success");
    else
        MessageBox("Invalid user info!", "Error",
                 MB_OK | MB_ICONERROR);
}
```

Be sure to invoke the parent class OnOK() function before using the data in m_Username and m_Password because it is the parent's OnOK() function that causes the data to be transferred. The OnOK() function in CDialog invoked UpdateData() with TRUE as the argument. Update-Data() then calls DoDataExchange(), which updates the m_Username and m_Password variables with the strings in the edit box.

The List Box Control

A list box control displays a list of strings in a scrollable window. There are two types of list boxes: single selection and multiple selection. Figure 8.15 shows a dialog with a multiple selection list box, which allows for more than one item to be selected. In a single selection list box, selecting an item deselects the other items.

Figure 8.15 A multiple selection list box.

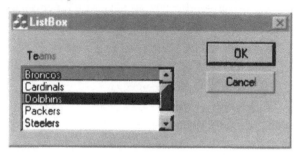

Use the List Box Properties window to select the ID and styles of a list box. Figure 8.16 shows the Styles tab of the properties window, which contains the Selection style of Single or Multiple.

Figure 8.16 The List Box Properties window.

With the other common controls discussed in this chapter, you could use the resource editor to create the control and rely on the DDX functions to transfer any data back and forth between your dialog class and the control. With list boxes, the resource editor is used to locate where the list box will be displayed. However, you need to an associate a CListBox object with the list box resource to initialize the strings in the list box. If the list box allows for multiple selections, then you also need to use the CListBox class to determine which items are currently selected. This section discusses how to initialize a list box and determine which item or items are selected.

Initializing a List Box

You cannot use the resource editor to determine the strings initially displayed in a list box. You need to create a CListBox object and invoke either its AddString() or InsertString() member function. This is typically done in the OnInitDialog() function, which is invoked by the framework when the dialog box is about to be displayed.

The following `OnInitDialog()` function was used to create the list box in Figure 8.15. The ID for the list box is `IDC_TEAMS`, and the `GetDlgItem()` function is used to return a pointer to the list box.

```
BOOL TeamDialog::OnInitDialog() {
    CDialog::OnInitDialog();
    //get a pointer to the list box
    CListBox * teams = (CListBox *) GetDlgItem(IDC_TEAMS);
    //add the teams
    teams->AddString("Broncos");
    teams->AddString("Packers");
    teams->AddString("Steelers");
    teams->AddString("Cardinals");
    teams->AddString("Dolphins");
    teams->AddString("Vikings");

    return TRUE;
}
```

All of the controls are windows, and you can use `GetDlgItem()` to get a pointer to any control using its ID. It is declared as:

```
CWnd* GetDlgItem(int nID);
```

Notice I had to cast the return value to a `CListBox` pointer because the return value is a `CWnd` pointer, which is a parent of `CListBox`. The `AddString()` function adds a string in sorted order if the list box uses the Sort style, otherwise the string is added at the end. Use `Insert-String()` to add a string at a particular index in the list box.

Single Selection List Boxes

If the list box uses the single selection style, then the `DDX_LBString()` function will transfer the selected string into a corresponding member variable. If no item was selected, the member variable will be a zero-length string. The following class includes a member variable for the selected team in the example in Figure 8.15.

NOTE: The CListBox is not required to determine which item is selected in a single selection list box.

```
class TeamDialog : public CDialog {
private:
   CString m_Team;
protected:
   virtual void DoDataExchange(CDataExchange*);
//remainder of class declaration
};

void TeamDialog::DoDataExchange(CDataExchange* pDX) {
   CDialog::DoDataExchange(pDX);
   DDX_LBString(pDX, IDC_TEAMS, m_Team);
}
```

To demonstrate the data exchange, I wrote a message handler for the LBN_DBLCLK message — generated when the user double-clicks in a list box. The message map entry to handle this message is the ON_LBN_DBLCLK() macro.

```
ON_LBN_DBLCLK(IDC_TEAMS, OnDblclkTeams)
```

The OnDblclkTeams() message handler displays a message box with the currently selected team. I needed to invoke UpdateData() to ensure that the currently selected team was stored in the member variable m_Team.

```
void CListBoxDlg::OnDblclkTeams() {
   UpdateData(TRUE);
   MessageBox(m_Team, "You selected...");
}
```

Handling a double-click in a list box is a common occurrence. The event usually results in an action similar to selecting the OK button.

Multiple Selection List Boxes

A multiple selection list box generates the same messages as a single selection, and the DDX_LBString() function can be used to transfer the currently selected item into a CString member variable. Knowing the currently selected item in a multiple selection list box, however, is not typically beneficial. For example, the currently selected item may have just been deselected, which is possible in multiple selection list boxes. For this reason, you often do not use data exchange with these list boxes.

Instead, what is more useful is to know all of the items currently selected. To do this, you need to use the functionality of the CListBox class. CListBox contains several member functions for obtaining and altering the selections of a multiple selection list box. For example, the GetSelCount() function returns the number of items currently selected. The Get-SelItems() fills an array with the indexes of the selected items.

To demonstrate these functions, the following OnOK() function displays the selected teams in the list box in Figure 8.15 (page 206):

```
void TeamDialog::OnOK(){
    CDialog::OnOK();
    CListBox * teams = (CListBox *) GetDlgItem(IDC_TEAMS);
    if(teams->GetSelCount() > 0) {
        int selected[6]; //there are 6 strings in the list box
        int numSelected = teams->GetSelItems(6,selected);
        for(int i = 0; i < numSelected; i++) {
            //get the string from the index
            CString buffer;
            teams->GetText(selected[i],buffer);
            MessageBox(buffer,"You picked");
        }
    }
    else {
        MessageBox("No teams were selected","Teams Dialog");
    }
}
```

If no teams are selected, then the message box informs the user of this. If one or more teams are selected, then a message box is displayed showing each team selected. The GetText() member function of CListBox is used to obtain the string value from the index. The selected array will be filled with the indexes of the selected teams.

The Combo Box Control

A *combo box* consists of a list of strings that are displayed in a drop-down list box. A combo box control looks like an edit control with an arrow to drop-down the list of strings. Figure 8.17 shows an example of a combo box control in a dialog box.

Figure 8.17 A combo box is a combination of an edit control and a list box.

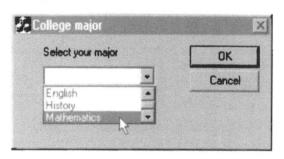

There are two ways to initialize the entries in a combo box. If you know the initial contents of the combo box each time it is displayed, then these strings can be made a part of the resource file by adding them using the Combo Box Properties window. This properties window has a Data tab, shown in Figure 8.18, where the strings can be entered.

Figure 8.18 The Combo Box Properties window can be used to enter the initial items of a combo box.

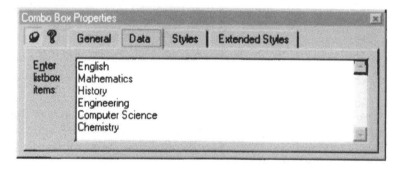

NOTE: When entering items in the Data window in Figure 8.18, you must press Ctrl-Enter to move down to the next line. Pressing Enter closes the properties window.

You can also add entries to a combo box using the AddString() and InsertString() member functions of the CComboBox class — similar to the technique used for list boxes. The following OnInitDialog() function shows how to add the items of the combo box in Figure 8.18:

```
BOOL MajorsDialog::OnInitDialog() {
    CDialog::OnInitDialog();
    CComboBox * majors = (CComboBox *) GetDlgItem(IDC_MAJOR);
```

```
CString entries [] = {"English","Mathematics","History",
         "Engineering","Computer Science","Chemistry"};
for(int i = 0; i < 6; i++)
  majors->AddString(entries[i]);


return TRUE;
}
```

There are two DDX functions for determining which item in a combo box is selected, depending on whether you want the index of the item selected or its actual value. The DDX_CBIndex() function obtains the selected index and uses a corresponding int member variable. The DDX_CBString() function transfers the selected string into a CString member variable. The following DoDataExchange() function associated the IDC_MAJOR combo box in Figure 8.17 with a m_Major member variable:

```
void MajorsDialog::DoDataExchange(CDataExchange* pDX) {
  CDialog::DoDataExchange(pDX);
  DDX_CBString(pDX, IDC_MAJOR, m_Major);
}
```

If no item in the IDC_MAJOR combo box is selected at the time the data exchange occurs, then the m_Major object will contain a zero-length string. The following OnOK() message handler displays a message containing the string selected in the combo box:

```
void CComboBoxDlg::OnOK() {
  CDialog::OnOK();
  if(m_Major.GetLength() > 0)
    MessageBox(m_Major, "You selected");
  else
    MessageBox("You did not make a selection","Warning");
}
```

Common Controls and ClassWizard

This chapter has discussed how to use controls in a dialog box. The dialog resource editor makes it a matter of visually laying out the controls in a dialog box to create the dialog's appearance. Much of the functionality of using a dialog box in your application revolves around the DoDataExchange() function, which links your controls to member variables of a class. As the chapter progressed, you probably noticed that the process of using controls in your application is similar for all controls.

Visual C++ contains a tool called ClassWizard that links the controls in a dialog box to member variables in your dialog class. ClassWizard also takes care of the details of filling in the DDX and DDV entries in the DoDataExchange() function. This can save you a lot of typing and allows you to quickly create dialogs and make them functional. To take advantage of ClassWizard, you need to be in an MFC project generated from AppWizard. The details of using AppWizard and ClassWizard are the topics of Chapter 10.

Chapter 9

The Document/View Architecture

Up until now, you have been learning how to develop MFC programs using two fundamental classes of the MFC architecture: CWinApp and CFrameWnd. The CWinApp class encompasses the thread and message handling portion of your application. The CFrameWnd class encompasses the window for your application. This chapter discusses two more classes that play an essential role in many MFC applications: CDocument and CView. These two classes form the basis of the document/view architecture.

This chapter discusses the relationship between documents and views in an MFC application, including the CDocument and CView classes. CDocument provides the basic functionality for a document — including opening and saving a document. The CView class is derived from CWnd and provides the basic functionality for viewing and altering the data of a document. Once you have an understanding of documents and views, the section "The CDocTemplate Class" (page 223) discusses how to create a relationship between the document, view, and frame window.

You will discover that writing a program using MFC involves spending most of your time coding and implementing the documents and views for the particular program that you are developing. Documents and views make your program unique, so understanding how to use them is an important step in learning MFC.

Documents and Views

Document/view architecture is based on the concept of separating the data in your program from how the user views the data. The *document* is the persistent data in your program. It is the data in your program that needs to exist after the user has quit the program. When the program is executed again later, the user can then open any document previously saved. The process of saving and restoring data is a built-in feature of the MFC architecture, and something users of Windows programs are familiar with.

For example, when you create a spreadsheet in Microsoft Excel, you can save the spreadsheet in a *.xls file. This file is an example of a document, and saving and retrieving the file is done using the File/Open and File/Save dialog. However, the concept of a document is not restricted to word processor and spreadsheet documents. Suppose you wrote a Solitaire program that allowed the user to quit the game with the intent of finishing the game later. The current state of the card game could be a document, and your program would provide the functionality to open and save these documents in a format that you determine. Your Solitaire program would use the File/Open and File/Save dialogs that users are familiar with. In other words, a document can be any data that you want it to be.

The advantage of using documents and views is that the application's data is separated from the user interface. When the data changes, the view is notified of the change and updates itself accordingly. You can also associate more than one view with a document. For example, a document might represent a stock's price changes during a day of trading. One view can display the prices using a bar graph, a second view can be used to display the prices in a line graph, and a third view lists the prices as text. When the price of the stock changes, each of the three views is notified and updates its display accordingly.

NOTE: A document has one or more views. However, this relationship does not go the other way. A view only has one document associated with it.

SDI vs. MDI

Document/view applications use either a single document interface (SDI) or a multiple document interface (MDI). The user can only open one document at a time using SDI. In other words, the current document must be closed before a different document can be opened. The Windows programs Notepad and Wordpad are examples of SDI programs.

The user can open multiple documents at one time using MDI. Each document is displayed in its own child window. Microsoft Word and Excel are examples of MDI applications. Chapter 10, "MFC AppWizard," focuses on writing SDI applications, with comparisons to MDI being discussed when relevant.

Most SDI applications consist of a single frame window to display the currently opened document. An MDI application typically consists of a frame window that can display multiple child windows. Each child window is itself a frame window. MFC provides classes for creating SDI and MDI applications that use the document/view architecture. The various classes involved are discussed in the next section.

The Classes of a Document/View Application

The following table lists the classes involved in developing an application that uses the document/view architecture.

CDocument	contains the data in your application
CView	provides a view for your document
CFrameWnd	provides the window around the view
CDocTemplate	associates a CDocument, CView, and CFrameWnd corresponding to a particular type of document
CWinApp	creates the CDocTemplate class

The application object creates a document template. The template object is responsible for creating the document and the frame window. The frame window creates the view or views associated with the current document. The remainder of this chapter discusses each of these steps in detail.

The CDocument Class

Documents are created by deriving a class from CDocument. CDocument provides the basic functionality for storing and retrieving a document's data in an archive and for updating the views. The document is represented as member variables of your class derived from CDocument.

For example, the following class is a document that represents the price and symbol of a stock. The price history is saved in a CArray object and the current price is a double. The class is derived from CDocument and overrides two virtual functions: OnNewDocument() and Serialize().

```
class CStockPriceDoc : public CDocument {
protected:
  DECLARE_DYNCREATE(CStockPriceDoc)
public:
  //member variables represent the data of the document
  CString m_StockSymbol;
  double m_CurrentPrice;
  CArray<double,double> m_PriceHistory;

  //member functions overriden from CDocument
  virtual BOOL OnNewDocument();
  virtual void Serialize(CArchive& ar);

  DECLARE_MESSAGE_MAP()
};
```

The DECLARE_DYNCREATE macro enables the CStockPriceDoc object to be instantiated dynamically at runtime, which happens when the document is read from a file. The DECLARE_DYNCREATE is used along with the IMPLEMENT_DYNCREATE macro — which needs to appear in the implementation file of the CStockPriceDoc as follows:

```
IMPLEMENT_DYNCREATE(CStockPriceDoc, Cdocument)
```

The OnNewDocument() function is invoked when a new CStockPriceDoc object is requested, and the Serialize() function is invoked during the opening and closing process. These two functions are now discussed in detail.

The OnNewDocument() Function

OnNewDocument() is invoked when the user selects File/New from the menu. The current document will be closed, allowing the user the opportunity to save the current document if it has been modified. OnNewDocument() is a message handler, but because it is virtual, you can override the function in your document without needing to add an entry in your document's message map.

In an SDI application, selecting File/New does not actually create a new document. Instead, the data in the current document is reset to represent an empty (new) document. OnNewDocument() is responsible for determining what it means for a document to be in a new state.

NOTE: In an MDI application, a new document object is instantiated for each object opened, so OnNewDocument() does not need to be overridden. Instead, you use the constructor in your document class to initialize the data of the document.

For example, the OnNewDocument() function in the CStockPriceDoc class clears the member variables by setting the price to 0.0, the stock symbol to an empty string, and removing all the prices from the price history array.

```
BOOL CStockPriceDoc::OnNewDocument() {
    if (!CDocument::OnNewDocument())
        return FALSE;
    //clear the member variables
    m_StockSymbol.Empty();
    m_PriceHistory.RemoveAll();
    m_CurrentPrice = 0.0;

    return TRUE;
}
```

Modifying a Document

What happens if the OnNewDocument() function is invoked and the user had not saved their changes? If their data was lost, you would have an unhappy user. MFC takes care of the details of ensuring that the document is saved before any data is lost, as long as your program notifies the framework of any changes made to the data. You need to mark a document's *modify flag* to TRUE if the data of the document has been altered by the user, and you also need to notify any views that the data has changed.

If a document has been saved and no changes in the data have occurred, then the modify flag is FALSE. Once changes are made to a document, the modify flag should be set to TRUE until the file is saved again. If the document is closed while the modify flag is TRUE, the user will be warned and prompted to save the file if they want. The SetModifiedFlag() is used to change the flag and is declared as:

```
void SetModifiedFlag(BOOL bModified = TRUE);
```

The bModified parameter specifies whether the document has been modified. Be sure to invoke this function in any of the "set" functions of the class, or any other function that changes the data. When the file is saved, the framework invokes SetModifiedFlag() for you with a FALSE argument.

Because a document can have more than one view, all views need to be notified when a change in the data occurs. After invoking SetModifiedFlag(), your document object should invoke UpdateAllViews(), which sends a message to each view that the data has changed. Each view can then take appropriate action depending on how the view is affected by the new data. The UpdateAllViews() function is declared as:

```
void UpdateAllViews(CView* pSender,
                    LPARAM lHint = 0L,
                    CObject* pHint = NULL);
```

The pSender parameter points to the view from where the modification came. If pSender is NULL, all views are notified. If pSender is not NULL, then the CView object it points to will not receive notification, but all others will. (In most situations, the view that generated the change will already know of the change, so receiving a notification will be unnecessary.) The lHint and pHint parameters can be used to send data to the views regarding the type of change that occurs.

The UpdateAllViews() function invokes the OnUpdate() member function of each view for the document. OnUpdate() is discussed in "The CView Class" (page 219).

To demonstrate the process of modifying the data of an object, suppose the stock price program changes the price of the stock using a function called OnNewStockPrice(). Any changes in the price of the stock should cause the bar graph, line graph, and text views to update their display. The following OnNewStockPrice() function shows the steps involved in changing the m_CurrentPrice member variable in the document class.

```
void CStockPriceDoc::OnNewStockPrice(double newPrice) {
  //update the data
  m_PriceHistory.Add(m_CurrentPrice);
  m_CurrentPrice = newPrice;
  //set modify flag to true
  SetModifiedFlag(TRUE);
  //update all views
  UpdateAllViews(NULL);
}
```

Because all views need to be updated, the argument for UpdateAllViews() is NULL. Be sure to set the modify flag to TRUE, so the user knows to save any changes to the document.

The Serialize() Function

The Serialize() function is invoked when the current document is being saved or when an existing document is being opened. Your code for storing and retrieving the document is placed in the Serialize() function, which is declared as:

```
virtual void Serialize(CArchive& ar);
```

The ar parameter is an archive that the document is being sent to or read from. This archive is typically a file on the user's computer. The framework intializes the CArchive object and associates it with the file selected from the File/Open or File/Save dialogs. The framework also handles the details of reading from or writing to the selected file.

Data is sent to the archive using the insertion operator (<<) and data is retrieved from the archive using the extraction operator (>>). Use the IsStoring() function of the CArchive object to determine if the serialization is being stored or retrieved.

The following function demonstrates the insertion and extraction operators by serializing a CStockPriceDoc object, defined earlier in this section. Notice that the data is retrieved from the archive in the same order it was sent to the archive.

```
void CStockPriceDoc::Serialize(CArchive& ar){
  if (ar.IsStoring()) {
    int size = m_PriceHistory.GetSize();
    ar << m_StockSymbol << m_CurrentPrice << size;
    for(int i = 0; i < size; i++)
      ar << m_PriceHistory[i];
  }
  else {
    int size = 0;
    ar >> m_StockSymbol >> m_CurrentPrice >> size;
```

```
    for(int i = 0; i < size; i++)
        ar >> m_PriceHistory[i];
    }
}
```

If IsStoring() is TRUE, then the archive represents the file to which to save the data. If the archive is being stored, then the user has selected to save the document and the stock's price, symbol, and history are sent to the archive. If the archive is not being stored, then the user has just selected an existing file to open, and the data is read from the archive and stored into the member variables. Be sure to retrieve the data in the same order it was stored, as the previous Serialize() function demonstrates.

As you can see, the document becomes an essential class in your application. All of the data that needs to exist beyond the life of your program needs to be accessible from the document class so it can be serialized.

The CView Class

A view is used to display the document to the user or provide an interface for the user to change the data of the document. A view is associated with only one document. The CView class — which is a child of CWnd — provides the basic functionality of a view, including keeping a pointer to the associated document. Your application will derive a class from CView or one of its child classes.

A typical view class will override the following inherited functions:

- GetDocument()
- OnUpdate()
- OnDraw()

A view does its drawing in the OnDraw() function. The view's OnUpdate() function is invoked from the UpdateAllViews() function in response to changes in the document's data. The view uses the GetDocument() function to retrieve a pointer to the associated document.

To demonstrate the usage of these functions, I will discuss the following class which creates a view for the CStockPriceDoc class discussed in the previous section. This particular view class contains strings that will be associated with member variables of the document class.

```
class CStockPriceView : public CView {
protected:
  DECLARE_DYNCREATE(CStockPriceView)
private:
    //member variables
    CString m_StockSymbol;
    CString m_StockPriceText;
    CString* m_History;
public:
    CStockPriceView();    //constructor
    //member functions
```

```
    CStockPriceDoc* GetDocument();
    virtual void OnDraw(CDC*);
    virtual void OnUpdate(CView*, LPARAM, CObject*);


    DECLARE_MESSAGE_MAP()
};
```

The GetDocument() Function

A view is associated with a single document, and the framework keeps a pointer to this document in the view's m_pDocument member variable. Your view needs to obtain this pointer to access the member variables of the document class. The GetDocument() function is declared as:

```
    CDocument* GetDocument() const;
```

Note that the return value of GetDocument() is of type CDocument*, so you will need to cast the pointer to the data type of your document class. Because your view invokes this function frequently, your view class can override GetDocument() to perform the necessary casting.

The following GetDocument() function for the CStockPriceView class illustrates a typical implementation of GetDocument() performing the necessary casting.

```
CStockPriceDoc* CStockPriceView::GetDocument(){
    return (CStockPriceDoc*)m_pDocument;
}
```

The OnUpdate() Function

Your view's OnUpdate() function is called from the document's UpdateAllViews() function. Within OnUpdate(), your view typically obtains a pointer to the document, updates the necessary view items, then invalidates the window so that OnDraw() is invoked.

OnUpdate() is declared as:

```
virtual void OnUpdate(CView* pSender,
                      LPARAM lHint, CObject* pHint);
```

The parameters for OnUpdate() are the arguments from UpdateAllViews() in the CDocument class. The pSender parameter is the view that modified the document, which will be NULL if all views are being updated. The lHint and pHint parameters contain user-determined information about the modifications that took place in the document.

The following function from CStockPriceView demonstrates the typical behavior of OnUpdate(). OnUpdate() converts the data in the CStockPriceDoc class to strings so they can be easily displayed by the view.

```
void CStockPriceView::OnUpdate(CView* pSender,
                        LPARAM lHint, CObject* pHint) {
  //get a pointer to the document
  CStockPriceDoc* pDoc = GetDocument();

  //update the symbol and current price
  m_StockSymbol = pDoc->m_StockSymbol;
  m_StockPriceText.Format("%f", pDoc->m_CurrentPrice);

  //update the price history
  if(m_History) {
    delete [] m_History;
  }
  m_Length = pDoc->m_PriceHistory.GetSize();
  m_History = new CString[m_Length];
  for(int i = 0; i < m_Length; i++) {
    m_History[i].Format("%f",
    pDoc->m_PriceHistory.ElementAt(i));
  }

  //invalidate the window
  CView::OnUpdate(pSender, lHint, pHint);
}
```

The CStockPrice::OnUpdate() function first obtains a pointer to the document using GetDocument(). Then, all of its member variables are updated using the current data in the document class. The view is invalidated by invoking the parent class OnUpdate(). Invalidating the window causes the OnDraw() function to be invoked, discussed next.

The OnDraw() Function

In the previous chapters, you've been shown how to draw in a frame window using the OnPaint() message handler. The OnPaint() function uses a paint device context for drawing. The OnDraw() function is similar to OnPaint(), except the OnDraw() function does not instantiate a device context. Instead, a device context is given to the OnDraw() function as its parameter:

```
virtual void OnDraw(CDC* pDC) = 0;
```

Notice that OnDraw() is a pure virtual function, meaning your class that inherits from CView must override this function. The pDC parameter is the device context where the drawing is to occur. The advantage of OnDraw() over the OnPaint() function is that OnDraw() can be used for drawing in any device context, not just a CPaintDC object. For example, OnDraw() can be used for printing a document by invoking it with a printer device context, then used for painting in a window by invoking it with a paint device context.

NOTE: Your view window will rarely override the OnPaint() message handler. Any painting that needs to occur can typically be done within OnDraw().

The following code from the CStockPriceView class demonstrates OnDraw() by displaying the stock symbol and price history in the view window.

```
void CStockPriceView::OnDraw(CDC* pDC)
{
  //display the stock symbol and price
  pDC->TextOut(10, 20, m_StockSymbol);
  pDC->TextOut(10, 50, m_StockPriceText);

  //display the price history
  for(int index = 0; index < m_Length; index++)
    pDC->TextOut(10, 80 + index*15; m_History[index]);
}
```

The CFrameWnd Class

The CFrameWnd class is the main window for your document/view application. This main window contains the menu bar, toolbars, and status bar of your application. Most importantly, the main window provides a container for the view to be overlayed in. The main window for the CStockPriceView is defined here:

```
class CMainFrame : public CFrameWnd
{
public:
  CMainFrame();
  DECLARE_DYNCREATE(CMainFrame)
protected:
  CStatusBar m_wndStatusBar;
  CToolBar m_wndToolBar;

  DECLARE_MESSAGE_MAP()
};
```

The implementation of the main frame class is similar to the other CFrameWnd classes discussed in the previous chapters.

The CDocTemplate **Class**

The CDocTemplate class is used to make the association between the document class, view class, and main frame. Your document/view application can allow for a single document to be opened at a time (SDI), in which case you use the CSingleDocTemplate class. If your application allows for multiple documents opened at a time (MDI), you use the CMultiDocTemplate class. We will now discuss how to create a document template for SDI. (Chapter 10, "MFC AppWizard," contains a discussion on creating an MDI application.)

The CDocTemplate class has a single constructor:

```
CSingleDocTemplate(UINT nIDResource,
                   CRuntimeClass* pDocClass,
                   CRuntimeClass* pFrameClass,
                   CRuntimeClass* pViewClass)
```

The parameter nIDResource is a resource ID used with the document type. It represents a string resource that contains information such as the title of the window, the document name, the document type, the file filter for the "Files of type" list, and the file filter extension. (When using Visual C++, you enter this information while running MFC AppWizard, discussed in .) For example, your stock price documents can have a *.stk extension. Files of this type can be associated with your stock price application.

The pDocClass parameter is the runtime class pointer of the document class. You use the RUNTIME_CLASS macro to obtain the CRuntimeClass pointer. Similary, pFrameClass and pView-Class represent the main frame and view runtime class pointers, respectively.

Your document/view application will typically instantiate a CSingleDocTemplate object within the InitInstance() method of the CWinApp class, as demonstrated in the following example:

```
BOOL CStockPriceApp::InitInstance()
{
  //create the document template for SDI
  CSingleDocTemplate* pDocTemplate = new CSingleDocTemplate(
      IDR_MAINFRAME,
      RUNTIME_CLASS(CStockPriceDoc),
      RUNTIME_CLASS(CMainFrame),
      RUNTIME_CLASS(CStockPriceView));

  //add the template to the application
  AddDocTemplate(pDocTemplate);

  return TRUE;
}
```

The AddDocTemplate() function is found in the CWinApp class and adds the document template to the list of available document templates that the application maintains. When a user opens a stock price document, the CStockPriceApp application will open the document, the CMainFrame window will display the CStockPriceView view, and the CStockPriceDoc will represent the data of the stock price document.

Summary

In order to fully understand and use MFC, you need to understand the document/view architecture. For example, the MFC AppWizard is an integral part of Visual C++ and relies heavily on documents and views. There are also design benefits to using documents and views because you can separate your data from how it is viewed.

The CDocument class is used to represent the data of your application. You use the CView class to create the views for the document and the CFrameWnd class to create a frame to contain the view. You then use the CDocTemplate class to create an association between the document, view, and main frame class. Your CDocTemplate object is then added to the list of document templates in your application class, which creates an association between your application and files with a certain extension. In the next chapter, you will see how to use the MFC AppWizard to create this association.

Chapter 10

MFC AppWizard

MFC applications typically fit into three categories:

1. Dialog-based The main window for the application is a dialog window. Dialog-based applications do not use the document/view architecture. Windows Dial-Up Networking is an example of a dialog-based application.

2. Single Document Interface (SDI) applications SDI applications use the document/view architecture and allow for a single document to be opened at a time.

3. Multiple Document Interface (MDI) applications MDI applications are similar to SDI applications, except that the application can open multiple documents at the same time.

The basic architecture of each type of MFC application is identical. For example, developing an SDI application involves writing a document, view, frame, and app class. Visual C++ comes with a tool called AppWizard that creates this basic architecture for the type of MFC application you are developing. For example, if you are developing an SDI application, the MFC AppWizard will generate the generic portion of your document, view, frame, and app class — allowing you to focus on your application and not spend time writing repetitive code.

This chapter shows you how to use the AppWizard in Visual C++ to create the workspace and project for an MFC application, and also to help you understand the code generated by the MFC AppWizard so you can take advantage of this powerful tool.

Starting the AppWizard

The MFC AppWizard is found on the Projects tab of the File/New dialog of Visual C++. Figure 10.1 shows an example of the projects in the New dialog found in the Professional Version of Visual C++. The actual list of available projects depends on your version of Visual C++.

To run the MFC AppWizard, perform the following steps:

1. Select "MFC AppWizard (exe)" in the list of available projects.
2. Enter a name for your project in the "Project name" window and change the Location, if desired.
3. Click the "OK" button.

Figure 10.1   Starting the AppWizard using the New dialog of Visual C++.

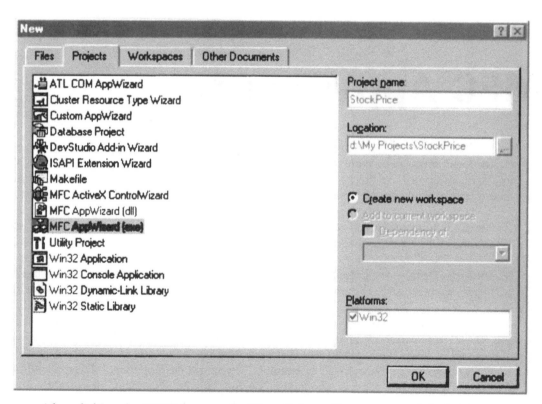

After clicking the "OK" button, the New dialog will go away and the MFC AppWizard will appear. Figure 10.2 shows Step 1 of the wizard, where you are asked to choose the type of MFC application to create.

Figure 10.2   Step 1 of the MFC AppWizard asks you to choose the type of MFC application to create.

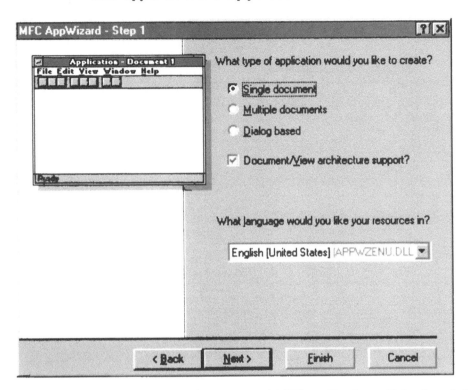

As I mentioned earlier, there are three types of MFC applications: dialog-based, SDI, and MDI. Notice Step 1 of the MFC AppWizard asks you to choose from one of these three choices. The wizard is different for dialog-based as compared to the SDI or MDI wizard. The remainder of this chapter discusses the wizard for dialog-based applications and the wizard for SDI and MDI applications.

Creating Dialog-Based Applications

Dialog-based MFC applications use a dialog as their main window. They are convenient for programs that do not use the document/view architecture. The dialog can be used to display information to the user and provide controls to interact with the user. Examples of dialog-based applications include the calculator program and Volume Control program that come with Windows. They provide controls for interacting with the user, but there are no documents to open or close. By selecting "Dialog based" in Step 1, the "Document/View architecture support?" checkbox is disabled.

Figure 10.3 Step 2 of the MFC AppWizard for Dialog-based applications.

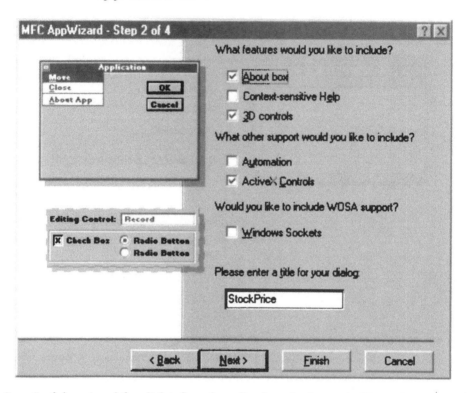

Step 2 of the wizard for dialog-based applications is shown in Figure 10.3. Step 2 allows you to select features of your application, such as:

- **About box** — Windows applications typically have an About option on the Help menu that displays a dialog containing version and other information about the application.
- **Context-sensitive Help** — AppWizard will generate a set of help files for using context-sensitive help.
- **3D controls** — Selecting this option provides shading for your controls, giving them a 3D effect.

You can also select support for technologies like:

- **Automation** — Select this option if you are using OLE automation.
- **ActiveX Controls** — Select this option if your application is going to use ActiveX controls.
- **Windows Sockets** — Select this option if your application is going to use Windows sockets, which allow for TCP/IP communication.

The last feature in Step 2 allows you to enter the title of your dialog — the text that will appear in the title bar. Select the "Next" button when you are finished to move on to Step 3, which is shown in Figure 10.4.

Figure 10.4   Step 3 of the MFC AppWizard for Dialog-based applications.

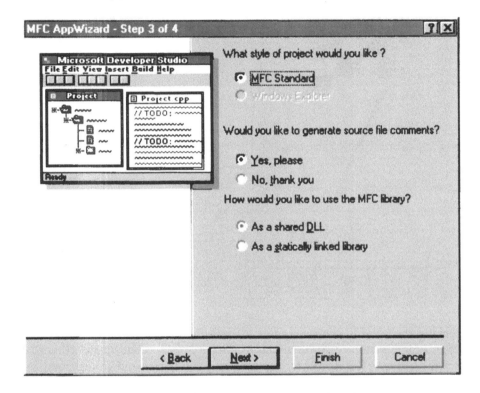

Step 3 begins by asking what style of project you want, but does not give you an option to change it from "MFC Standard," which provides the architecture of a standard MFC application. The next question allows you to specify whether the AppWizard should generate comments in your source code or not. In the beginning of your MFC development experience, you will find that the comments are extremely helpful in understanding the generated code and also in determining where to place your own code.

The final question in Step 3 asks if you want the MFC library to be linked statically or as a shared DLL. If you know your target platform is going to have the MFC DLL installed, then sharing the DLL creates a smaller executable. The advantage of a statically-linked DLL is that it does not need to be installed on a client's machine because the DLL is contained in the executable (which results in a larger executable file).

Once you select the options of Step 3, select the "Next" button. Figure 10.5 shows Step 4 of the wizard, which displays the names of the classes it is going to generate for you. The only option you can change in Step 4 is the name of the app class being generated.

Figure 10.5 Step 4 of the Dialog-based AppWizard shows the names of the classes being generated for you.

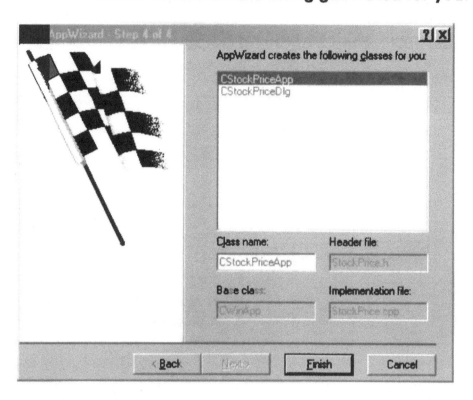

Clicking the "Finish" button causes a confirmation screen to be displayed. Figure 10.6 shows an example of the confirmation screen for a project called StockPrice. Clicking "OK" finishes the wizard. The AppWizard generates a workspace and project, and also generates the classes for your dialog-based application.

The AppWizard generated the following three classes in the StockPrice example:

CStockPriceDlg	A child of CDialog, this class represents the main window of the application. You will notice methods for initializing and painting the window, as well as the DoDataExchange() method for mapping fields of this class to controls in the dialog.
CStockPriceApp	A child of CWinApp, this class represents the application class. It contains the InitInstance() method, which instantiates the dialog and displays it.
CAboutDlg	A child of CDialog, it represents the About dialog. This class will not be generated if you selected not to have an About box.

Figure 10.6 The confirmation screen of AppWizard shows the files it will generate.

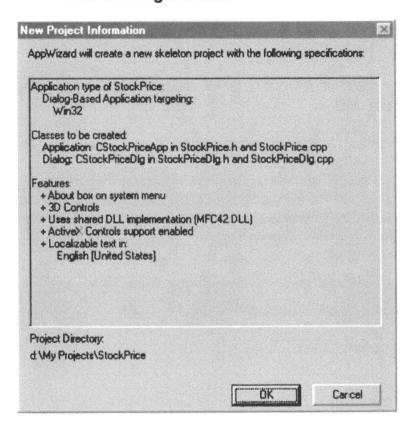

Look through the source code of these classes generated by AppWizard. After reading the previous chapters of this book, the generated code will look familiar to you. Of course, there are plenty of added methods and statements that AppWizard generates, but these are typically for your benefit. For example, the wizard generates debugging preprocessor directives and adds constructors and destructors to your classes. The following code is the CStock-PriceApp class generated by AppWizard.

```
// StockPrice.cpp : Defines the class behaviors for the application.
//

#include "stdafx.h"
#include "StockPrice.h"
#include "StockPriceDlg.h"
```

```
#ifdef _DEBUG
#define new DEBUG_NEW
#undef THIS_FILE
static char THIS_FILE[] = __FILE__;
#endif


/////////////////////////////////////////////////////////////////////////
// CStockPriceApp

BEGIN_MESSAGE_MAP(CStockPriceApp, CWinApp)
  //{{AFX_MSG_MAP(CStockPriceApp)
      // NOTE - the ClassWizard will add and remove mapping macros here.
      //    DO NOT EDIT what you see in these blocks of generated code!
  //}}AFX_MSG
  ON_COMMAND(ID_HELP, CWinApp::OnHelp)
END_MESSAGE_MAP()


/////////////////////////////////////////////////////////////////////////
// CStockPriceApp construction

CStockPriceApp::CStockPriceApp()
{
  // TODO: add construction code here,
  // Place all significant initialization in InitInstance
}


/////////////////////////////////////////////////////////////////////////
// The one and only CStockPriceApp object

CStockPriceApp theApp;


/////////////////////////////////////////////////////////////////////////
// CStockPriceApp initialization

BOOL CStockPriceApp::InitInstance()
{
  AfxEnableControlContainer();
```

```
// Standard initialization
// If you are not using these features and wish to reduce the size
// of your final executable, you should remove from the following
// the specific initialization routines you do not need.

#ifdef _AFXDLL
    Enable3dControls();            // Call this when using MFC in a shared DLL
#else
    Enable3dControlsStatic();      // Call this when linking to MFC statically
#endif

    CStockPriceDlg dlg;
    m_pMainWnd = &dlg;
    int nResponse = dlg.DoModal();
    if (nResponse == IDOK)
    {
        // TODO: Place code here to handle when the dialog is
        //  dismissed with OK
    }
    else if (nResponse == IDCANCEL)
    {
        // TODO: Place code here to handle when the dialog is
        //  dismissed with Cancel
    }

    // Since the dialog has been closed, return FALSE so that we exit the
    //  application, rather than start the application's message pump.
    return FALSE;
}
```

Notice how the comments direct you where to add your own code and where *not* to add code. For example, you can add initialization code in the CStockPriceApp's constructor, but you can not add any statements to that portion of the message map that is maintained by the ClassWizard. In the InitInstance() function, a CStockPriceDlg is instantiated, its DoModal() method is invoked, then the return value is checked in an if/else statement. You can modify any of the code in the InitInstance(), although it is more likely that you will simply add code in the denoted areas.

Projects generated by AppWizard can be built and executed without any additional code from you. Much of the work you do with dialog-based applications is in creating the layout of the dialog, which can be done using the Resource Editor. In other words, with AppWizard and the Resource Editor, you can rapidly develop a dialog-based application by focusing on solving your problem and not on writing the repetitive MFC architecture code.

Creating SDI/MDI Applications

In Step 1 of the MFC AppWizard (see Figure 10.2, page 227), you are prompted to choose the type of MFC application you want to create. If you select Single Document or Multiple Documents, the wizard creates a workspace and project for developing SDI or MDI applications that take advantage of the document/view architecture. Figure 10.7 shows a new project called MyWordPad that will use the SDI architecture.

Figure 10.7 Creating an MFC application that uses the Single Document Interface.

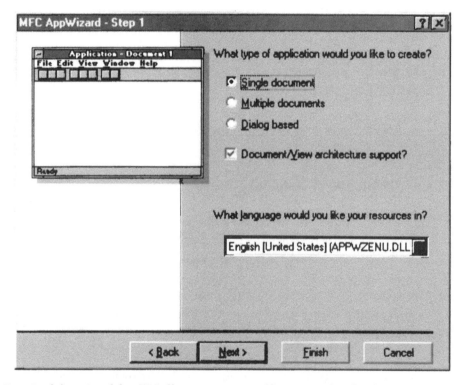

Step 2 of the wizard for SDI allows you to specify settings for database support (see Figure 10.8). You have four options:

- **None** — Select this option if your application is not going to use databases.
- **Header files only** — Select this option if you want AppWizard to generate the header files and linked libraries for database support. You will be able to efficiently add classes to your application to represent recordsets.
- **Database view without file support**— In addition to generating header files and linked libraries, the AppWizard will generate classes for a record view and a recordset. "Without file support" means the generated document class will not contain serialization capabilities.

- Database view with file support — This option is similar to the previous choice, except that the generated document class will contain serialization capabilities.

Selecting either of the settings that provide database views enables the "Data source..." button. Clicking this button allows you to select the database location, type of database, and options about the recordset.

Figure 10.8   Step 2 of the MFC AppWizard for SDI applications allows you to specify database support.

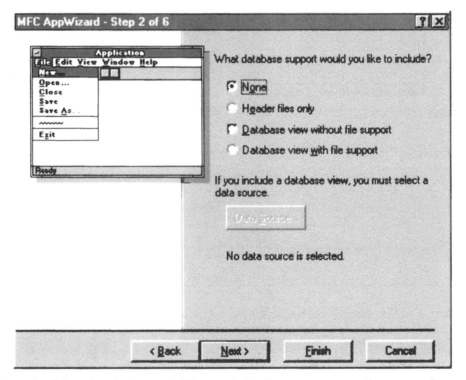

Step 3 of the wizard, shown in Figure 10.9, allows you to specify support for compound documents, automation, and ActiveX controls. The example in Figure 10.9 is not using any of these options. (A discussion of object containers and servers, automation, and ActiveX controls is beyond the scope of this book.)

Figure 10.9   Step 3 of the MFC AppWizard for SDI applications allows you to specify support for compound objects and automation.

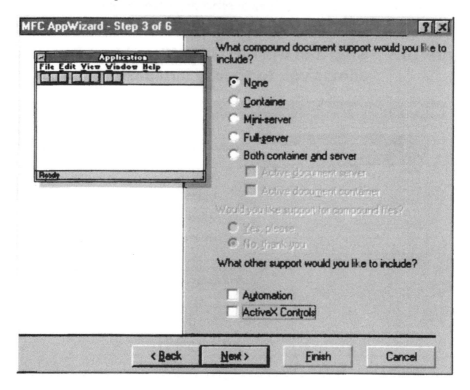

Step 4 of the wizard, shown in Figure 10.10, allows you to specify features about the application you are developing and the types of files that will be associated with your application. You can specify the following settings:

- **Docking toolbar** — Select this option if you want the main frame window to contain a toolbar that can be docked to the frame. You can also specify the look of the toolbar by answering the "How do you want your toolbars to look?" question. The toolbar will contain buttons for creating, opening, and saving a document, as well as cut-and-paste buttons and printing buttons.

- **Initial status bar** — Select this option if you want your main frame window to contain a status bar. The status bar will contain indicators for NUM, CAPS, and SCROLL lock, as well as a message line for displaying tooltips and help items.

- **Printing and print preview** — Select this option if you want printing and print preview features added to your view class.

- **Context-sensitive Help** — AppWizard will generate a set of help files for using context-sensitive help.

- **3D controls** — Selecting this option provides shading for your controls, giving them a 3D effect.

- MAPI (Messaging API) — Select this option if your application needs support for sending and retrieving email.
- Windows Sockets — Select this option if your application is going to use Windows sockets, which allow for TCP/IP communication.

Figure 10.10 Step 4 of the MFC AppWizard for SDI applications allows you to specify settings about the frame window and the types of files associated with your application.

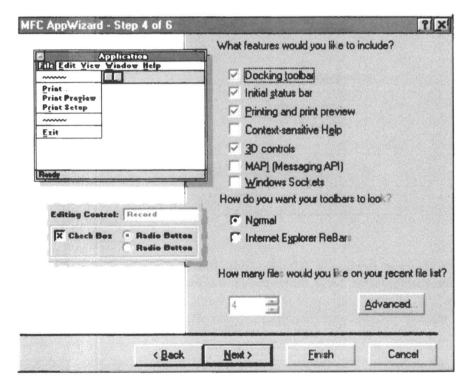

You can specify how many files appear in the recent file list. The recent file list appears at the bottom of the File menu and allows for easy access to recently-opened documents.

Clicking the "Advanced..." button displays the Advanced Options dialog shown in Figure 10.11. Use the Advanced Options dialog to specify the file types that are to be associated with your application. You enter the file extension of the files associated with this application in the "File extension" edit box. Filling in a file extension automatically fills in the "Filter name" edit box.

Figure 10.11 The Advanced Options dialog allows you to specify the file types associated with your SDI application.

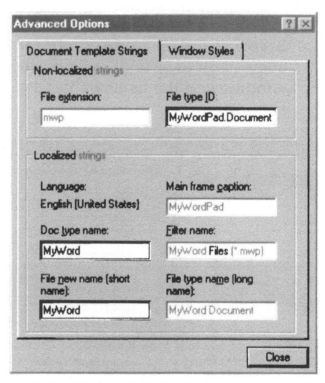

You can also specify the Window Styles for the main frame window in the Advanced Options dialog. Figure 10.12 shows the various settings you can choose in the "Main frame styles."

Figure 10.12 The Advanced Options dialog allows you to specify window styles for the main frame window.

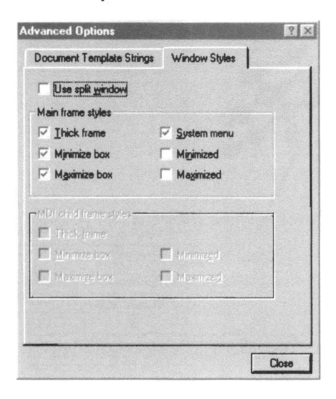

Step 5 of the wizard for SDI and MDI applications is identical to Step 3 of the wizard for dialog-based applications (see Figure 10.4, page 229). The options are the same and were discussed earlier in "Creating Dialog-Based Applications" (page 227).

Figure 10.13 shows Step 6 of the wizard. Step 6 displays the files to be generated by the AppWizard. You can also specify the base class of the application's view class. In the example in Figure 10.13, the base class for the view was changed from CView to CeditView. This will create a view that consists of an edit field similar to Microsoft's Wordpad.

Figure 10.13 Step 6 of the MFC AppWizard for SDI applications shows the classes to be generated.

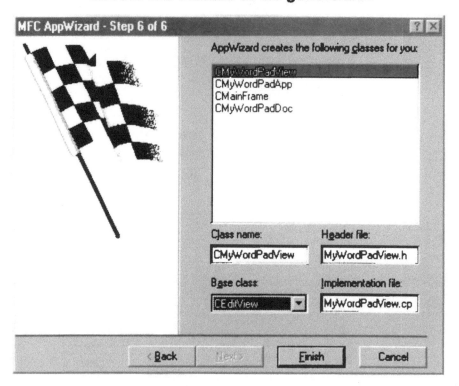

Selecting "Finish" in Step 6 displays a confirmation window similar to the one shown in Figure 10.6 (page 231). The confirmation window displays the files to be generated and the various settings you selected throughout the wizard. Clicking the "OK" button causes the wizard to generate the classes as well as a workspace and project.

The AppWizard generated the following five classes in the MyWordPad example:

CMainFrame	A child of CFrameWnd, this class represents the main frame window of the application.
CMyWordPadApp	A child of CWinApp, this class represents your application class. It contains the InitInstance() method where the CSingleDocTemplate object is instantiated and the main frame window is displayed.
CMyWordPadDoc	A child of CDocument, this is your document class in the document/view architecture. It contains the OnNewDocument() and Serialize() functions.
CMyWordPadView	A child of CEditView, this is your view class in the document/view architecture. It contains the GetDocument() and OnDraw() functions, as well as functions for printing the document.
CAboutDlg	A child of CDialog, this class represents the About box of your application.

The MyWordPad application is a fully-functional text editor that does not require any additional coding on your part. The parent class of CMyWordPadView — CEditView — handles the functionality of editing the text, cut-and-paste, printing, and print preview. Figure 10.14 shows the MyWordProgram application opening a document. Notice the File/Open dialog filters the documents using the "MyWordFiles (*.mwp)" filter.

Figure 10.14 The MyWordPad application filters the documents using the *.mwp filter.

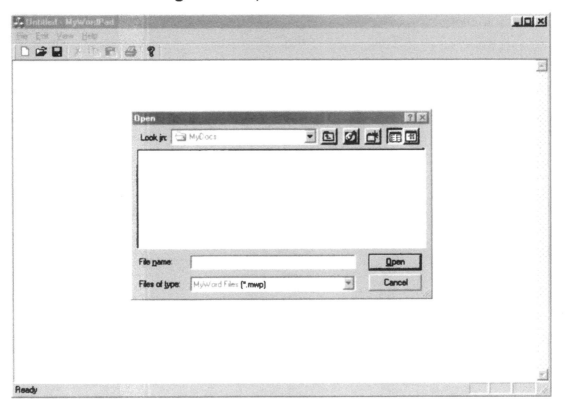

Conclusion

The MFC AppWizard is an integral feature of Visual C++. In real-world development, you will rely heavily on the AppWizard to generate the foundation of your applications. You can combine the AppWizard with other Visual C++ tools like the Resource Editor and the ClassWizard to develop high-end, sophisticated GUI applications with much of the code generated for you.

In order to fully appreciate the power of AppWizard, you need to understand the code being generated for you. My goal in writing this book was to provide you with the information necessary to be able to use AppWizard and understand what it is doing for you. It took nine chapters to cover the material, which shows how steep the learning curve is for MFC programming. I hope you now have an understanding of the MFC architecture and the roles of the main frame, the application class, and the document/view architecture.

Index